BRIDGEPORT

Picture Research by Neil S. Swanson

"Partners in Progress" by Sharon L. Cohen

Produced in cooperation with the
Business/Industry Council
of Fairfield County

Windsor Publications, Inc.
Northridge, California

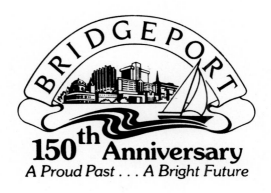
BRIDGEPORT
150th Anniversary
A Proud Past . . . A Bright Future

ONLY IN
BRIDGEPORT

An illustrated history
of the
Park City

GOODYEAR

WEST END MOVING & STORAGE CO.
LOCAL & LONG DISTANCE

FURNITURE & PIANO MOVING

NAGY MEATS

SCHINE SHOES

GAMWING LAUNDRY

SILVERS JEWELRY

Lennie Grimaldi

Windsor Publications, Inc.—History Book Division

Publisher: John M. Phillips
Editorial Director: Teri Davis Greenberg
Design Director: Alexander D'Anca

Staff for *Only In Bridgeport: An Illustrated History of the Park City*
Editor: Lane A. Powell
Assistant Editors: Laura Cordova, Marilyn Horn
Editorial Development: Lynn Kronzek
Director, Corporate Biographies: Karen Story
Assistant Director, Corporate Biographies: Phyllis Gray
Editor, Corporate Biographies: Judith Hunter
Layout Artist, Corporate Biographies: Mari Catharine Preimesberger
Sales Representative, Corporate Biographies: Fred Sommer
Editorial Assistants: Kathy M. Brown, Marcie Goldstein, Pat Pittman,
    Sharon Volz
Designer: J.R. Vasquez
Layout Artist: Susan L. Wells

Library of Congress Cataloging-in-Publication Data

Grimaldi, Lennie, 1958-
    Only in Bridgeport.

    Bibliography: p. 299
    Includes index.
    1. Bridgeport (Conn.)—History. 2. Bridgeport (Conn.)
—Description. 3. Bridgeport (Conn.)—Industries.
I. Title.
F104.B7G74   1986   974.6'9   86-9100
ISBN 0-89781-169-0

Published 1986
Printed in the United States of America
First Edition

Contents

CHAPTER I
The Birth of Bridgeport   **11**

CHAPTER II
The People   **31**

CHAPTER III
Spirit, Mind, and Voice   **49**

CHAPTER IV
Barnum's the Name   **67**

CHAPTER V
All That Brass   **95**

CHAPTER VI
The Park City   **127**

CHAPTER VII
Jasper McLevy   **151**

CHAPTER VIII
Politics, Police, and Perpetrators   **173**

CHAPTER IX
Fighting the Image   **191**

CHAPTER X
Partners in Progress   **225**

Patrons   **298**

Bibliography   **299**

Index   **300**

This postcard of Pleasure Beach Park (circa 1900) best describes the once-great amusement park. The park featured a carousel, miniature train ride, Ferris wheel, roller coaster, and pool. Courtesy, Robert Clifford Collection

Preface

When Windsor Publications chose me to write this book the instant shouts of joy were as quickly followed by the silence of reality. Over the course of eight years I had written who knows how many newspaper and magazine articles on Bridgeport—a city whose unending supply of stories has saved my freelance career from extinction. There is always something to write about in Bridgeport—neighborhoods, politics, crime, ethnic diversity. But a book, now that's frightening.

The first question I asked myself was: where do I start. And oddly enough it would be the same question a million people would ask me during the course of my research. The first person I visited was David W. Palmquist, who has headed the Historical Collections of the Bridgeport Public Library for more than thirteen years. There he was in his office, cup of coffee in hand, pondering my question.

"Why not start at the beginning," he said. Palmquist, I had come to learn as a reporter, knows just about everything about Bridgeport, "Except where the money is buried." I have a pretty sound feeling that if he knew where to find it, he'd share that with Bridgeport too. Palmquist explained that most everything I needed was located in the library, and pointed me to books and articles on Bridgeport's early history. It was the beginning, as he said, and from there on, except where he could confirm for me what others couldn't, I was on my own.

For practically every weekday for the next year the Historical Collections became my stairway to Bridgeport's history. I've never been much for climbing stairs, but the sixty-stair climb from the library's first floor to the Bishop Room was part of my daily attachment to the library, a spiral journey to the top.

During my journey I learned enough about Bridgeport to write several books. The city's history is a magnificent blend of Yankee ingenuity and working-class ethnics forming a reservoir of faces and stories. Names such as P.T. Barnum, Elias Howe, Harvey Hubbell, Nathaniel Wheeler—the men who helped build a town that at first didn't want to become a town, but had to when Stratford, which owned the property within the present boundaries of the city, cast Bridgeport from under its

The two towers of the county courthouse on Bridgeport's Golden Hill Street are visible at right in this panoramic photograph (circa 1890). The courthouse was completed in 1888. When the building was enlarged in 1917, one tower was relocated to give the building a more balanced look. Courtesy, Historical Collections, Bridgeport Public Library

control. That is what this book is about, the story of an unwanted tiny community and its efforts to become a major city.

To say that this is the definitive history of Bridgeport would be a gross misrepresentation. Such an effort is possible, but three or four years and just as many volumes would be what it would take to complete it. Nevertheless, *Only In Bridgeport* covers Bridgeport's history within the themes of the book's chapters and hopes to offer a look at the city's past so we all can understand the city a little better.

There are many people of present-day Bridgeport who offered the same kind of contributions and time to this book as the people who contributed to Bridgeport's history. They number probably more than 100 and include David Palmquist and his staff; Jim Motavalli and John Slater, who allowed me to write this book at the editorial offices of the *Fairfield County Advocate*; Steve Winters, who opened up the library of the *Bridgeport Post*; Jim Callahan, Christine Janis, and Michael J. Daly for their editorial direction; A.H. Saxon, Charles Brilvitch, and Lew Corbit for their historical genius; Neil Sherman of the Bridgeport Chamber of Commerce; my friend Tom Bucci who allowed me to write this book while I was supposed to be his mayoral campaign press secretary; and Kate "eat a peach" Flanagan for her encouragement.

I thank them and thank you—the people of Bridgeport.

For
Dad, Mom, Julie
and
The Captain

Isaac Sherman, Jr., Bridgeport's first mayor, symbolizes the city's birth and the period that launched Bridgeport's rise as a major city. Sherman owned a lucrative saddlery business during his days as mayor, but twelve years after he left office he died bankrupt. Courtesy, Historical Collections, Bridgeport Public Library

CHAPTER I

The Birth of Bridgeport

"We do most solemnly protest against this resolve (the formation of the town of Bridgeport)."

*—Enoch Foote, town moderator,
June 11, 1821*

Isaac Sherman, Jr., had a lot to think about on October 3, 1836. Five months earlier the Connecticut Legislature had designated Bridgeport to become a city on this day, and now, under the new charter, voters had a job to do. Bridgeporters, and Sherman—who that day would be elected the city's first mayor—were looking toward the future: toward the day when the ferocious fires that had been destroying their livelihoods would die out, and when streets would be free of garbage, carts, and animal droppings. Sidewalks would be repaired and the city's harbor would be dredged to make way for larger vessels sailing to and from the West Indies and nearer East coast ports. The improvements, though needed, would be costly. It was an earlier time of taxpayer grumbling. Sherman was determined that he would be the one to keep the city going in the right direction.

The city's first day was biting cold, much too cold for Sherman to be out walking. But he was a politician and he wasn't about to miss the chance to be seen by the voters in his best top hat and black satin bow tie. He stepped outside his frame house at the corner of Division and Beaver streets—now one of the city's busiest intersections at Park and Fairfield avenues—and brooded.

Sherman broke off from his thoughts. Standing on his front steps while the city went out to vote wasn't going to get him elected. As he approached the schoolhouse to cast his vote, he waved to well-wishers and went inside. It wouldn't be until ten o'clock that night that he would make Bridgeport history as the city's first mayor.

But within a year—at the end of his first and only term—Sherman was back in his saddlery business. He left Bridgeport politics, disillusioned by the bureaucratic red tape that kept him from achieving the great things he had in mind on that cold October day. Twelve years later, bankrupt and debt-ridden, he died of cholera in Freeport, Illinois.

Though Sherman's precedent-setting position leaves him known only to present-day trivia buffs, never to be included among prominent Bridgeporters like P.T. Barnum and Jasper McLevy, he became a symbol of the city's birth and of the period that catapulted Bridgeport's rise as a big city—the period of the harbor and the railroad.

*   *   *

Years before even a settlement existed at what would later become Bridgeport, the land was a fertile plain of loamy soil bounded by vast bodies of water, which would later serve to transport Indian-chasing settlers.

Over 200 years before Isaac Sherman, Jr., died, his colonial descendants discovered a village of 500 Pequonnock Indians, who took their name from the "clear fields" where they had settled and farmed years earlier. The area's reservoir of resources—thick forests, abundant fish and wildlife, a mild climate, and waterways such as the Pequonnock River—had drawn the Pequonnock tribe from their northern locations.

The Pequonnock was one of five tribes of the Paugussett nation—a group of blood-related tribes that once controlled much of the southwestern part of Connecticut. In 1637 English colonists met the Pequonnock tribe for the first time in the Pequot War, a conflict caused by the Indians' trading problems with the English and Dutch. The war, fought near the Mystic River along the state's eastern shore, killed hundreds in the tribe and brought a bloody end to the Pequot's power, forcing the tribe to flee westward. A group of Pequot refugees reached what later would become Stratford and were joined by a number of Pequonnock Indians who aided them against the colonists in a later battle. It was while the colonists were pursuing the tribes that the colonists became aware of the excellent areas for settlement along the Connecticut coast.

The tribes flourished in the warmer southern New England climate. Roasted, boiled, and fresh corn dominated the Indian diet. They braided the husks into mats for sleeping or covering houses, and used cobs for scrubbing. The Indians ate a wide range of animals killed by bow and arrow, and trapped, snared, and hunted in communal drives.

Skins and feathers were used for clothing and decoration, and as tools. They ate fresh and saltwater fish caught in weirs strung across streams or speared from shore or from canoes. For the winter months, corn was dried and buried in pits in woven sacks or baskets. Even fish and shellfish caught in times of abundance were dried for use in other seasons. Indians drank only water until the colonists introduced them to corn whiskey.

Indian settlements were always near cornfields or fishing, hunting, and gathering areas. A typical home was a dome-shaped wigwam made by planting a circle of flexible poles into the ground and bending the tops together to form a dome-like frame. It was then covered with bark, hides, or woven mats, leaving a doorway and rooftop smoke hole. Simple furniture, mats, skins, woven items, and a few wooden bowls and spoons filled the wigwam.

Not everything went smoothly for the Indians during this relatively quiet period. The

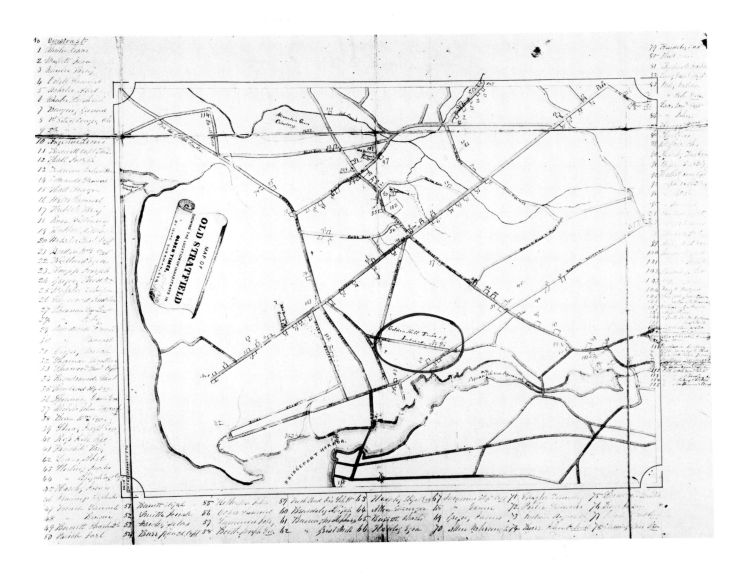

This map of Stratfield highlights the eighty-acre reservation of
the Golden Hill Indians, which sprawled along present-day
Washington Avenue. The first such reservation established in
Connecticut, the General Assembly ordered the Indians to the
land in 1659. Courtesy, Historical Collections, Bridgeport Public Library

The main attraction at Captain's Cove Seaport is the H.M.S. Rose. The original Rose was built in England in 1756 for the seven-year war with France and Spain. Following its restoration it will sail in the Statue of Liberty Centennial-Op Sail '86. Photo by Neil Swanson

lack of a common language between the tribes made it difficult for them to form solid bonds, and left room for a great deal of animosity. The strong tribes dominated the weak and entered into loose alliances to strengthen themselves against enemies.

The arrival of white men from Massachusetts settlements reinforced the inter-tribal rivalry rather than promoting mutual support. In fact, the Indians greatly outnumbered the colonists for a few years, and, had they joined forces, they could have driven them out of the area. But the colonists exploited the rivalries, playing tribes off against each other, weakening the Indian power and halting the threat to white settlement in Connecticut. This "divide and conquer" policy throughout the years drove the Indians farther westward.

In the meantime, upstate colonists were watching the southwestern part of the state with great interest. In 1639, the General Assembly commissioned Connecticut's Deputy Governor Roger Ludlowe to establish the settlement of Pequonnock, to include the lands east of the Uncoway River (what is now Ash Creek), and extend as far north as King's Highway and as far south as Long Island Sound.

But Ludlowe, an enterprising colonist, never made it. As he and four other pioneers headed south with their livestock, they heard that some competing settlers were planning a plantation west of the Pequonnock area. Ludlowe took claim to the land before they did and promptly settled the village of Uncoway, which would be known as Fairfield by the following year.

"Some others intended to take up said place who had not acquainted the court with their purpose," Ludlowe told the General Court in October 1639 by way of explanation—or apology. The court reprimanded Ludlowe, and a committee headed by Governor John Haynes traveled to Pequonnock and Uncoway to investigate.

Pequonnock was settled by other colonists after Ludlowe's diversion to Uncoway, and the governor administered an oath of fidelity to the Pequonnock planters. He ordered them to send one or two deputies to the next General Court for instruction in the formation of their own local court. Haynes and Ludlowe were ordered by the General Court to determine the boundaries between Pequonnock and Uncoway.

* * *

Ludlowe enjoyed Uncoway so much that he stayed around as part of a four-man team "to execute justice there as cause shall require," which sometimes meant hanging anyone he deemed a witch. Witch hangings were by no means a daily occurrence, but they did happen from time to time when superstitious townspeople found a woman bearing "witch signs," sometimes nothing more than a birthmark, mole, freckle, or scar. To avoid suspicion, many women covered anything that might invite a noose fitting.

In 1653, settlers came from miles around to attend the hanging of Fairfield's Goody Knapp, a suspected witch whom one historian described as nothing more than a simple-minded woman. (*Goody* and *Goodwife* were terms indicating a rank of social stature granted to the common woman of the time.) The testimony of Goody Odell, a midwife who examined Knapp and reportedly spotted "witch marks," sealed the poor woman's fate. The beginning of the end was a "confession" by convicted Stratford witch Goody Basset who, before her death, suggested "others who hold their heads full high" were no different than she. This confirmed colonists' belief that other witches abounded.

The hysterical Knapp refused to confess but was given a speedy trial and declared guilty by Ludlowe. She was executed just northwest of an Indian field, now the site of the Burroughs Home at 2470 Fairfield Avenue. Many women crowded around her body when it was cut

In 1653, settlers came from miles around to witness the hanging of Goody Knapp. Settler Roger Ludlowe declared Knapp a witch based on the testimony of another woman who was declared a witch. Illustration by Don Almquist. Courtesy, Historical Collections, Bridgeport Public Library

down from the gallows, anxious to peek at the witch signs. A friend of the deceased, Goodwife Staples, shook her head and said, "They were naught but such as she herself or any woman had." At that remark, another woman countered, "Aye, and be hanged for them, and deserve it too."

Goodwife Staples' tongue nearly dug her own grave as Ludlowe accused her of being a witch. But her infuriated husband sued Ludlowe on behalf of his wife for defamation of character. Staples won the suit, his wife won acquittal, and Ludlowe left the colonies forever.

* * *

Ludlowe's departure caused him to miss much of the newlywed period between the Indians and the white settlers—a time when both realized they were stuck with each other and resolved to make the best of it. Nevertheless, curiosity and distrust remained between the two groups.

Country Road and King's Highway, the same North and Boston avenues now traveled by thousands every day, were Indian trails that joined Fairfield and Stratford. The first house built between those towns was owned by Thomas Wheeler at Black Rock Harbor in 1644. Wheeler was so concerned about the possibility of an Indian uprising that he built a small fort by his house and equipped it with two guns aimed at the harbor and the Indians.

But forts such as Wheeler's didn't always keep the Indians at a respectful distance. They were being caught in a squeeze between the expanding settlements of Fairfield, to the west, and Stratford, to the east. Because many Indians had an intense desire to learn more about the white man, it wasn't uncommon for a settler to look up from his chores and find an Indian peering right back at him. But before any major disruptions between the two groups occurred, the General Assembly in 1659 ruled that Stratford's parcel of land known as Golden Hill (that lay within the Pequonnock area) should be given to the Indians. The eighty-acre parcel today lies within Bridgeport on Washington Avenue, and was the first such reservation established in Connecticut.

Since Stratford was ordered to hand over

property to the Indians, the court also ruled that Fairfield should compensate its neighbor with $100 worth of beef, pork, wheat, and peas. In return for the reservation, the Indians promised never to steal any cattle, corn, or peas, and to maintain their fences so cattle wouldn't break through to destroy settlers' crops.

To keep the peace, settlers were forbidden to sell arms, ammunition, liquor, horses, or boats to Indians. Indians were forbidden to enter the settlers' houses or handle their firearms. Any Indians prowling near settlers' homes after dark could be shot.

Regardless of the new rules, by the early 1700s all of the tribes in the Paugussett nation had been disturbed enough by contact with white men to move west. The remaining Golden Hill Indians complained to the General Assembly about losing parts of their reservation through white encroachment and illegal land sales. To compensate, the court granted the Indians a supplemental land parcel on Corum Hill, in Huntington, Connecticut. But white settlers continued to move into the Golden Hill area, driving out the Indians. In 1769, with but a few wigwams remaining, settlers invaded the reservation, claimed all but six acres, and forced out every Indian by tearing apart their wigwams. Town authorities took no action.

In 1854 the tribe bought a twenty-acre reservation in Trumbull and for the next 100-plus years battled in court to retain their land. In June 1979 the tribe purchased a sixty-nine-acre strip in upstate Colchester—an effort to maintain a natural environment incorporating riding trails, timber management efforts, and wildlife habitats as federal and state authorities stepped up protection to the Indians and their property. The present-day history buff would be hard-pressed to find concrete remains of the Indians' life in Bridgeport. But while few Indian relics may be unearthed between the high-rise buildings and paved roads, the Indians' legacy survives in names such as the Housatonic and

Pequonnock rivers, Golden Hill Street, and Chopsy Hill, named after an Indian whose wigwam stood in that North End area.

*　　*　　*

From the mid-1600s to the pre-Revolutionary War period, the Bridgeport area became a prosperous farming community, resplendent with cornfields and occasionally visited by foreign vessels carrying cargoes of livestock and wheat. The settlers lived in unpainted oak clapboard houses with sloping roofs. Many of the men engaged in agriculture or seafaring trades; others were millers, blacksmiths, and tanners. Besides churches and a schoolhouse, the only other public building was a tavern on the site of present-day 2354 North Avenue. Legend alleges that General George Washington stopped off at the tavern in 1775 while on his way to Boston to take charge of the Continental Army.

Pequonnock underwent several name changes between 1694 and its designation as Bridgeport borough in 1800. In 1694 it became Fairfield Village; in 1701, Stratfield; and in 1798, Newfield. The first was prompted by the formation of a school. In 1694, while part of the settlement was still owned by Fairfield, many citizens complained to the General Court that the four miles their children had to travel to attend school in the center of Fairfield was much too far. In response, the court allowed the citizens to establish a school and the settlement became known as Fairfield Village. Residents took on all educational expenses for the forty-seven students and separated themselves from the Fairfield educational system. At the same time, the settlers also engaged their own minister and were allowed to set up their own local government. Seven years later, in 1701, the village became Stratfield, and a road, now State Street, was built through Stratfield to the Pequonnock Harbor, opening up a route between Fairfield and Stratford along the shore.

The residents of Stratfield during the American Revolution were far removed from the battles. Stratfield was still a quiet farming community considered too small for plunder. A few local settlers fought in the war, such as Captain Thaddeus Bennett, a shoemaker and farmer, and Nathaniel Fayerweather, also a farmer. One resident, Dr. Lyman Hall, a minister ordained in Stratfield in 1749, went on to become one of the signers of the Declaration of Independence. But the majority stayed close to home to tend their families and properties.

The Revolutionary War period brought growth for the village of Stratfield. From the close of the war, a whole new community sprouted—including a public ferry, the first bridge, and a newspaper. Stratfield became Newfield, and was formally recognized in 1798 by the Connecticut General Assembly upon maintaining a fire engine company. Nevertheless the village of Newfield still belonged to Stratford.

Two years later, the General Assembly incorporated Newfield as a separate borough, making it the state's first borough, and giving residents their first degree of independence from the larger community of Stratford. The area was declared the Borough of Bridgeport—taking its name from the old Lottery Bridge that connected it to Stratford. The borough was given the responsibility of caring for its own streets, and was granted most of the privileges extended to towns, except representation in the General Assembly and the right to vote in their own borough. To vote, residents still had to travel the five miles to Stratford.

Bridgeport borough, with its wealth of foreign and coastal sea trade, began a period of remarkable growth. A census of the borough in 1810 counted 1,089 residents, two churches, 123 houses, and eighteen sailing vessels engaged in trade with the West Indies. Exports included livestock, wheat and rye flour, Indian meal, corn, oats, pork, butter, and cider. Manufactured articles included beaver hats, rope, saddles, boots and shoes, cabinetwork, and

Isaac Sherman, Sr., uncle to Bridgeport's first mayor, invested money in a saltworks that pumped saltwater from the Pequonnock River into vats using a windmill near the bank. Courtesy, Historical Collections, Bridgeport Public Library

carriages. There were two tanneries, three printing offices, two weekly newspapers, one pottery, and forty-three stores.

But the War of 1812 brought all that economic activity and progress to a halt. Few ships left the relative safety of the Pequonnock River for fear of being seized by the British. Blockades by British ships made necessities, such as flour, a luxury. But several townspeople—who saw the war as an inconvenience because it interfered with shipping—rowed a small boat to New York City to get a fresh supply of flour. The British fired on them but missed, and became so infuriated that they fired on Grover's Hill, a military detachment in Black Rock.

On February 22, 1815, news of the peace between Great Britain and America launched a parade of events in Bridgeport that included cannon firing, bell ringing, and a ball at Knapp's Hotel at Wall and Water streets.

The war's aftermath left a massive salt shortage and many communities learned to make their own. Isaac Sherman, Sr., uncle to Bridgeport's first mayor, invested money in a saltworks located north of Gold Street and west of the present Congress and Water streets. At the works, saltwater was pumped from the harbor into vats by a windmill near the bank. Bridgeporters used homemade salt for many years, but the undertaking was unprofitable and dried up due to one major fault: the salt works was located near the river and the harbor water was too diluted with fresh water from the river's tributaries.

Soon, Bridgeport became financially sound again, perhaps too sound for some. The borough's saddlery and carriage industry and West Indies trade had started to boom, and Stratford's influential citizens feared that Bridgeport's economic strength would some day give it the balance of power. So Stratford unceremoniously dumped Bridgeport from under its control, and despite violent protests from its residents, Bridgeport borough became a town in 1821.

*   *   *

"We do most solemnly protest against this resolve," said town moderator Enoch Foote in

Bridgeport's transportation in the late 1800s included horse-drawn trolleys such as the one shown here on Main Street heading toward Seaside Park. Courtesy, Historical Collections, Bridgeport Public Library

1821 during the first official town meeting. Renegade Bridgeporters complained bitterly to the General Assembly that they were "deprived of their lawful name as town (Stratford) and have another imposed upon them all without their consent."

They claimed the lines of division were unjust as they were getting but one-fourth of the actual territory of Stratford. Bridgeport now had a seacoast of less than 1,000 feet, while Stratford had five miles on the coast and ten miles on the Housatonic River. And Stratford received half of Bridgeport's harbor while it unjustly divided the lands so three-fourths of the bridges (and their upkeep expenses) were in Bridgeport. Park Avenue remained the western boundary of the city until 1870 when the state legislature extended it to include the portion of Fairfield lying east of Ash Creek.

Meanwhile, as Bridgeport carried on in its cramped surroundings, its citizens soured on the town's form of government and decided that it needed all the privileges of an incorporated city, including the power to borrow money to build a railroad. A petition of incorporation was approved in May 1836 to take effect the following October, and the city's boundaries were enlarged so that the eastern line was extended to Yellow Mill Creek to include what would later become East Bridgeport.

Though Bridgeporters were still harboring bad memories of Stratford cutting them loose, the city was considered a thriving community and showed potential as an industrial center, confirming Stratford's earlier fears. Some waterfront businessmen owned their own wharves and small boats, and sailed between Bridgeport and New York and sometimes Boston. Stores of every kind filled downtown, including shops advertising women's shawls from Paris, and specialty shops dealing exclusively in hats, clothes, and hand-sewn boots.

But one thing was missing: a railroad. The world's newest and fastest way to travel had so far eluded the residents and merchants of

The first trains of the Housatonic Railroad Company steamed into Bridgeport Harbor in 1840 and were of great importance to the busy commercial area. These trains handled freight arriving by ship from the West Indies and more local ports such as New York, Boston, and Baltimore. Oyster and whaling boats used the harbor as well. Courtesy, Historical Collections, Bridgeport Public Library

Bridgeport and luring it to the area became the chief reason for the city's incorporation. Progressive Bridgeporters were anxious for a rail line into Bridgeport to carry on trade that had never before been possible, and knew that incorporation would give them the authority to borrow money to build a line.

In March 1837, just five months after its incorporation, Bridgeport passed a resolution pledging aid to the Housatonic Railroad Company. The state legislature had earlier granted incorporation papers to Enoch Foote, William Peete, and W.C. Sterling of Bridgeport, allowing them to form the railroad company and grant a charter with permission to build a line into Bridgeport. The railroad had been connected from Boston to Albany with a Connecticut line to New Milford. Alfred Bishop, a Danbury native who tired of farming in New Jersey, settled in Bridgeport and became president of the Housatonic, and the most persistent figure in the drive to locate a terminal of the Housatonic Railroad in the city. Bishop and company built the line from the Massachusetts border, just south of Sheffield, to New Milford, Connecticut, and south into Bridgeport.

Work on the railroad began in July 1837, and in less than three years, chiming church bells and thundering cannons ushered in the first railroad steam engine.

Train travelers suffered many inconveniences in the early days of the railroad. Sometimes the weight of a passing train would force track spikes to pop up and poke through the train floor. Railroad employees wielding sledge hammers would watch the track for stray spikes, and would drive them back into the rail if they spotted one sticking up. The wood-burning engines sprayed sparks over the passengers, and fires were frequent. The traveling coaches were hard and uncomfortable and springs were scarce.

Stopping, with the use of a hand or foot brake, was not easy. Sometimes when the train reached the station, several strong porters

Alfred Bishop settled in Bridgeport and became a major force in attracting the Housatonic Railroad to the city. Courtesy, Historical Collections, Bridgeport Public Library

seized the end of the train and heaved while the station agent thrust sticks of wood through the wheel spokes. Locomotives often broke down and horses and oxen were hired to drag the cars to the nearest station and repair shop. Accidents were frequent. Bridgeport had street-level tracks, and several pedestrian fatalities occurred until the tracks were elevated onto the present viaduct system around 1900.

The railroad and the harbor transformed the city into a great industrial center. Though much hullabaloo was made of the railroad, the harbor and seafaring trades were of equal importance to Bridgeport's evolution. In 1836, numerous vessels sailed between Bridgeport and New York, Boston, Baltimore, and the West Indies. Several whaling companies were formed, including the Bridgeport Whaling Company, which had four boats proclaiming the "prosecution of whale and other fisheries in the Atlantic and Pacific Oceans." Whaling expeditions sometimes lasted two years with a net capture of thirty to forty whales. Spectacular crowds assembled at the water's edge to welcome mariners home from their voyages—voyages that sometimes left many men at sea.

During the port's early days, a store and wharf were built by Philip Nichols at one end of Pembroke Street, and just before the American Revolution, sea-going cargo was handled on the west side of the harbor at the mouth of the Newfield Harbor.

It wasn't until the work of harbormaster Captain John McNeil, years later, that Bridgeport's harbors became revered throughout the East Coast. In 1846 Captain John Brooks, Charles Middlebrooks, and Charles Rockwell, officers of the steamboat *Nimrod,* asked if their steamer could enter the harbor over the outer bar at night, something that was not normally done. Since the channel was sixty feet in width at low tide, determining the exact location of the channel during darkness was crucial and delays would inconvenience passengers who had to connect with the Housatonic train for Albany. Abraham A. McNeil (the future harbormaster's father) had the idea to position a small rowboat with a mast bearing a signal light off the outer bar. The steamer advancing to port followed the light for direction, and Bridgeport's first lighthouse became operational. But many crucial improvements still had to be completed before large crafts could enter the harbor.

In 1888 John McNeil asked the Army Corps of Engineers for money to widen the harbor channel as far as Black Rock and Cedar Creek so manufacturers could bring their freight to within a few yards of their factories instead of carting it the two to three miles from Bridgeport's East Side. The request was approved, and the work was done at the expense of the Beardsley Dredging Company, which reim-

bursed itself by selling the dredged gravel to owners of oyster grounds. About l00,000 cubic yards of gravel were excavated.

McNeil then planned construction of a breakwater to extend from near the point of Welles Tongue (near the current United Illuminating Company plant) to the inner beacon, with as large an area of the north dredged as needed to supply protection for all crafts against storms. It would also afford crafts of all classes a harbor out of the way of incoming and outgoing vessels.

The plan fostered a large oyster industry, yielding $350,000 to $400,000 per year, of which $60,000 reached the coffers of local merchants. Construction of the breakwater also saved many shoreside property owners from damaging winds and crashing waves. Steamers moored safely at docks in the mouth of the lower bay.

Bridgeport's old railroad depot on Water Street, circa 1890. Elevation of the tracks in 1900 onto the present viaduct system brought an end to the many pedestrian fatalities and injuries. Courtesy, Historical Collections, Bridgeport Public Library

Above: *In January 1893, hundreds of Bridgeporters journeyed on ice to the Bridgeport lighthouse when the harbor froze solid. This lighthouse, built in 1871, replaced an earlier effort—a small rowboat with a mast bearing a signal light. Courtesy, Historical Collections, Bridgeport Public Library*

Above right: *This view of East Bridgeport and the harbor, from the roof of the Security Building in 1905, shows the industrial growth during the early 1900s. The many smokestacks and ships in the harbor are evidence of this period of rapid growth. Courtesy, Historical Collections, Bridgeport Public Library*

McNeil widened and deepened the harbor, raised beacons, and installed lighthouses regarded as some of the best equipped and maintained in Long Island Sound. The lighthouse at Penfield Reef was described by McNeil as the "key" to navigating Bridgeport harbor for vessels bound from New York. Bridgeport harbor became one of the finest on the Atlantic coast—annual water-borne commerce reached more than one million tons by the 1890s.

*   *   *

While Bridgeporters adjusted to the beginning of the city's industrial revolution, some farsighted entrepreneurs—such as Phineas Taylor Barnum and General William H. Noble—began to take advantage of its potential for growth. Most of the eastern side of Bridgeport (actually still within Stratford's boundaries at the time) was owned by General Noble, a wealthy land developer who bought the land from Stratford and planned to subdivide it and build streets. Barnum bought 700 acres at $200 each from Noble and together they laid out Washington Park and presented it to the city. The park is still located on Washington Avenue.

Barnum went on to create an innovative financing plan for residents who could not afford to buy outright their own homes. His project encouraged people to make payments on a house and lot and secure ownership at the expiration of the payments. The plan helped develop the city, and brought new residents and the first industrial establishments to the area.

One company Barnum's plan attracted was owned by Elias Howe, the inventor of the first working sewing machine which he manufactured in a factory built at Howe and Kossuth streets in 1863. Factories joining Howe's included the Wheeler and Wilson Sewing Machine Company, The Bridgeport Brass Company, the Warner Brothers Company, the Bullard Company, the Bridgeport Machine Tool Company, and the Southern New England Telephone Company.

Bridgeport banking, begun in 1806, flourished from the economic expansion and Bridgeport's status attracted some big-name politicians. In 1860 Abraham Lincoln addressed a large crowd in Washington Hall during a campaign visit and reportedly tasted his first fried oyster dinner at the Bridgeport home of Frederick Wood. In 1864 President Lincoln's call to arms during the Civil War effort drew an overwhelming re-

sponse as seven regiment companies were organized in Bridgeport.

In the mid-to-late-1800s fires destroyed numerous buildings and upset years of planning. On December 12, 1845, a midnight blaze in George Well's oyster saloon on Bank Street changed the course of the city's business section, forcing an overnight move from Water Street to the present downtown district on Main Street. The fire engulfed Bridgeport at a vulnerable time—low tide—when pipes from fire engines filled with mud as fire fighters tried to pump water from the river.

When it was over, half the downtown area was burnt to the ground, including 800 barrels

The work of Bridgeport harbormaster Captain John McNeil initiated harbor development, including a breakwater to supply protection for all crafts, such as the steamer Doris, *shown here in 1893. Courtesy, Historical Collections, Bridgeport Public Library*

Left: *Elias Howe, Jr., the inventor of the first working sewing machine, made his machines in a factory at Howe and Kossuth streets. P.T. Barnum lured Howe to the city during Barnum's development of East Bridgeport. Courtesy, Historical Collections, Bridgeport Public Library*

Right: *Sewing machine partners Nathaniel Wheeler and Allen Wilson left Middletown, Connecticut, to occupy a building (shown here in 1890) on East Washington Avenue in 1856. Wheeler and Wilson earned credit for making the sewing machine a commercial success by reducing the cost of its manufacture. Courtesy, Historical Collections, Bridgeport Public Library*

Below: *Elias Howe, Jr., successfully defended his 1845 sewing machine design against patent infringers, and twenty years later began production in this large building at Howe and Kossuth streets, which had a dock for shipping the machines to New York buyers. Courtesy, Historical Collections, Bridgeport Public Library*

Above: *The Fairfield County Courthouse (as seen from the roof of the Security Building in 1905) was built in 1888, to replace the original courthouse, now McLevy Hall, built in 1853-54. Courtesy, Historical Collections, Bridgeport Public Library*

Below: *On December 12, 1845, a midnight blaze in a saloon on Bank Street destroyed half of the Water Street downtown area, as this outline shows. The business district was forced to be moved to the present downtown district on Main Street. Courtesy, Historical Collections, Bridgeport Public Library*

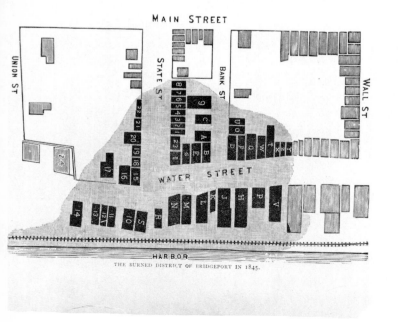

THE BURNED DISTRICT OF BRIDGEPORT IN 1845.

of flour, 100 barrels of mackerel, and great quantities of leather goods, groceries, meats, carpets, and clothing. Forty-nine buildings were destroyed and forty families were left penniless. After losses were totaled, Water Street merchants moved to Main Street for a new start.

One of the city's most gruesome blazes began in a hat factory on Crescent Avenue on June 8, 1877. Eleven people died in the fire, and editorials in the *New Haven Palladium,* the *New York Tribune,* and the *New York World* denounced Bridgeport's negligence in not providing an adequate water supply for fire emergencies. Another fire, six years later, gutted Elias Howe's sewing machine factory, crippling the company financially although production continued for many more years.

Despite fires, deaths, and crushed businesses, Bridgeport again rebuilt itself into a bustling city with the aid of Irish residents who had first begun immigrating following the potato famines of the 1840s. By 1850 about one out of seven Bridgeport residents had been born in Ireland.

Bridgeport's industrial growth during this period was followed by geographic growth as well. With a population nearing 20,000 in 1870, the West End and Black Rock were annexed from Fairfield. In 1889 Bridgeport reached its present bounds when the East End and West Stratford were annexed. A railroad, a renewed harbor, and geographic extension came in handy for Bridgeport's next stage—the tide of immigration.

Large stores such as Dorsen's "Modern Department Store" did a booming business on Main Street in 1915. Courtesy, Historical Collections, Bridgeport Public Library

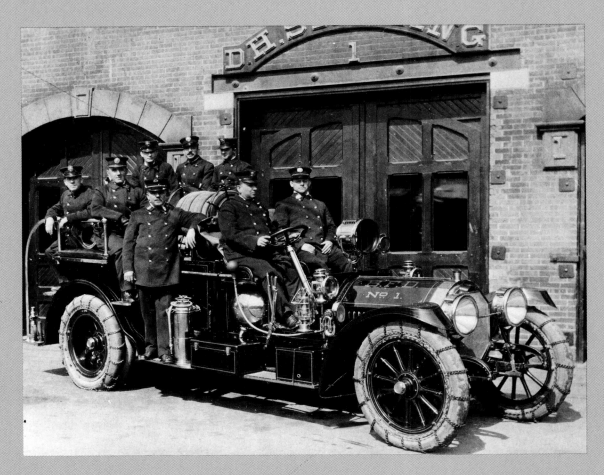

The administration of Clifford B. Wilson, lasting from 1911 to 1921, marked a progressive period in Bridgeport. Wilson motorized the fire and police departments and paved much of the city. His administration also established school dental programs and the city's recreation department. Pictured above is the Bridgeport Fire Department's Engine Company #1, circa 1920. Courtesy, Historical Collections, Bridgeport Public Library

CHAPTER II

The

People

"Bridgeport had so many ethnic groups that the joke in Boston was, 'They don't speak English there.'"

—*Charles J. Stokes,*
professor of economics,
University of Bridgeport

In 1978, Tom Quach thought he had as much a chance of escaping Communist-controlled Saigon for America as he had of "flying to the moon."

"Everybody was looking for a way to leave," the native Vietnamese said. "The Communists controlled you. Things were so bad that if a lamp-post could walk it would escape."

Quach is one of Bridgeport's most recent immigrants. He had worked for the Exxon Corporation in South Vietnam, but after the Viet Cong takeover things got so bad that Quach and his wife were confined to their home, their food was rationed, and many of their possessions were confiscated.

The one concession the Communists granted was mailing Quach's letters, but generally only after they were censored. Fearful of being branded a spy and arrested, Quach could not petition the government for emigration papers. He instead successfully explored transfer options with his employer, the Exxon Corporation in Paris, which provided Quach with money and food and sent him through a training program. He stayed in France for about a year until his brother, who had arrived in Bridgeport many years before, contacted Deacon Joseph Farley, director of Ethnic and Cultural Services

In the early 1900s the city's population grew by thousands. Organized labor cut the workday from twelve to eight hours, and in 1915 the city was subjected to roughly 100 strikes. These workers for the T.J. Pardy Construction Company built the famous twin theatres of Sylvester Z. Poli in 1921. Courtesy, Historical Collections, Bridgeport Public Library

for the Diocese of Bridgeport, which had recently begun a program to resettle refugees. Quach and his wife Kim arrived in Bridgeport in August 1979. His first job was as a store manager for Cumberland Farms in Bridgeport. Athough he spoke little English he swayed the store owners to hire his wife, brother, and nephew so they could operate the store as a family. He and his wife took some courses at the University of Bridgeport, saved their pennies, and with his brother chipped in to buy a house on Iranistan Avenue. They have twin girls born in Bridgeport.

Today Tom Quach works for Deacon Joseph Farley, the man who helped bring him to Bridgeport. Together they have relocated hundreds of refugees in the Bridgeport area through the Catholic Center, supplying clothes, food, and housing, and guiding them through educational programs and monitoring their progress.

"I'm an American citizen now," says Quach. "You could not understand the feeling I have, knowing a few years ago it was nothing but a dream. I want to kiss the ground when I think about it. It's a totally new life."

*   *   *

Tom Quach's story has a precedent in the tales told by thousands of immigrants and refugees who have come to Bridgeport since the 1840s to escape hunger, joblessness, or war in their home countries.

Bridgeport has undergone numerous changes in 150 years—it's been a Yankee farming community, the arms and munitions center of the country during wartime, a seaport and railway center, one of Connecticut's smallest towns, and the state's largest city. The changes were the result of the passage of time and the growth of technology, and mirrored progress in the rest of the country. Yet the one consistent factor steering these changes hasn't changed at all: Bridgeport's ethnic diversity.

"Bridgeport has had many nicknames be-

stowed on it throughout history," wrote Herb Geller, whose *Ethnic History* series appeared in the *Bridgeport Sunday Post* from October 1977 to February 1980. "It has been called the Park City, Industrial City, Harbor City, and even Circus City, but one name this community deserves above all is the Ethnic City."

Should a visitor be whisked around town, he or she would catch a glimpse of many of the world's cultures in eighteen square miles. As many as sixty ethnic groups have settled in Bridgeport during the past 150 years. Bridgeport today has a predominantly Italian and Irish North End, Portuguese in the Hollow, blacks on the East Side, and a Hispanic West

Patrick Coughlin, an early Irish settler in Bridgeport, set a new standard for immigrant groups arriving in Bridgeport by becoming the city's first Irish-born mayor. The new arrivals recognized that real power rested with the vote, and they were quick to register and exercise that right. Courtesy, City of Bridgeport

Side. There are Eastern Europeans, including Hungarians, Poles, Lithuanians, Ukrainians, Slovaks, Albanians, and Rumanians, recently joined by the new wave of immigrants and refugees from Cambodia, Laos, and Vietnam. The city's ethnic festivals include a St. Patrick's Day Parade, Columbus Day Parade, Puerto Rican Day Parade, and an international folk festival honoring all ethnic groups. It may be that if Bridgeport ever realized the great spirit of its cultural diversity, every day would be a Fourth of July celebration.

Bridgeport, as one of America's magnet cities, has attracted millions of starving, tired, and persecuted immigrants hopeful for a job and a new way of life. A look at Bridgeport's population trends shows the story of the foreign surge. But the statistics hardly tell the entire story behind Bridgeport's immigrants, as each face reflects deprivation, turmoil, war—and new hope.

Bridgeport Population Growth	
1830	2,800
1840	4,570
1850	7,560
1860	13,299
1870	19,835
1880	29,148
1890	48,868
1900	70,996
1910	102,054
1920	143,555
1930	146,716 —Immigration restrictions
1940	147,121
1950	158,709

* * *

The Irish were the first foreign group (after the English) to settle in Bridgeport, and were the most important contributors during the city's early years. Hundreds of thousands of Irish poured into the United States in the late 1840s after a blight fell upon their potato harvests. More than half the Irish people had become homeless wanderers, living on bark and berries while despair spread over their land. News of the disaster sparked a wave of sympathy, and Americans sent shiploads of food worth nearly one million dollars—a great sum in those days. But it wasn't nearly enough. Stricken Irish families fled their land in masses to the United States. Over one-and-a-half million immigrated by 1860, more than all the world had sent since 1776.

Until their great move to Bridgeport in the late 1840s, the Irish community numbered only 100 or so. But the colony was large enough

to have constructed St. James Cemetery (1829) and St. James Church (1843), the third Catholic church built in Connecticut. The Irish initially settled around Middle Street and in the South End, the two oldest parts of town. Later they filtered into the Hollow and the East Side, courtesy of the land made available by P.T. Barnum and General Noble.

The Irish influence couldn't have come at a better time for Bridgeport, a city with plans. The railroad had already been completed by the time the Irish arrived in Bridgeport, but the Irish helped to build Bridgeport's factories and aided railroad improvements, filling the industrial East's ever-mounting demand for labor.

The Irish, like many of the other ethnic groups that would follow, encountered a solid wall of prejudice and open hatred. They were given the lowest paying and most difficult jobs, and poverty was their common denominator. Nevertheless, they won admiration through their persistent hard work and warm-hearted humor. The Yankees were still—and would remain for many years to come—the financial establishment and held a solid grip on the city. Financial and business decision makers were almost always Yankees. But the Irish recognized that real power rested with the vote, something they were denied in their native land. They registered as quickly as possible. Because of their large families, they sought jobs with steady incomes, particularly in the public service areas. The Irish were cops, firemen, and teachers, and their jobs often were political appointments.

Patrick Coughlin, one of the first Irish settlers in Bridgeport, became the city's first Irish-born mayor in 1888. But it wasn't until the election of Denis Mulvihill in 1901 that the Irish gained serious political clout. Mulvihill, born in Tralee, Ireland, in 1838, personified the rise of the early immigrant. He labored as a stoker at the Wheeler and Wilson Sewing Machine Company and appealed to voters with such battle cries as, "Who made the world? Denny Mulvihill with his pick and shovel."

Such a gift of gab launched the Irish to positions of power. In the early 1900s the Irish brain of Bridgeport was Republican Town Chairman John T. King, who convinced members of the Ancient Order of Hibernains, newly ensconced on Washington Avenue, to elect Clifford B. Wilson, an English descendant, mayor. Wilson served from 1911 to 1921 and many credit him as Bridgeport's most progressive mayor of all time. Bridgeport then was a horse-and-carriage town dependent on trolley car transportation. Anticipating the arrival of the automobile, Wilson took Bridgeport out of the dirt by paving most of the city. He also motorized the police and fire departments, built the city's first emergency medical clinic,

Denis Mulvihill, known as the stoker mayor, was Bridgeport's first workingman's mayor, laboring at the Wheeler and Wilson Sewing Machine Company. "Who made the world? Denny Mulvihill with his pick and shovel," was his rallying cry. Courtesy, City of Bridgeport

instituted dental programs in schools, developed Seaside Park, and established the city's Recreation Department.

One of the great Irish contributions to Bridgeport is St. Vincent's Hospital, organized by the Irish clergy in 1905 and staffed mostly by Irish-American doctors and nurses. The Irish also made a major contribution to Bridgeport's nightlife district, what Richard Howell, a reporter at the long-gone *Bridgeport Herald*, called "Bohemia," because city residents would wander in and out of the piano and fiddler music halls. At the turn of the century these establishments lined Middle and Water streets. Bill Sheridan was noted for his Black and Tan saloon, in which both blacks and whites congregated. The Alhambra Music Hall was run by Jimmy McNally, where Bert Green, one of the first ragtime pianists, performed. Morris

Above: *By the turn of the century, Bridgeport's electric trolley system began replacing the city's horse-drawn variety, and personified growth and modernization. Bridgeport's greater work force and factories had created the need for newer transportation. Courtesy, Historical Collections, Bridgeport Public Library*

Facing page: *The trusty Bridgeport Department of Public Works, two of its workers shown here in 1917 at Clinton and Fairfield avenues, was prepared for practically all sanitation emergencies. Photo by Lew Corbit, Sr. Courtesy, Historical Collections, Bridgeport Public Library*

King and Tom Tobin owned the Star Cafe, and George "Needles" Downing ran the Tremont Hotel (for a time the home of ex-bare knuckles champion John L. Sullivan).

Howell wrote that Water Street watering hole faithfuls would sometimes walk across the street and drop off the dock. "Some were fished out and some drifted out with the tide into Long Island Sound, never to be heard of again."

The Irish maintained a numerical leadership among all immigrant groups in Bridgeport for six decades (until about 1920, when the Italians surpassed them). By World War I, Bridgeport had become home to numerous other ethnic groups, including Germans, Lithuanians, Hungarians, and Poles. The immigrants had nothing more than enough money to reach Bridgeport, where they found little in the way of family and social services.

But work was their salvation and work they did. The firearm, brass, electrical, valve, and machine tool industries which catapulted Bridgeport to economic prominence were dependent largely on the labor of these ethnic groups. But practically every new group was subjected to cruel treatment due to their naivete and ignorance of the English language (particularly the German population, one of the city's leading ethnic groups). Often Ital-

Above: "Bohemia" is how newspaperman Richard Howell described Bridgeport saloons because people would wander in and out of the watering holes along Middle and Water streets, Bridgeport's nightlife district at the turn of the century. Courtesy, Robert Clifford Collection

Below: The Remington Arms plant, Bridgeport's massive anchor of the Arsenal of Democracy, was the largest factory complex in the United States. This photo, shot from Boston Avenue, shows the complex under construction in 1915. Photo by Lew Corbit, Sr. Courtesy, Historical Collections, Bridgeport Public Library

ians were victimized by the *padrone and barracks* system. On the promise that they would receive jobs, they were offered cramped housing in old carriage shops, which featured deplorable sanitary conditions and provisions at exorbitant prices. Special agents from the Department of Labor closed down such an operation in January 1900 at an old shop on Railroad Avenue, adjoining the Barnum & Bailey Circus winter headquarters.

Economic prosperity came to Bridgeport during the war years, sparked by the 1915 construction of the Remington Arms Company, which was born out of the Union Metallic Cartridge Company plant established in Bridgeport in 1867. When war broke out, the U.S. government capitalized on the arms plant and Bridgeport's labor force, which in less than a year built thirteen interconnected, five-story buildings on Boston Avenue and Bond Street. It became the largest single factory in the country, occupying 77.6 acres and covering 1,680,000 square feet. The Browning machine gun and Colt automatic pistol were manufactured at Remington Arms, which produced seven million rounds of ammunition a week, two-thirds of all ammunition produced in the United States for the allied forces. More than 20,000 people worked in the plant and Bridge-

The Union Metallic Cartridge Company, established in 1867, packed quite a wallop. When World War I broke out, the United States government capitalized on Bridgeport's labor force and backed the construction of the Remington Arms Company, which was born out of Union Metallic. Courtesy, Robert Clifford Collection

*This 1915 photo shows Bridgeport's Animal Rescue League
ambulance transporting a sick horse along Park Avenue. While
motorized vehicles were beginning to play a larger role in commerce and transportation, keeping horse power in shape was
still essential. Courtesy, Historical Collections, Bridgeport Public Library*

port became known as the Arsenal of Democracy of the industrial world.

Bridgeport's ethnic groups supported the war with an outburst of patriotism. But Bridgeport also suffered the pains of rapid growth. While tens of thousands flocked to Bridgeport for work, the city was the main target of labor's drive to go from a twelve- to an eight-hour work day. Roughly 100 strikes marred the city during the summer of 1915, with immigrant groups leading the revolt. The war boom caused a critical housing shortage, and the government pressed attics and basements into service. The Bridgeport Chamber of Commerce, established in 1915 from the Board of Trade (1876), organized the Bridgeport Housing Company, which built a series of war workers' housing projects. The U.S. Housing Corporation built 470 single- and multiple-family dwellings in Bridgeport, and created a local innovation: the one-family attached row house. Higher tax rates, increased property valuations, and growing bond issues were needed to finance additional schools, street lighting, police and fire protection, and expanded city services such as trolley lines to factories.

The great prosperity that propelled Bridgeport through the war years collapsed after the conflict ended. The loss of war orders sent the city into a slump. By 1920 the average hourly wage for unskilled labor—laborers, helpers, and handymen—had fallen to forty-six cents an hour. Toolmakers did better at eighty cents an hour, but female workers, whose positions in the manufacturing field included machine operators, inspectors, and assemblers, earned roughly thirty-seven cents an hour. For the first time in sixty years Bridgeport experienced a decline in immigration due to loss of available jobs and because of new government restrictions enacted in 1921 and 1924 limiting eastern and southern European immigration.

These restrictions left the Italians as the dominant population group in the city. Be-

tween 1890 and 1930, 80,000 Italians came to Connecticut. Like most of the immigrant groups, Italians, particularly those from southern Italy, came here primarily to escape homelessness and poor economic conditions. The arrival of the southern Italians triggered a rivalry which persists today among the various Italian groups, and in some parts of Bridgeport it still makes a big difference which province of Italy an Italian's mother or father came from. For instance, former Mayor Leonard Paoletta's family descends from Castelfranco, a mountain village about fifty miles northeast of Naples. The man Paoletta defeated in 1981, John Mandanici, was of Sicilian heritage. To this day there remains a competition between the two Italian provinces, and it was mirrored in the fire the two candidates breathed at each other during the 1981 mayoral campaign.

Italian-American Colonel Henry Mucci became Bridgeport's most honored World War II Army officer when he led 121 Rangers on a daring raid twenty-five miles into Japanese-occupied territory. Mucci and his men rescued 513 Allied troops from an enemy prison camp in the Philippines during the raid. In 1974 Bridgeport's section of Route 8 was named for him.

Bridgeport's population peaked at about 158,709 in 1950, but Mayor Jasper McLevy claimed a population of nearly 170,000 in the mid-1950s. The influx of blacks during and after World War II, and Hispanics in the fifties and sixties, accounted for the increase.

Bridgeport's immigrant groups organized many associations, such as the Ancient Order of Hibernians, The Bridgeport Deutsche Schulen, the Bridgeport Schwaben Veiren, The Germania Singing Society, St. Patrick's Society, the Danish Benevolent Society, The Trinacria Society, the Italian Community Center, and the Jewish Community Center. The ethnic groups also formed their own communities, in some respects preserving the ways of the

Fred Atwater, who defeated John T. King's machine in 1921, is something of a trivia question. He has the distinction of being Bridgeport's last one-term mayor. King received a measure of revenge in 1923 when William Behrens (facing page), a butcher by trade, defeated Atwater for the first of his three terms. Courtesy, City of Bridgeport

old country. In the early 1900s, for example, the Park City had seven different newspapers published in Italian, three in Hungarian, and one each in German, Yiddish, and Slovak.

Father Stephen J. Panik, born in Slovakia in 1893, came to Bridgeport in 1912 and be-came a determined advocate for housing the poor and the working class. Father Panik, the pastor of Saints Cyril and Methodius Roman Catholic Church, was named chairman of the newly formed Bridgeport Housing Authority in 1936 and led the establishment of the Fa-

Stephen J. Panik was born in Slovakia in 1893. He came to Bridgeport in 1912 and took over for his cousin Gaspar at St. Cyril & Methodius Roman Catholic Church in 1933. Panik served the church for twenty years till his death on November 22, 1953. Father Panik was the man behind the Father Panik Village Housing Project for the poor. The project was completed in 1941. Photo by B. Brignolo, Brignolo Studios. Courtesy, Historical Collections, Bridgeport Public Library

ther Panik Village housing project in 1941. In the 1930s, the East Side neighborhood bounded by Hamilton Street and Crescent, Pembroke, and Waterview avenues—known as Hell's Kitchen—suffered from unacceptably high housing density and was noted as a high-risk fire hazard. Backed by federal money, several city blocks were cleared to immediately upgrade apartment housing and living conditions for thousands. The housing project opened as Yellow Mill Village, but years later Panik's success would deteriorate into a crime-ridden complex.

Other past examples of the city's wide-ranging ethnic flavor include the White Eagles, a Polish semipro baseball team; Syrian and Lebanese stores that featured Arabic food; and South End Greek candy stores and restaurants. The Hungarian community, the second largest in the country, played gypsy music in restaurants in the West End, the section of the city once called Hunk Town. Some of the foreign flavor dissolved as families moved to the suburbs and as ethnic groups adopted American lifestyles. But the city has managed to retain a large part of its ethnic flavor. The new wave of refugees is a result of the U.S. government's policy of granting political refugee status almost exclusively to people from Communist nations. Bridgeport now has six Vietnamese stores, a Korean food store, a Cuban bakery, and a Ukrainian arts and crafts shop.

These neighborhoods have sown a crop of unique foreign-born characters. A Bridgeport tradition of many years' standing finds foreign-born Italians, Portuguese, and Hungarians lined alongside the railroad tracks on Housatonic Avenue waiting for grape vendors during the fall wine-making season. These old-fashioned wine brewers with their caps and baggy pants drive out in their pickup trucks and station wagons to buy grapes to make wine, continuing a family tradition. They wait for Joseph Visconti, who's sold the California grapes for

seventeen years, to open his thirty-foot trailer so they can sample the grapes and slip him orders on pieces of paper, because many of them do not speak English.

The South End has the city's heralded smiling hot dog man Skirmantas Rastas, whose family left economically-ruined Lithuania for the United States in 1949. Rastas is renowned for selling thousands of hot dogs each year at Pleasure Beach, Seaside Park, Beardsley Park, and from his other concession stands in the city. Another side of Rastas shows his talent for turning depressed tenements into restored Victorian gingerbreads, helping to rejuvenate Bridgeport's South End.

Bridgeport's neighborhoods have remained a bargain bazaar. The Park City still offers fifty- to seventy-five-cent beers at neighborhood bars such as Dolan's Corner, the Shamrock Pub, the Bon Ton, and Sol's Cafe—and together they reflect the city's ethnic mix.

The city has had its share of ethnic tensions in various overcrowded neighborhoods, however. In 1981, as Laotians moved into an East Side Puerto Rican neighborhood, a fire set in an apartment building killed a Laotian woman. The Laotians blamed the Puerto Ricans, but differences were settled through the help of the International Institute of Connecticut. This social agency grew from the YWCA (formed circa 1900) with a mission to relocate foreign-born women. Today the Bridgeport agency aids hundreds of refugees and immigrants each year through counseling, resettlement, employment, job training, language education, and a wide variety of other social services.

The U.S. Immigration and Naturalization Service no longer keeps a breakdown on immigrants entering Connecticut, but Myra Oliver, executive director of the International Institute, says her agency serves populations from sixty different nationalities. "We in Bridgeport help the foreign-born," says Oliver. "Bridgeport is still a city of immigrants."

Another Bridgeport institution who has been around longer than most can remember is Lew Corbit of Corbit's Studio. The studio was founded in 1900 by Lewis H. Corbit, Sr., and Lew Corbit has been following in his father's footsteps since 1934, recording Bridgeport's growth and people. Courtesy, Corbit's Studio

Just as today, schools at the turn of the century had school bands. The Lincoln School Band seen here circa 1900 wasn't a typical school band as known today, but was a Fife and Drum Corps. If you look carefully you'll see that the band members have fifes under their arms. Courtesy, Robert Clifford Collection

CHAPTER III
Spirit, Mind, and Voice

"No Fear—No Favor—We Do Our Part—The People's Paper"
—Bridgeport Herald *slogan*

The immigrant groups that settled in Bridgeport arrived with deep religious feelings that had accompanied them through their lives of poverty, war-born dislocation, and political unrest. Today, Bridgeport has some 150 churches, synagogues, and missions that link its people to their cultures and communities.

Bridgeport's early churches were Congregational, Episcopal, and Baptist. Methodism came to Bridgeport in 1789. The first Catholic Mass was said in 1830 and the first Catholic church dedicated in 1843. The first Universalist church was organized in 1845; the Presbyterian church was founded in 1853; the first Jewish congregation was established in 1859; and the first Lutheran church opened in 1887.

While Bridgeport's church activities are today generally confined to services, prayer, and an occasional evening of church-basement bingo, the church in the days of the Yankee settlers served an additional, quite different function. The church was the most important building in the community—a sort of all-purpose center. Prayers were said, psalms read, town meetings conducted, disputes settled. Basically, any and every problem that involved the community was aired in the church or meetinghouse. Church officers were appointed, including tax collectors, a treasurer, a school committee, a constable, a secretary, and selectmen, who set taxes which supported the church and school. The constable was the busiest town official. He chased after thieves, Sabbath breakers, and those who spent too much time drinking. But for many years this would be the spot where all local affairs were settled.

In 1695 the community, then called Fairfield Village, erected the First Church of Christ in Stratfield. The church's dedication came the year after the community had estab-

lished its first school, and the church was built for similar reasons. Since the settlers who lived in Fairfield Village, between Fairfield and Stratford, were troubled by the difficult trips to either town to attend church, the legislature granted approval for them to build their own house of worship. The new building was on Park Avenue, and the Reverend Charles Chauncey became the first pastor. He was a busy one at that, baptizing more than 400 children. In those days, the booming sound of a drum summoned people to church, until bells were installed in 1774. Church services during the winter months could get uncomfortable in the cold, drafty, and unheated meetinghouse, especially when the sermon ran three to five hours, as it did on occasion. This church was the predecessor of today's United Congregational at Park Avenue and State Street, making it the oldest church in Bridgeport.

In the 1800s Broad Street became known as Church Row. The churches shown in this circa 1836 woodcut are, from left to right: the First Congregational or North Church, built 1807; St. John's Episcopal, built 1801; and the Second Congregational Church, built in 1830. Woodcut by John Warner Barber. Courtesy, Historical Collections, Bridgeport Public Library

Below: *Founded in 1807, the First Congregational Church (First Church of Christ in Stratfield) is the oldest in the city. In 1830 the congregation split and a group formed the Second Congregational Church. By 1916, differences had been settled and the United Congregational was formed. The church above is the First Congregational or Old North Church as it appeared around 1910. The church was built in 1850. Courtesy, Historical Collections, Bridgeport Public Library*

Above: *Though the original church was built in 1748, this 1888 interior photo of St. John's Episcopal shows the structure built in 1873-75 on Fairfield Avenue. In early Bridgeport, churches were the most important building in town. Town meetings were held, town officials were appointed, and disputes were settled in those meeting places. Courtesy, Historical Collections, Bridgeport Public Library*

Walter W. Curtis has served as Bishop of the Diocese of Bridgeport since 1961. In 1963 Bishop Curtis led a drive to establish a commuter college now familiar to all as Sacred Heart University. Photo by Frank W. Decerbo. Courtesy, Post Publishing Company

The second church in the area, St. John's Episcopal, founded in 1748, now stands on Fairfield Avenue. The First Baptist Church was erected in 1837 on Broad Street and now is located on Washington Avenue. It has increased neighborhood minority attendance through a department which ministers to Spanish-speaking worshippers. The emergence of many churches by 1837 produced Bridgeport's "Church Row" on Broad Street. In succession came the Second Congregational, the First Baptist, the First Congregational, the Episcopal, and the Methodist churches.

Today Walter W. Curtis, Bishop of the Diocese of Bridgeport (which encompasses all of Fairfield County) is the spiritual leader of some 325,000 Catholics, the most populous of all Bridgeport denominations. The Diocese of Bridgeport was formed from the Diocese of Hartford by Pope Pius XII in September 1953. The Most Reverend Lawrence J. Shehan, auxiliary bishop of Baltimore, was named the first bishop.

Bridgeport's first Catholic mass was celebrated by Father James Fitton of Boston in the Middle Street home of James McCullough, a leader of the tiny Irish colony which dedicated St. James Church in 1843. St. James became the predecessor of St. Augustine Cathedral, the seat of the Diocese of Bridgeport, after the construction of the new church on Washington Avenue in 1868. The first members of Bridgeport's Irish community are buried in St. James Cemetery on Grove Street.

In 1874, three Roman Catholic churches served Bridgeport: St. Augustine's; St. Mary's on Pembroke Street, built in 1857; and St. Joseph's on Catherine Street, built in 1874. As the new century approached, the Catholic population surge resulted in the construction of several new churches, including St. Michael the Archangel on Pulaski Street and St. Patrick's on North Avenue, both built in 1889; St. John Nepomucene on Jane Street in 1891; and St. Anthony of Padua on Colorado Avenue in 1892.

By 1930, Bridgeport had more than 100 houses of worship, their congregations working and sacrificing for several years, dependent on local support and contributions from the numerous ethnic groups.

The Hungarians formed The Hungarian Reformed Church in 1894, and the Lithuanian St. George's Church on Park Avenue was chartered in 1859. But recent times have seen many churches renovated, dissolved, moved, or displaced because of industrial development. Many minority congregations have purchased vacated church buildings or erected their own. Messiah Baptist, a black-congregation church on Arch Street, was replaced by an $800,000 building a short distance from the Arch Street church that was razed during the Congress Street redevelopment program in the 1960s. The oldest black church in Bridgeport is Bethel African Methodist Episcopal Church on Grove Street, formed in 1826 by blacks who had escaped southern slavery and found refuge in Bridgeport before Abraham Lincoln's Emancipation Proclamation.

*   *   *

Founded in 1826, the Bethel African Methodist Episcopal Church is the oldest black-congregation church in Bridgeport. Now located on Grove Street, the church was formed by escaped slaves from southern states. Photo by Neil Swanson

The formation of the first school followed the same pattern as the first church's establishment. In 1650, the Connecticut Code of

Now a Park Avenue garage complete with a basketball hoop, this simple one-room building is thought to be the oldest existing schoolhouse in the United States. It was built in 1738 in Fairfield County and the last teacher there was Ellen M. Spear. Courtesy, Historical Collections, Bridgeport Public Library

Laws required that every township of fifty or more households must provide a school where children could learn to read and write. The Village of Pequonnock was far from either Fairfield or Stratford, so before 1678, the children of Pequonnock had to travel several miles to one of those towns to attend school. Parents, in particular, grew tired of the long trips, so the general court allowed them to organize their own school, which had forty-seven students the first year. The villagers were responsible for funding the institution, which had a curriculum and disciplinary standards that make today's standards seem lax.

Students not only had to haul their books to school, they had to supply wood for fuel. Failure to bring wood to school led to merciless teachers banishing pupils to the coldest, darkest corner of the schoolroom. School days, including Saturdays, were generally eight hours of long, constant work. No study halls, no physical education, no nap periods. The children of the colonists were first required to learn the alphabet, syllables, and the Lord's Prayer from a "hornbook," a thin piece of wood about five inches long and two inches wide which had a cover sheet of printed letters. The printed page was covered with a thin sheet of yellowish horn which allowed the letters to be read. A strip of brass fastened the paper and the horn to the wood, which had a string hole so the hornbook could be carried around the pupil's neck or to the side.

Most students wouldn't dare cheat or talk out of place. Breaking those rules brought swift consequences, not easily forgotten. Schoolmasters were ruthless and had many a torture tool, including the birch rod, the walnut stick, and a stick with heavy leather straps. Perhaps the most feared was the flapper, a piece of heavy leather with a hole in the middle. When the flapper came down, a blister the size of the hole was raised on the flesh. Whipping the soles of students' feet, forcing them to sit on a unipod, or gagging them with a stick were other disciplinary methods.

Punishment became less severe as the school system progressed. By 1796, when the settlement was known as Stratfield, three schools had been erected, funded by money given to Connecticut from the sale of lands in Pennsylvania and Ohio to repay losses in the Revolutionary War. By 1876, Bridgeport's eleven school districts, which collected their own taxes, were consolidated under one governing body—the Board of Education. H.M. Harrington served the first of his fourteen years on the board as superintendent of schools.

The new management didn't waste any time upgrading the school system. New schools were needed during the school board's early days, but until it overcame a cash flow problem, stores and dwellings were rented as temporary classrooms. Within one year, a public high school opened on Prospect Street with Charles D. Peck serving as principal. Two

The Prospect School was built in 1877-88 on Prospect Street and by the turn of the century it held grades one through eight. In 1963 the school was demolished as part of Mayor Samuel Tedesco's downtown redevelopment project. Courtesy, Historical Collections, Bridgeport Public Library

The forty-three ninth grade students from room five in this photo (1898) are an indication of the overcrowding the city's schools experienced at the turn of the century. The huge increases by 1899 caused the Board of Apportionment to order a yearly tax of one mill to fund new schools. Courtesy, Historical Collections, Bridgeport Public Library

years later a training school for teachers was housed in the same building.

The Board of Apportionment in February 1899 passed a resolution ordering a tax of one mill to erect buildings for educational uses. By 1920, Bridgeport's school board had moved into its new quarters at 45 Lyon Terrace (the present site of City Hall). It instituted medical inspection and free kindergartens, built fire escapes in schools, and built a high school on Congress Street, known years later as Congress Junior High School. Still, Bridgeport schools were overcrowded during World War I from the mass of immigrant children. In the 1920s, married female teachers struggled against a school board ruling that married women whose husbands earned a decent living could not be kept in the system. Superintendent of Schools Carroll Reed suggested that married teachers were motivated by a desire for luxuries.

Classes in the thirties and forties, although cramped, offered some much-needed harmony from the discord of the Depression and World War II. Ukulele clubs, harmonica bands, and boys' glee clubs were formed. Students from Maplewood School aided the war effort by manning war bond booths and packing Christmas boxes for USO distribution to armed services hospitals. In the late 1950s, severe overcrowding in the three city high schools forced the school board to inform students from Trumbull and Monroe that Bridgeport could no longer accomodate them. Mayor Jasper McLevy was criticized for continued slashing of the educational budget, which left schools in disrepair and teacher salaries low. But, the 1960s saw more school construction resulting in four new facilities: the Read, Blackham, Roosevelt, and Columbus schools. The influx of blacks and Hispanics drastically changed the composition of the student population, and busing was implemented.

These events of the 1970s perhaps affected the school system more than any other municipal department. School officials found themselves explaining why city tests scores were among the worst in the state. A desegregation suit brought against the city by the NAACP, the Spanish-American Coalition, and many parents, forced U.S. District Court Judge Ellen Bree Burns to oversee ten years of sweeping changes to complete racial balance in the schools' population. In July 1976 Geraldine Johnson was named the first black superintendent of schools; two years later she came face to face with the longest teachers' strike in Connecticut history when Mayor John C. Mandanici couldn't make progress in negotiating a new contract. After repeated warnings to return to work, the Superior Court ordered 200 teachers to jail. They were incarcerated at

Camp Hartell, a National Guard facility in Windsor Locks, Connecticut, for thirteen days until they agreed to return to work.

"The strike was the saddest event in Bridgeport educational history," said James Connelly, the present superintendent of schools. "The school system hit rock bottom."

Fallout from the strike included the transfer of about 1,000 Bridgeport students from public to private schools. The strike was instrumental, however, in the passage of a binding arbitration law to prevent future teacher strikes.

Today the Bridgeport school system administers 20,000 students, thirty-one elementary schools, three high schools, three alternative schools, and one special education facility, all sharing a yearly budget of fifty million dollars.

Bridgeport's college days began in 1927, when Dr. E. Everett Cortright, Dr. Alfred C. Fones, and James H. Halsey pushed for the

Originally the Bridgeport High School built in 1882, this building served as the Congress Junior High School after the new Bridgeport High School was constructed on Lyon Terrace in 1916. Courtesy, Historical Collections, Bridgeport Public Library

formation of the Junior College of Connecticut. These men took the lead in raising money for the school, recruiting students and faculty, and developing educational opportunities. In 1947 with an enrollment of 3,000, the school was rechartered as the University of Bridgeport, and three years later all operations were moved to a twenty-two-acre campus at Seaside Park. Today the university boasts a law school and the Carlson Library, named after longtime benefactors William and Philip Carlson, founders of the Metropolitan Body Company.

In 1963, the Most Reverend Walter W. Curtis, Bishop of Bridgeport, led the drive to establish a commuter college for students who chose not to attend boarding schools. Sacred Heart University, on north Park Avenue near the Bridgeport line in Fairfield, has since served as an ideal opportunity for students outside Bridgeport to attend a university nearer their homes. In addition, Fairfield University, founded as part of the Fairfield College Preparatory School started by the Society of Jesus in 1942, has become one of the finest institutions of higher learning in the country.

Mirroring the formation of community colleges around the country in the 1960s, the Stratford Board of Education and the State Commissioner of Higher Education established Housatonic Community College in 1966. It operated from Bunnell High School in Stratford before relocating to the former Singer Building on Barnum Avenue in Bridgeport. The college won immediate cultural acclaim through its founding of the Housatonic Museum of Art.

The one Bridgeport institution of learning that transcends all others is the Bridgeport Public Library at Broad and State streets. The library, headquartered in the Burroughs Building, is the largest library system in Connecticut, containing 500,000 volumes. About 40,000 people pass through the doors of the downtown building each month to visit the reference and newspaper rooms, the children's department, the Popular Library, and the exhibition areas. The Klein Porcelain Room displays Chinese porcelain, paintings, etchings, and a Rembrandt, all donated by former library director Milton Klein. The library's Henry A. Bishop Room has been the home of the Historical Collections for fifty years, and the technology and business department is one of the finest in New England. The city's library system includes four neighborhood branches and a bookmobile.

The Bridgeport library system grew out of the urging of twelve-year-old Stiles Middlebrook, who wrote in 1830 "that some source of reading material should be at the disposal of the people of Bridgeport." Middlebrook would slip such letters under the office door of the *Weekly Farmer,* which published them. The immediate result was the formation of a library on Wall Street by a group of city leaders led by Alanson Hamlin, the foremost lawyer of the city. The Bridgeport Library Association was formed in 1850 and city leaders such as P.T. Barnum, Hanford Lyon, Philo C. Calhoun, and Frederick Wood regularly donated books and thousands of dollars to the library. Within twenty years, the library had 8,500 books and dozens of newspapers and magazines as it settled into its new quarters in the Wheeler Building at Main and Fairfield, built by Nathaniel Wheeler of the Wheeler and Wilson Sewing Machine Company. In 1883, Catharine Burroughs Pettengill, whose father had made a fortune through his fleet of vessels in foreign trade, willed $100,000 toward the construction of a new library. The current

Originally founded in 1880, the Bridgeport Public Library's first permanent home was in the Burroughs building (pictured here circa 1880) on the corner of Main and John Street. Now the largest public library in Connecticut, it is housed today at Broad Street in a building erected in 1927. Courtesy, Historical Collections, Bridgeport Public Library

Before occupying the top three floors of the Burroughs building, the Bridgeport Public Library was located temporarily in the Wheeler building at Main and Fairfield. The circulation room seen here in the Burroughs building circa 1890 was one of the many specialty rooms. Courtesy, Historical Collections, Bridgeport Public Library

Facing page, top right and bottom: What is today known as the Dinan Center was once called the Hillside Home Hospital. Founded in 1915, a survey by the National Civic Federation called it "an outstanding example of the trend toward scientific and humane care for the destitute poor." Half of the inmates were foreign born. The hospital, seen here circa 1917, was virtually fireproof and had it's own kitchen, laundry, bake shop, and barber shop. Superintendent of the Department of Public Welfare Anges P. Thorne was praised by Mayor Fred Atwater for the facility's operation. In 1930 the average patient population was 314. Courtesy, Historical Collections, Bridgeport Public Library

federal-style building was completed in 1927.

Catharine Pettengill also co-founded Bridgeport Hospital along with two other women, Frances Pomeroy and Susan Hubbell. The women acted in response to an urgent call by Dr. George F. Lewis for an institution to handle accident cases and serious illnesses. City patients had been cared for in the basement of what later became police headquarters. The new hospital opened in November 1884, with P.T. Barnum as the first president and Dr. Lewis as the first physician in charge. That first year 148 patients were treated. Now the 650-bed facility annually treats some 23,000 patients. The hospital is acclaimed for its burn unit and its link with the Rehabilitation Center of Eastern Fairfield County formed in 1935.

St. Vincent's Medical Center formally opened on June 28, 1905, following a call for a new Catholic hospital. Ann Bohan, a par-

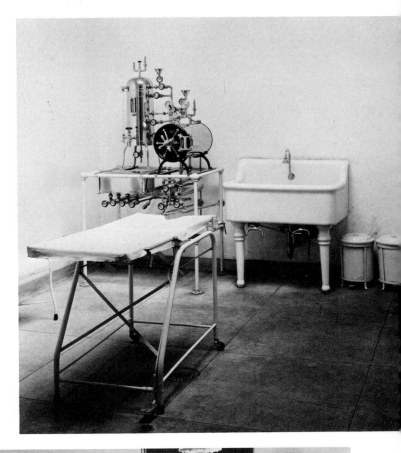

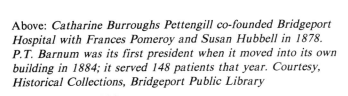
Above: *Catharine Burroughs Pettengill co-founded Bridgeport Hospital with Frances Pomeroy and Susan Hubbell in 1878. P.T. Barnum was its first president when it moved into its own building in 1884; it served 148 patients that year. Courtesy, Historical Collections, Bridgeport Public Library*

BRIDGEPORT HERALD.

VOL. 9. No. 581.   BRIDGEPORT, CONN. SUNDAY, NOV. 17, 1901.   PRICE FIVE CENTS.

THE LARGEST CIRCULATION IN THE STATE.

FLYING MACHINE FACTORY
THE LATEST OF
BRIDGEPORT'S INDUSTRIES

Gustave Whitehead, Inventor of Only Practical Air Ship, Engaged in Building Soaring Carriage Which Will Be Placed on the Market in Spring and Sell For About the Same Price That a High Grade Automobile Brings. Night and Day Forces Working. Fifteen Mechanics and Two Engineers Employed at the Flying Machine Works.

ADMITTANCE TO SHOP REFUSED.

New York Man of Money Backing the Project and Already $10,000 Has Been Placed at the Disposal of the Inventor A Good Family Machine With Seating Capacity For Six Will Cost About $2,000. Inventor Whitehead Will Fly From Bridgeport to New York

WILL USE NEW MOTIVE POWER.

IF THE PLANS of his financial backer materialize and the indications are that they will, Gustave Whitehead, the flying machine inventor will shortly experience the pleasure of having his product manufactured on a large scale and Bridgeport will win the distinction of possessing the most unique and modern industry in the whole civilized world.

Upwards of $10,000 have already been expended by the capitalists who have interested themselves in Mr. Whitehead believing as he does himself that the problem of aerial navigation has been solved. It would be foolhardy to presume that Mr. Whitehead could succeed in obtaining such an amount of capital without first giving the possessing of some assurances that his invention had reached the state of perfection.

No one realizes any more than Mr. Whitehead himself that the general...

RADICAL CHANGE IN BRIDGEPORT'S
STREET CAR SERVICE PROPOSED

Connecticut Railway and Lighting Company May Inaugurate the Pole System of Making Stops Belief That Better Time Can be Made With This System in Force.

FOR THE PUBLIC TO DECIDE.

FRIEND PROVES FALSE
AND HUSBAND SUES

Walter M. Conway Sues Arthur Gross for $25,000 Damages For Alienation of His Wife's Affections.

FAMOUS IRONMASTER
TWISTED IN ROMANCE

(Special to the Herald.)
NEW YORK, Nov. 16.

WALTER M. CONWAY, proprietor of the largest summer hotel in Bethel Haven, Conn., and who is said to have inherited more than $1,000,000 from his father, who was one of the best known men in the wholesale dry goods district at the time of his death, has brought suit for absolute divorce and also one for $25,000 damages for alienation of his wife's affections against Arthur Gross, who is a member of the Greenwich summer colony.

Gross is an insurance adjuster in this city and is wealthy in his own right having inherited $250,000. It is said from the estate of his father, the late Peter Gross, who was an ironmaster.

VISITED THEATER,
SAW ELOPEMENT,
FOLLOWED SUIT

Miss Beulah Shelley and William V. Leary Weaved Impressed With an Elopement They Saw at the Theater That They Went Straightaway to a Minister and Were Made One.

BRIDE'S MOTHER WAS
FORGIVING BUT PAPA
WAS HOT AT FIRST

Wedding Had Been Set for Easter But the Young People Took Time by Both Forelocks and Stole a March on Well Laid Plans.

BRIDE RETURNS TO
FORMER POSITION

DROPPED DEAD,
DELIRIUM TREMENS

Child Saw Her Father Fall to the Floor and Asked Ambulance Surgeon if He Would Soon be Well Again.

FRANK DARK A
HARD DRINKER

FRANK DARK, a Slavonian, died of delirium tremens at his home, 175 Church street, Bridgeport, shortly after two o'clock last night.

THE REPUBLICAN MACHINE
WAS HOT AFTER
DIRECTOR WILLIAMS HEAD

They Had Him at the Atlantic Hotel Where They Tried to Force Him to Resign So That Merle Cowles Could Succeed Him.

He Turned Them Down

The Machine Men Pointed Out to Him That He Would Have to Go and That Merle Cowles, if Made Director By Mayor Stirling Might Hold the Office By Not Leaving Himself Liable For Charges of Any Kind. Mr. Williams Was Firm and Held On.

THERE IS A Republican politician in Bridgeport who has the least bit of sympathy for Director of Public Works Williams. Herald reporters were unable to find...

DIRECTOR WILLIAMS

ishioner of St. Patrick's Church, willed $14,000 to the Reverend J.B. Nihill for the new hospital. The facility was the first in Bridgeport to adopt an eight-hour work schedule for nurses instead of the customary twelve-hour work day. The hospital today is a 391-bed facility. Park City Hospital, organized in 1926, has grown from a tiny 35-bed unit to a larger 200-bed facility. All three hospitals care for Bridgeport and the surrounding communities, including Fairfield, Westport, Easton, Trumbull, Monroe, and Stratford.

* * *

Bridgeport has been a newspaper town since Lazarus Beach, a local Stratfield printer, decided villagers needed a documented source to spread gossip about new bridges, stores, and streets. In 1795 he established the weekly *American Telegraph and Fairfield County Gazette* which was distributed by riders on horseback. Subscriptions sold for $1.50 a year and the circulation was about 800.

Bridgeport's first daily paper was the *Republican Farmer,* founded in 1810. Just about everything was recorded with a touch of Yankee humor. The front page was one gray mass of poetry and advertising, and daily events generally were reserved for pages two and three. Pictures and fancy layouts were light-years away—this paper didn't even have headlines. In a typical edition of the 1830s, residents saw an ad plugging "Dr. Bowen's remedy for the piles," and a few columns away appeared a story about rats as big as cats creating havoc. "No devices which human ingenuity can plan for their destruction have been left untried," proclaimed the paper. Numerous ads selling flour, cheeses, guns, boots, and saddles covered the rest of the front page. Page two might have covered a local fire, a shipwreck in Cape Cod, or a flight of locusts ravaging the East Indies.

Soon many papers sprouted in Bridgeport,

some for a brief time only, including the *Connecticut Courier* in 1810, the *Bridgeport Republican* in 1830, the *Spirit of the Times* in 1831 (later the *Bridgeport Standard*), and the *Bridgeport Chronicle* in 1848.

Bridgeport had many other dailies and weeklies that passed quickly. When the newsprint settled in the 1920s, four newspapers competed for supremacy: *The Farmer,* the *Times-Star* (consolidated from the *Times* and *Star* in 1926), the *Bridgeport Sunday Herald* (est. 1890), and the *Bridgeport Post* (est. 1883). News carriers were sure never to drop off the wrong paper on someone's doorstep, as each paper was easily distinguishable by its own distinctive style.

The Farmer retained much of the early-day flavor, the *Time-Star* was known for its diverse sports section, and *The Bridgeport Post* succeeded on its local coverage. But the paper everyone talked about, even if they hated it, was the *Herald.* Richard Howell, the paper's editor and publisher for more than twenty years, was noted for his intriguing sports writing and his reports on Bridgeport's nightlife. His 1928 book, *Tales from Bohemia Land,* chronicled Bridgeport's tavern characters as seen by their drinking partner, Richard Howell. In 1929, the paper was sold to Leigh Danenberg, whose daring news style, exposure of Bridgeport corruption, and campaigning for governmental change catapulted the *Herald*'s reputation as a scandal sheet. "No Fear—No Favor—We Do Our Part—The People's Paper," boasted the front page slogan.

Danenberg owned the paper, but Harry Neigher was "Mr. Herald." His column, "Bridgeport Night Life," appeared for forty-two years and jabbed at every gin mill, every celebrity, and every socialite divorce in town. When the legendary mobster Dutch Schultz took residence at the Stratfield Hotel, Neigher cracked, "Dutch Schultz has given the Bridgeport Police Department 24 hours to get out of town."

Such columns lured residents right from church to line up outside the *Herald* plant on Lafayette Street, listening for the pounding of the presses and smelling the wet ink while waiting for the day's edition. The newspaper did not maintain popularity with advertisers, however, and ceased publication in 1974, leaving *The Bridgeport Post* as the dominant paper in the city. The *Post* and its sister papers *The Telegram* and *The Sunday Post* flourish as the city's family newspapers, reporting a heavy dose of local news ranging from city government and civic groups to teen-age birthday parties. The only smidgen of local competition for the *Post* comes from the *Fairfield County Advocate*. The *Advocate* is an iconoclastic weekly, part of a chain of alternative papers based in Hatfield, Massachusetts. Its inclination towards muckraking—clearly extreme from the mainstream approach of the *Post*—has led it to take on some of the city's powerful interests (including the *Post* itself). Some people see it as the *Herald* reborn. However, in 1984, the *Advocate* toned down its rebel image and increased its arts coverage.

The early sketches of Bridgeport's two most famous cartoonists appeared for many years in the *Post*. Al Capp, born Alfred C. Caplan, attended Bridgeport High School and ten years later, during a hitchhiking trip through the South, won inspiration for his "Li'l Abner," which was syndicated by hundreds of newspapers. Warren Harding High School graduate Walt Kelly, employed by the *Post* as a cartoonist, later used many Bridgeporter names in his "Pogo" series, created while he drew for the *New York Star* in 1943. Kelly's P.T. Bridgeport, an arrogant swamp creature in a straw hat, caricatured Bridgeport's first citizen, P.T. Barnum. Kelly died in 1973 and "Pogo" was continued by his wife, Selby Kelly, until 1975.

Radio came to Bridgeport in 1926 with the founding of radio station WICC (call letters Industrial Center of Connecticut), which remains the most popular station in Bridgeport. Depression-era radio filled the airwaves with logs of local programming. A typical day would include *Bridgeport Post-Telegram* news flashes, record-request hours, live performances by the Chocolate Dandies Orchestra, and performances by local baritone Thomas Wall or pianist Patsy Stoccatore. Mayors Edward T. Buckingham and Jasper McLevy would highlight municipal affairs. One highly-acclaimed show, hosted by Sheriff Edward A. Platt, featured an all-talent show for inmates direct from the local jail which was heralded for improving inmate morale. Some listeners even responded with job offers to first offenders.

WICC and newcomer WNAB (now WJBX), founded in 1941, were fierce competitors on the early airwaves. An underground railroad seemingly connected the two, as many of the popular disk jockeys worked first for one station and then the other. Since New York radio played a big factor, Bridgeport had its share of radio successes due to the competition. Bob Crane, who later found stardom with television's *Hogan's Heroes,* was Bridgeport's most famous disk jockey of the 1950s. Crane added a new dimension to radio, interjecting one-liners between record-spinning. Crane also played the drums and often talked his way into performing with bands at the Pleasure Beach Ballroom. Crane left WICC for Los Angeles and *Hogan's Heroes* in the mid-1960s.

The big items in the fifties and sixties were Dick Alexander, one of the few black announcers of the time and an announcer with a large teen audience; and Alan Brown, an Arthur Godfrey sound-alike who insisted Godfrey imitated him. At present, Bridgeport's most famous voice is Tiny Markle, whose orchestra played frequently at the Pleasure Beach Ballroom in the 1950s before he entered radio as a record spinner, later to become the long-time talk show host for WNAB and now for WICC.

Tiny Markle, whose band played at the Pleasure Beach Ballroom in the 1950s, is Bridgeport's most famous voice. In 1926 WICC (Industrial Center of Connecticut) was founded to provide the city's listeners with news flashes, live broadcasts, and music by request. Photo by Dennis Bradbury

Bridgeport's first adventure into television came in the mid-1950s. Radio station WICC operated a UHF television station, but since UHF television was almost nonexistent and an adaptor was needed for fine tuning, the station had few viewers. WICC's owner, Ken Cooper, appealed to the Federal Communications Commission to take the station off the air until a new buyer was found, because the station had no viewers. The FCC wasn't convinced. To prove his point, Cooper hired Bob Crane to go on the air and hold up a $100 bill. The first person to call the station, said Crane, would win the $100. No one called.

Within a few weeks a trade publication ad proclaimed: "Television station WICC has proven conclusively that it has no viewers." The station was taken off the air.

Jenny Lind, a great mid-nineteenth century soprano, was lured to America to tour for P.T. Barnum to establish him as a legitimate cultural empressario. Barnum's advance publicity turned out thousands to greet Lind when she arrived in New York in late 1850. Courtesy, Historical Collections, Bridgeport Public Library

CHAPTER IV

Barnum's the Name

"There's a sucker born every minute"

—*origin unknown*

"The Prince of humbug," they called him. "The Shakespeare of advertising," "the king of adjectives." He was a man with a genius for inspiring lucrative curiosity, like a circus parade lures spectators to the paid admission of the big top. He could convince hundreds of thousands to step right up and inspect the 160-year-old nurse of George Washington, the bearded lady, the smallest man in the world. With whirlwind tours of circus freaks, exotic animals, and human feats, he cranked out humbug by the yard.

Phineas Taylor Barnum knew better than anyone else in creation that every crowd had a silver (dollar) lining. Barnum was the master myth maker, and he's still a favorite subject of playwrights and authors because he was so up-front and amiable about his humbuggery. "There's a sucker born every minute," is a Barnum quote entrenched in cliche history. Now nearly 100 years after his death it's in some ways fitting and in other ways sad that he is most esteemed and credited for that often-parroted apocryphal expression. If he ever said it, no historian has ever been able to document it. The statement may have found its place as a corruption of a Barnum suggestion or attributed to Barnum by one of his circus rivals.

The real legacy of Barnum—showman, circus innovator, author, philosopher, humanitarian, public servant, humorist, and even Bridgeport mayor—has been clouded over by the obfuscation of the man's many promotions. That old huckster impression lingering these many years overshadows his contributions to the entertainment profession and to Bridgeport. But as Barnum said, "I don't care what they say about me if they only say something."

Beneath the charm and extravagance of his circus persona is a man whose contributions to Bridgeport are unmatched. Barnum is quite simply the single most important contributor to the city's history. He developed thousands of acres of city property, converting farm and pasture land into choice building lots; enabled the working class to purchase land and houses through an innovative payment system; donated a large part of Seaside Park, one of the first waterfront parks in the country; attracted numerous manufacturing companies; served as the president of Bridgeport Hospital, the local water company, and the Pequonnock Bank (a predessesor of Connecticut National); donated the money to establish the Barnum Museum; established Mountain Grove Cemetery; and provided funding for Bridgeport schools, the library system, parks, and other civic ventures. Another side of Barnum was his drive to grant blacks the right to vote and his sympathy for the woman's rights movement.

Bridgeport's first citizen is best explained by his biographer A.H. Saxon: "P.T. Barnum has the paradoxical distinction of being one of America's best-known least-understood phenomena."

*　　　*　　　*

East Bridgeport was P.T. Barnum's "pet" project. He wanted to remind anyone who passed through the East Side that he had planned the district. There's Barnum Avenue; Hallett Street (the maiden name of his first

wife, Charity); and Caroline, Helen, and Pauline streets, named for three of his daughters. Noble Avenue is named for Barnum's land developer partner, William Noble. In 1851, five years after Barnum took up residence in the city following his discovery of Charles Stratton (Tom Thumb), Barnum purchased a tract of farmland from Noble. Together they laid out streets, reserved several acres for a park (Washington Park), and initiated the sale of lots. For the next two decades Barnum urged people to invest in a new home and offered a unique incentive. "It is evident," Barnum commented in the *Bridgeport Standard,* "that if the money expended in rent can be paid towards the purchase of a house and lot, the person so paying will in a few years own the house he lives in, instead of always remaining a tenant."

Anyone who could furnish in cash, labor, or material, 20 percent of the amount needed for the construction of a home, would be loaned the rest of the money at 6 percent interest by Barnum, who would be repaid in small weekly, monthly, or quarterly sums. Upon completion of the payments, the residents owned the house. The average cost of a house was roughly $1,500.

Barnum wrote in his autobiography that "it is much better that every person should somehow manage to own the roof he sleeps under. Men are more independent and feel happier who live in their own houses; they keep the premises in neater order, and they make better citizens."

They also made P.T. Barnum richer—the entrepreneur reserved the sale of some lots until after the price of the real estate increased.

Phineas Taylor Barnum, the most important individual contributor to Bridgeport's history, is shown here in 1875 during his only term as the city's mayor. Barnum developed thousands of acres of city property, helped the working class to purchase land and homes through a unique payment system, and attracted numerous manufacturing companies, in addition to many other achievements. Courtesy, City of Bridgeport

Born July 5, 1810, in Bethel, Connecticut, P.T. Barnum was the oldest of five children in a family so poor that he attended his father's funeral in borrowed shoes. Courtesy, Historical Collections, Bridgeport Public Library

Land that Barnum purchased less than forty years earlier for $200 had increased in value to more than $3,000 by 1885. Nevertheless, the townspeople and the *Standard* were behind his admitted "profitable philanthropy" approach. "Barnum may make money by the operation," wrote the *Standard* in 1864, "Very well, perhaps he will, but if he does, it will be by making others richer, not poorer; by helping those who need assistance, not by hindering them, and we can only wish that every rich man would follow such a noble example, and thus, without injury to themselves, give a helping hand to those who need it. Success to the enterprise!"

Barnum's farsightedness also produced thousands of jobs in an industrial development led by the Wheeler and Wilson Sewing Machine Company and Elias Howe's sewing factory. Barnum was constantly planning new real estate deals. The *Standard* reported in 1886 that Barnum had made 1,637 real estate transfers since May 30, 1846, the year he purchased the tract of land to build his orientalstyle mansion, Iranistan.

But not every Barnum business decision proved timely. Though his East Bridgeport plan was ultimately successful, Barnum lost a bundle trying to resettle there the struggling Jerome Clock Factory. By the time the costly venture failed in 1856 he was $500,000 in debt and bankrupt.

Barnum always looked at "the bright side," however. Writing in 1869, by which time he was solvent again, he observed that "My pet city, East Bridgeport, was progressing with giant strides . . . That piece of property, which, but eight years before, had been farmland, with scarcely six houses upon the whole tract, was now a beautiful new city, teeming with life, and looking as neat as a new pin."

*   *   *

Before Barnum ever gave much thought to such a place as Bridgeport, he was halfway through his life. Barnum was born July 5, 1810, in Bethel, Connecticut. He was the son of Philo Barnum, a tailor, farmer, and tavern keeper. His grandfather, Ephraim Barnum, was a captain in the Revolutionary War. P.T. was the eldest of five children in a family so poor that he attended his father's funeral in borrowed shoes. In 1826 his father died and Barnum accepted a job as a clerk in a Brooklyn, New York, store. Shortly after, he took a job as a clerk in a porterhouse before returning to Bethel in 1828 with $125 to his name. In

Bethel he established a retail fruit and confectionary store. The next year he married Charity Hallett and opened a lottery office.

Barnum's first great test as a promoter came when he turned his attention to the newspaper business and circulated on October 19, 1831, the first issue of *The Herald of Freedom,* a muckraking sheet which fought "bigotry, superstition, fanaticism and hypocrisy." Barnum was arrested for libel three times in three years; the third time sent him to jail for sixty days after he accused a Bethel deacon of being "guilty of taking usury of an orphan boy." Barnum's jailing won him praise and mushroomed the popularity of his paper, which continued to publish despite his incarceration.

Townspeople gave Barnum a parade upon his release. He sold his paper and a mercantile business in 1834 and moved to New York where he launched his showman career with the hiring of an old black woman, Joice Heth, who he claimed to be 161 years old and once George Washington's nurse.

Barnum exhibited Heth and several other attractions for several months, then joined Aaron Turner's traveling circus as ticket seller, secretary, and treasurer, which prepared Barnum for circus life. After a brief stint with his own traveling show he returned to New York, worked at various jobs, and went broke. Barnum had not a cent to his name, but he built up a reservoir of moxie and convinced some friends to

Page 72: *P.T. Barnum launched his showman career with the unveiling of an old black woman, Joice Heth, whom he claimed was 161 years old and once George Washington's nurse. Courtesy, Historical Collections, Bridgeport Public Library*

Page 73: *Late-nineteenth century trade cards often used a popular person or place to attract attention to a product. Bean's Dry Goods store used P.T. Barnum's face to sell dry and fancy goods. Hood's Sarsparilla used the circus to attract customers to the special qualities of that remedy. Photo by Neil Swanson. Courtesy, Robert Clifford Collection*

GREAT ATTRACTION
JUST ARRIVED AT HINGHAM.
☞ FOR A SHORT TIME ONLY. ☜

JOICE HETH,
NURSE TO
Gen. George Washington,

(The father of our country,) who has arrived at the astonishing age of **161** years! will be seen at HINGHAM for a SHORT TIME ONLY, as she is to fill other engagements very soon.

JOICE HETH is unquestionably the most astonishing and interesting curiosity in the World! She was the slave of Augustine Washington, (the father of Gen. Washington,) and was the first person who put clothes on the unconscious infant who in after days led our heroic fathers on to glory, to victory and freedom. To use her own language when speaking of the illustrious Father of his country, "she raised him." JOICE HETH was born in the Island of Madagascar, on the Coast of Africa, in the year 1674 and has consequently now arrived at the astonishing

Age of 161 Years!

She weighs but forty-six pounds, and yet is very cheerful and interesting. She retains her faculties in an unparalleled degree, converses freely, sings numerous hymns, relates many interesting anecdotes of *the boy* Washington, the red coats, &c. and often laughs heartily at her own remarks, or those of the spectators. Her health is perfectly good, and her appearance very neat. She was baptized in the Potomac river and received into the Baptist Church 116 years ago, and takes great pleasure in conversing with Ministers and religious persons. The appearance of this marvellous relic of antiquity strikes the beholder with amazement, and convinces him that his eyes are resting on the oldest specimen of mortality they ever before beheld. Original, authentic and indisputable documents prove however astonishing the fact may appear, JOICE HETH is in every respect the person she is represented.

The most eminent physicians and intelligent men in Cincinnati, Philadelphia, New-York, Boston and many other places have examined this *living skeleton* and the documents accompanying her, and all *invariably* pronounce her to be as represented 161 *years of age*! Indeed it is impossible for any person, however incredulous, to visit her without astonishment and the most perfect satisfaction that she is as old as represented.

☞ A female is in continual attendance, and will give every attention to the ladies who visit this relic of by gone ages.

She was visited at Niblo's Garden New York, by *ten thousand persons* in two weeks.———Hours of exhibition from 9 A. M to 1 P. M. and from 3 to 6 and from 7 to 9 P. M.—Admittance 25 cents—Children 12½ cents.

☞ For further particulars, see newspapers of the day. ☞ Over

Above: *Barnum's first mansion, Iranistan, was built in 1848 and cost about $150,000 to complete. It was a replica of the Oriental Pavilion of George IV. Painting by A.B. Guernsey. Courtesy, P.T. Barnum Museum*

Right: *Little was saved in the 1858 fire that destroyed Barnum's Iranistan mansion. However, this exhibit in the P.T. Barnum Museum contains some of the furniture from that home. Photo by Neil Swanson. Courtesy, P.T. Barnum Museum*

Facing page, top: *Bridgeport became the circus capital of the world when P.T. Barnum selected the city to be his winter headquarters. Courtesy, Robert Clifford Collection*

Facing page, bottom: *In 1842 P.T. Barnum opened his American Museum in New York City. The museum, on the corner of Anne and Fulton streets, contained animals, oddities of nature, and such attractions as the Fejee Mermaid and the Wild Men of Borneo. Courtesy, P.T. Barnum Museum*

Left: *In 1880 Barnum joined with James A. Bailey to create the Barnum and Bailey Circus. Photo by Neil Swanson. Courtesy, P.T. Barnum Museum*

Facing page: *For a mere fifty cents in 1855 you could own the music to P.T. Barnum's "National Poultry Show Polka." Courtesy, Historical Collections, Bridgeport Public Library*

Above: *Thousands bought tickets to see the celebrated soprano, Jenny Lind. Lind gave ninety-five concerts in nineteen cities in less than one year. Courtesy, Historical Collections, Bridgeport Public Library*

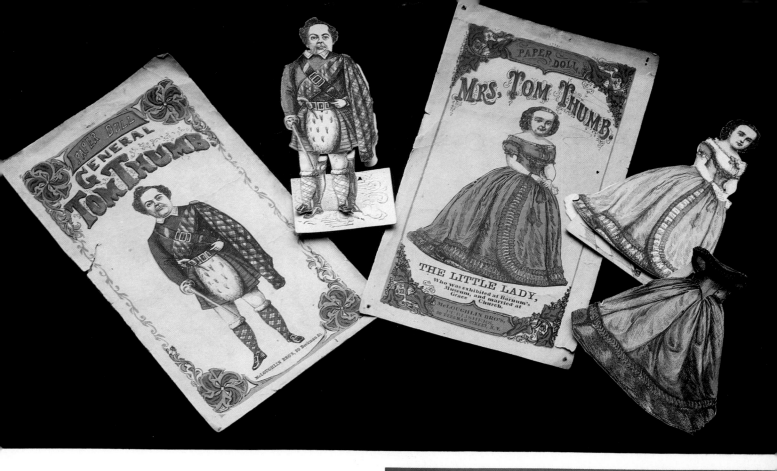

Above: *This pipe (about the size of a matchbook) and many other personal belongings of Tom Thumb (Charles Stratton) are on display at the P.T. Barnum Museum. Photo by Neil Swanson. Courtesy, P.T. Barnum Museum*

Facing page: *This poster of "The General" was likely used as a promotional piece following his appearances before Queen Victoria. Courtesy, Historical Collections, Bridgeport Public Library*

Top: *Paper doll figures of Tom Thumb and his wife were available from Barnum's circus. Several sets of clothes were included with each doll, and it was possible to dress Thumb in many of the costumes he wore when he performed for Queen Victoria. Photo by Neil Swanson. Courtesy, P.T. Barnum Museum*

Above: *These are some of the clothes and costumes belonging to Charles and Lavinia Stratton. The six-inch ruler indicates the small scale of the clothing. Photo by Neil Swanson. Courtesy, P.T. Barnum Museum*

Charles S. Stratton,

KNOWN AS

PHOTOGRAPHED BY E. T. WHITNEY & CO., NORWALK, CT.

GENERAL TOM THUMB.

The smallest man alive. Born in Bridgeport, Conn., January 4th, 1838. He has appeared three times before Her Majesty Queen Victoria, and also before most of the crowned heads of Europe. His performances have been witnessed by upwards of Twenty Millions of Persons.

WHITNEY & CO., have the General's assurance that this is the last picture he will have taken in character. They will furnish copies by mail, in each or all his characters, for 25 cents each. Direct, E. T. WHITNEY & CO., Photograph and Fine Art Gallery, Norwalk, Conn.

The "smallest man alive" poses for the last time in character, circa 1860. Since he was four years old, Charles Stratton traveled the world with P.T. Barnum, entertaining millions. Copies of this photo were available for twenty-five cents. Courtesy, Historical Collections, Bridgeport Public Library

back his purchase of the American Museum. He filled his newest prize with numerous odd attractions, including the Fejee Mermaid (a combination monkey and fish), the Wild Men of Borneo, the bearded lady Josephine Clofullia, and Chang and Eng, the original Siamese Twins. Barnum became a national favorite.

But the attraction that catapulted the big man to international fame was Bridgeport's own twenty-five-inch boy, Charles S. Stratton, better known as Tom Thumb.

Barnum met Stratton in November 1842 while visiting his brother, who operated the Franklin Hotel in Bridgeport. Barnum had

heard of a remarkably small child, and at my request, my brother Philo F. Barnum, brought him to the hotel. He was not two feet high; he weighed less than 16 pounds, and was the smallest child I ever saw that could walk alone; he was a perfectly formed, bright-eyed little fellow, with light hair and ruddy cheeks, and enjoyed the best of health. He was exceedingly bashful, but after some coaxing, he was induced to talk with me and he told me that he was the son of Sherwood E. Stratton of Bridgeport, and that his own name was Charles S. Stratton. After seeing him and talking with him, I at once determined to secure his services from his parents and to exhibit him in public.

Barnum hired Stratton, who was just four years old, for three dollars a week plus traveling and board expenses for his mother. (Stratton's parents were normal sized.) In December 1842 Barnum "announced the dwarf on my museum bills as 'General Tom Thumb.'" (Though

Barnum often referred to Stratton as his dwarf, he was actually a midget. Midgets are proportioned normally, but on a smaller scale.) Barnum devoted numerous hours educating and training his tiny prodigy for singing and dancing. Tom Thumb had a "great deal of native talent" and Barnum hired him and his parents for a year at seven dollars per week, plus fifty dollars at the end of the engagement to exhibit him anywhere in the country. As Tom Thumb became a public favorite, it wasn't long before Barnum upped his weekly salary to twenty-five dollars. Barnum for a time was reluctant to contract Tom Thumb for any great length of time for fear he would grow and force him to abort his smallest-man-on-earth campaign.

It turned out that Barnum's biggest problem with the midget was counting the money he made from him. (Tom Thumb reached a height of only forty inches.) The pair spent three years in Europe, including London and Paris, where Thumb played and danced before the "crowned heads of Europe." He even performed for Queen Victoria at Buckingham Palace.

In 1862 Barnum hired another midget, Lavinia Warren of Middleboro, Massachusetts. Stratton and Warren were married February 10, 1863, in New York and resided in a mansion at Bridgeport's Main Street and North Avenue. The Tom Thumb Conservatory, as it was known, was demolished in 1952 to make room for a parking lot for City National Bank. Tom Thumb established Barnum as the most celebrated showman of the times, and in turn Barnum became Bridgeport's greatest public relations man.

While Barnum delighted in all the attention, he urgently wanted to be recognized as an impresario of "legitimate" performers. The "Swedish Nightingale" Jenny Lind, the most celebrated European soprano, represented a much different kind of Barnum showcase. In 1848, Barnum completed his innovative oriental-style home Iranistan, and featured it on his letterhead in a pitch to bring Lind to the United

Facing page: *On September 1, 1850, Barnum introduced to America the "Swedish Nightingale," Jenny Lind, the celebrated European soprano. In less than a year, Lind concert receipts totaled more than $700,000. Courtesy, Historical Collections, Bridgeport Public Library*

Right: *Charles Stratton catapulted P.T. Barnum to international fame after Barnum met Stratton in November 1842 while visiting his brother, Philo, who operated the Franklin Hotel in Bridgeport. Courtesy, Historical Collections, Bridgeport Public Library*

Below: *Barnum and Tom Thumb spend three years in Europe, including London and Paris, where Thumb entertained royalty. Courtesy, Historical Collections, Bridgeport Public Library*

States. Lind surmised that she wanted to visit a place that had such a beautiful house. Before she had even set foot in America, Barnum started an avalanche of publicity and thousands covered the wharves in New York to watch her arrival on September 1, 1850. Lind gave ninety-five concerts for Barnum in nineteen cities in less than a year. The receipts totalled more than $700,000.

*   *   *

By 1850, Barnum's home life centered on Bridgeport; its transportation and nearness to New York was just what he wanted.

"Its situation as the terminus of the Naugatuck and the Housatonic railways, its accessibility to New York, with its two daily steamboats to and from the metropolis, and its dozen daily trains of the New York and Boston and Shore Line railways are all elements of prosperity which are rapidly telling in favor of this busy, beautiful, and charming city."

It was in the last thirty years of his life that Barnum's architectural work infused the city with beauty. He teamed up with two English brothers, George and Charles Palliser, to design and build inexpensive single-family "Model Gothic Cottages" in the area of Main, Broad, Whiting, and Atlantic streets. The brothers' first project was laid out over what had been the municipal cemetery on Cottage Street. Barnum advocated the establishment of a rural park-like burial ground, got state approval, and raised the funds to transfer the 4,000 interments to the new Mountain Grove Cemetery. Many people complained about the transfer of their relatives and friends, as truckloads of bodies were hauled over to Mountain Grove by George W. Pool, a retired butcher hired by Barnum. Pool apparently had little regard for matching the deceased with the correct headstone, and it seems he didn't empty the old municipal cemetery when he made the transfers; even in recent years from time to time

skeletons and headstones have been dug up among the houses at the old Cottage Street location.

"The cottages they designed here between 1874 and 1878, of the most fashionable architectural lines and unbelievably modest price tags, were a smashing success with homebuyers," said Charles Brilvitch, a Bridgeport architectural historian, of the Pallisers' and P.T.'s project. "They began replicating this success all over town, and soon all of Connecticut was clamoring for Palliser houses."

Brilvitch, for one, is quite familiar with the Barnum myth. He resides in one of Bridgeport's architectural beauties, the Octagon House, built in 1856 by clothier Nathan Gould at Barnum Avenue and Harriet Street. Numerous newspaper accounts credit Barnum with building the house and charging the curious twenty-five cents to see "a round house on a square lot."

The Pallisers wrote design books with basic patterns, signaling the emergence of mail-order architecture in America. In 1880, Barnum and the Pallisers started a new South End development, building mansion-scaled Victorian duplexes. They saved money on foundation costs and the houses remained affordable for the working class. In 1982 the block bound by Austin, Gregory, and Atlantic streets and Myrtle Avenue was officially listed as a Historic District in the National Register of Historic Places.

Barnum constantly looked for ways to beautify Bridgeport. In 1863, he proposed that Bridgeport's shore on Long Island Sound, at that time strewn with rocks and boulders, should be cleared out, opened along the entire waterfront, and transformed into a park. He predicted that such an improvement would increase the taxable value of the property in the area, enrich the city treasury, be an attraction to visitors, and increase development.

Barnum felt that "it dwelt upon the absurdity, almost criminality, that a beautiful city

Barnum's third Bridgeport home, Waldemere, completed in 1869, remains today as separate residences at Atlantic and Rennell streets in Bridgeport and One Pauline Street in Stratford. Courtesy, Historical Collections, Bridgeport Public Library

Phineas Taylor Barnum and Charles Stratton (shown here circa 1844) enjoyed enormous, worldwide success. Stratton began working for Barnum at age four, appearing first at Barnum's American Museum in 1842. Courtesy, P.T. Barnum Museum

like Bridgeport, lying on the shore of a broad expanse of salt water, should so cage itself in that not an inhabitant could approach the beach."

Barnum faced stiff opposition from many "old foggies," who complained that people anxious to see salt water and inhale the breeze from the sound could take boats at the wharves. Barnum convinced several landowners to donate land and he purchased and donated about $20,000 worth of land himself. Hundreds of workmen graded inaccessible approaches to the beach and laid out walks and drives. The rocks and boulders over which Barnum had attempted to cross by foot and horseback were used to build a seawall. Paths were opened, trees planted, and a bandstand and Civil War Soldiers' and Sailors' Monument were erected. Barnum presented this new improvement to the city and called it Seaside Park. "I do not believe that a million dollars, today, would compensate the city of Bridgeport for the loss of what is confessed to be the most delightful public pleasureground between New York and Boston," Barnum wrote.

In the summer of 1866, with Barnum's wife's health declining, a physician recommended that the family move nearer to the seashore. Barnum's first house, Iranistan, had burned to the ground in 1857. A few years later he built his dream house, the elegant Lindencroft, which was adorned with statuary and fountains, trees and shrubbery and beautiful flowers. Lindencroft was sold July 1, 1867. He moved into his completed house Waldemere (Woods by the Sea) in June 1869, another house built with the highest in comfort,

keeping in mind always that houses are made

to live in as well as to look at, and to be homes rather than mere residences. So the house was made to include abundant room for guests, with dressing rooms and baths to every chamber; water from the city throughout the premises; gas, manufactured on my own ground; and that greatest of all comforts, a semi-detached kitchen, so that the smell as well as the secrets of the cuisine might be confined to its own locality.

Two sections of Waldemere remain today as separate residences, one at Atlantic and Rennell streets, and the other at One Pauline Street in Lordship, across Bridgeport's harbor, the residence owned by actress Nancy Marchand. Barnum's last Bridgeport mansion, Marina, was built in 1889 for his second wife, Nancy Fish, after the death of Charity. The University of Bridgeport eventually acquired Marina and demolished it in 1961 to build the Marina Dining Hall.

* * *

It wasn't until the last twenty years of his life that Barnum's circus won international fame, nevertheless the tireless worker served one term as mayor in 1875, winning by 200 votes over Democrat Frederick Hurd. Barnum, a staunch Democrat until his friendship with Republican Abraham Lincoln, won the election as a Republican despite the Democrats' 500-voter majority. Democratic chants branded him a flimflam showman who cared nothing for public service.

Barnum was truly one of Bridgeport's first progressive mayors, fighting for numerous public improvements (including an abundant, citywide water supply), called on the police department to crack down on vice, and successfully warred against Sunday liquor sales. Barnum vehemently spoke out against the drinking of alcohol and often spoke of reform. "Caring for all, partial to none," was one of his mayoral slogans.

A vintage Barnum publicity stunt: in 1888 the Stratford Avenue Bridge was replaced by a new iron structure. To assure everyone of its safety, Barnum paraded a dozen elephants weighing some thirty-six tons onto the bridge. Barnum, hatless and white haired, is standing in the middle of the group. The hatless man standing next to Barnum is Patrick Coughlin, Bridgeport's first Irish mayor. Photo by Corbit's Studio. Courtesy, P.T. Barnum Museum

"Before there can be any reform in Bridgeport," he told an alderman, "there will have to be a few first-class funerals."

Barnum possessed good humor and had a razor-sharp wit. At one of his temperance lectures, a heckler asked whether alcohol hurt a man internally or externally. Barnum shot back, "Eternally."

"Spiritous liquors of the present day are so much adulterated and doubly poisoned that their use fires the brain and drives their victims to madness, violence and murder," he told the Common Council.

The money annually expended for intoxicating liquors, and the cost of their evil results in Bridgeport, or any other American city where liquor selling is licensed, would pay the entire expenses of the city (if liquors were not drank) including the public schools, give a good suit of clothes to every poor person of both sexes, a barrel of flour to every poor family living within its municipal boundaries, and leave a handsome surplus on hand. Our enormous expenses for the trial and punishment of criminals, as well as the support of the poor are mainly caused by this traffic. Surely then it is our duty to do all we can, legally, to limit and mitigate its evil.

Barnum sapped every ounce of mayoral power and the magic of his words to lead Bridgeport. He fought persistently with the Common Council in defending the Board of Police Commissioners' right to maintain the ultimate authority in the police department. During his

farewell speech to the council, he urged all to hold no grudges.

Occasional thunder and lightning are needful to the preservation of a pure atmosphere. If those who invoke the hurricane are prompted by pure and disinterested motives, their action will be approved. I am glad to believe that you have endeavored to study and promote the best interests of the city. In my efforts to be faithful to duty, I have never felt the slightest personal animosity, and I entertain for each and every member of this Council sincere wishes for their happiness and all the public approval which their actions merit.

And now, gentlemen, as we are about to close our labors in a harmonious spirit, and bid each other a friendly farewell, we have like the Arabs, only to 'fold our tents and silently steal away,' congratulating ourselves that this is the only 'stealing' which has been performed by this Honorable Body.

*   *   *

Barnum's circus career took off in 1870 with the formation of his immense circus. "The Greatest Show On Earth" consisted of a museum, menagerie, and eventually a grand three-ring circus that required 500 men, numerous horses, and a seventy-car freight train to transport it through the country. Bridgeport became the circus capital of the world when Barnum selected it as the winter headquarters—the site was a ten-acre lot in the West End along Wordin Avenue, Norman Street, and Railroad Avenue. Daily, downtown Bridgeport was treated to visits from the most famous circus characters, including William F. "Buffalo Bill" Cody.

On November 20, 1887, an evening fire destroyed the winter headquarters, killing nearly all the animals except for several elephants and a lion which escaped into the streets and nearby barns. Barnum's "sacred" white elephant

was killed in the blaze. Barnum, the eternal optimist, immediately began erecting another winter headquarters.

"I am not in show business alone to make money. I feel it my mission, as long as I live, to provide clean, moral, and healthful recreation for the public to which I have so long catered," Barnum explained.

Throughout his life, Barnum was cursed by fires; his Iranistan home, New York museum (twice burned), and winter headquarters all were hit by fire. In 1880 Barnum formed a partnership with circus associate James A. Bailey, who carried on the circus after Barnum's death. The Barnum and Bailey Circus was sold to the Ringling Brothers in 1907, and the new owners moved the headquarters to Sarasota, Florida, in 1927.

Even in the last years of his life Barnum never lost his enthusiasm for a masterful publicity stunt. One of his last Bridgeport gimmicks took place in 1888. The Stratford Avenue Bridge was replaced by a new iron structure and Barnum assured everyone of its safety by parading twelve elephants weighing thirty-six tons onto the bridge.

In the fall of 1890, a stroke confined Barnum to his home. In his final letter to his partner James Bailey, the Greatest Showman on Earth reflected on his career:

Never cater to the baser instincts of humanity, strive as I have always done to elevate the moral tone of amusements, and always remember that the children have ever been our best patrons. I would rather hear the pleased laugh of a child over some feature of my exhibition than receive as I did the flattering compliments of the Prince of Wales. I am prouder of my title 'The Children's Friend' than if I were to be called 'The King of the World.'

I regret exceedingly that my bodily weakness prevents my being present at the exhibition in New York, for I veritably believe that if I

*Just as in the first Barnum Festival Parade in 1949, there is
always a best float among floats. The Lycoming Girls Club
won best float award in the Barnum parade in 1962. Their
float featured a Gemini capsule orbiting the earth. The girls'
costumes were truly space-age for 1962. Bridgeport Brass president Herman W. Steinkraus conceived of the festival as a way
to reunite the city, then suffering a postwar slump. Courtesy,
Historical Collections, Bridgeport Public Library*

In 1949 Bridgeport saluted the greatest showman on earth with the Barnum Festival. The King and Queen event, Tom Thumb competition, Jenny Lind Concert, grand parade, and the midway, shown here at Seaside Park, represent some of the special features associated with the Barnum tribute. Courtesy, Historical Collections, Bridgeport Public Library

could again see the rows of bright-faced children at our matinees and observe their eyes grow round with wonder or hear their hearty laughter, it would do me more good than all the medicine in the world.

I am too weak to write more now, but let me entreat you to never allow the honorable and honestly acquired title of 'The Greatest Show on Earth' to be in any way disgraced or lessened in fame. Go on as you have begun and I know you will continue to prosper.

Barnum died five days later on April 7, 1891. The public and press reacted with intense sorrow. "The death of Barnum ends a unique career, and no singular combination of traits and talents survives to compete with his memory," wrote the *New York Tribune*. "It is probably safe to say that not more than half a dozen persons now living, including reigning sovereigns, are known by name to so many millions of their fellow beings as was Barnum."

"The death of P.T. Barnum may not 'eclipse the gaiety of nations,' but it takes out of the world one who has added more to this gaiety than perhaps any other man who has ever lived," noted the *New York World*.

"Bridgeport has long since outgrown the influence of any one man, but still so far as civilization has penetrated, Bridgeport has been associated with his name and is known as the city in which he made his home," wrote the *Bridgeport Standard*.

Bridgeport has indeed outgrown the influence of any one man, but no man has had more influence on Bridgeport than P.T. Barnum, a man who cherished friendships with Abraham Lincoln and Mark Twain, a man so famous that he wrote of receiving letters from foreign countries addressed simply "P.T. Barnum, America" and a man who made Bridgeport a better place to live.

Barnum lives on in Bridgeport; no less than forty businesses, streets, and enterprises are named for him or his family, including Barnum Avenue, Barnum School, and of course, the Barnum Museum and the Barnum Festival. Playwright Mark Bramble even captured Barnum in a Broadway show of the same name in 1980.

In life and in death, Barnum has benefited Bridgeport. He willed the money for the museum that recalls the step-right-up spieling of his circus life. It is there that hundreds of thousands have rediscovered Tom Thumb, Jenny Lind, and P.T. himself. "Barnum's the most important 19th Century figure in the development of Bridgeport," said museum curator Robert Pelton.

In 1949, so that Barnum's "kind acts may live forever," Bridgeport saluted the showman with the Barnum Festival, an idea generated by Bridgeport Brass executive Herman W. Steinkraus. It includes the King and Queen event, the Jenny Lind Concert, the Tom Thumb competition, and numerous other special features, capped by the grand parade, all saying thanks to the Greatest Showman on Earth and Bridgeport's first citizen.

Barnum's impact was worldwide. During one of his visits to England, Barnum listened to the Bishop of London making a farewell speech. The Bishop closed by saying, "I hope I shall see you in heaven." Barnum smiled and answered, "You will if you are there." So will all of Bridgeport.

With Pleasure Beach Amusement Park on the horizon, the Lake Torpedo Boat Company yard, at the foot of Seaview Avenue, is seen here in 1922. Owner Simon Lake submitted a submarine design to the U.S. War Department in 1893, but the government decided against construction at that time. Courtesy, Historical Collections, Bridgeport Public Library

CHAPTER V
All That
Brass

"Industria Crescimus— By Industry We Thrive"

—city motto, adopted 1875

When Bridgeport's city fathers introduced this city motto saluting the development of Barnum's East Bridgeport, few could have realized that some forty years later their city would have clearly earned its reputation as the industrial center of the country. If the true worth of a city is measured by how much it has contributed to progress, then the contribution of Bridgeport's labor force, inventiveness, and industrial prominence have left its mark nationwide. Bridgeport has boasted of being the sewing machine and corset capital of the world, and it was the armament center of the nation during the two world wars. Its manufacturing produced an assortment of offbeat and progressive firsts, including model trains, luxury cars, aerosol sprays, and undergarments. Its Yankee ingenuity invented the pull-chain light socket, and the micrometer, which is used in various industries to measure small distances and diameters. Add to that the aviation genius of Igor Sikorsky and the enterprising Dymaxion automobile design of R. Buckminster Fuller.

*   *   *

Barnum's East Bridgeport set the tone for citywide manufacturing, and the race was led by the sewing machine industry. After Barnum's Jerome Clock Factory failed, sewing machine partners Nathaniel Wheeler and Allen

Wilson left Middletown, Connecticut, to occupy the clock factory's East Washington Avenue building in 1856. Ten years later Elias Howe, Jr., of Spencer, Massachusetts, who had successfully defended his 1845 sewing machine design against patent infringers, manufactured machines from a large building at Howe and Kossuth streets which had a dock for shipping machines to New York buyers. Wheeler, Wilson, and Howe revolutionized the clothing industry, and sewing machine manufacturing remained Bridgeport's major industry through the end of the nineteenth century.

The city of Bridgeport was just thirty years old at this time and was making its first giant step in rapid growth, advancing from its earlier comb and hatmaking and patent leather industries, and the anchoring carriage and saddlery industries.

Of the early sewing machine entrepreneurs,

Sewing machine manufacturing in Bridgeport was the city's major industry through the end of the nineteenth century. This drawing of the machine made by partners Allen B. Wilson and Nathaniel Wheeler in 1852 was the beginning of the industrial revolution that put Bridgeport on the map. Courtesy, Historical Collections, Bridgeport Public Library

The Singer Sewing Machine Company absorbed the Wheeler and Wilson Company in 1905. Singer was the first to offer installment plan purchasing, which put the sewing machine within the reach of nearly everyone. Courtesy, Historical Collections, Bridgeport Public Library

Wheeler won the credit for making the machine a commercial success through simplified machine operation and improvements that reduced the costs of manufacture. Singer, which absorbed the company in 1905, introduced an installment-buying sales system which further supported the industry. By train and commercial freighter, thousands of sewing machines left Bridgeport as the nation's population and demand for clothing burgeoned during the Civil War. Another Bridgeport company of national importance was the Union Metallic Cartridge Company, founded in 1867. The New York dealer of munitions located its plant on Pauline Street in East Bridgeport and manufactured arms during the Civil War.

The mid-nineteenth century also was a growth period for banking. Between 1850 and 1860 three banking institutions were chartered that became the forerunners of today's Citytrust. People's Bank was chartered in 1842, and Mechanics and Farmers Bank was chartered in 1871. The Connecticut National Bank had its

*This twenty-six-piece marching band from the Wheeler and
Wilson Factory posed for this postcard photo in the late 1800s.
Parades were popular and all the major industries had a band.
Before becoming a heavily industrial city, Bridgeport factories
produced hats, patent leather, and was the home of a number
of saddlery and carriage shops. Courtesy, Robert Clifford Collection*

People's Bank, on the corner of Main and Bank streets, was chartered in 1842. The First National Bank occupied the second floor of this building, seen here circa 1870. Courtesy, Historical Collections, Bridgeport Public Library

attracting capital and promoting business interests in the city.

The Bridgeport Brass Company, incorporated in 1865, operated from a sprawling plant on Housatonic Avenue. It got its start from the brass-framed hoop skirts which became popular in the 1860s. When styles changed in 1870, the company concentrated on making kerosene lamps and parts, and later it made the first flat copper sheets for photoengraving purposes and a variety of brass parts for plumbing equipment, automobile tire valves, shell casings, and parts for flashlights. America's first micrometer originated in the brass shop. During World War II, Bridgeport Brass invented the DDT aerosol bomb, used in tropical jungles to destroy disease-carrying insects. After the war, the product was marketed for commercial use

Originally built in 1806 (shown being remodeled in 1856), the Bridgeport Bank was the first organized bank in Bridgeport. Courtesy, Historical Collections, Bridgeport Public Library

beginning as the first banking institution in Bridgeport, organized as the Bridgeport Bank in 1806.

In 1860, Bridgeport's ninety-six manufacturing establishments employed 2,196 males and 1,131 females. The sewing machine and carriage making companies together employed 1,000 people.

The men who ran these companies were the most go-getting of an extremely dynamic breed of early entrepreneurs who, during the emergence of steam power, advanced Bridgeport toward its most spectacular growth period. Brass, machine tool, and corset companies would make Bridgeport a world leader in those fields and, years later, the electrical equipment industry would join their ranks. The expanding industrial climate was aided in 1875 by the founding of the Board of Trade, which was active in

98

Right: *Workers here trim edges in the final process of manufacturing sheet brass in 1909. Beginning with brass hoops for skirts in the 1860s, Bridgeport Brass later produced parts for brass lamps, shell casings, and tire valves. Courtesy, Historical Collections, Bridgeport Public Library*

Below: *Bridgeport Brass invented the DDT aerosol bomb during World War II. DDT was used to kill disease-carrying insects, and after the war the product took off with dozens of commercial applications. Courtesy, Historical Collections, Bridgeport Public Library*

THE FOUR MOST POPULAR CORSETS IN AMERICA.

DR. WARNER'S CORALINE CORSET.

THIS is by far the most popular dollar Corset ever introduced. It has been before the public over five years, and has rapidly grown in sales, which are now in excess of 3000 Corsets daily. This immense success is due to the superiority of Coraline over whalebone as a stiffener for Corsets, and to the excellent quality of these Corsets. This Corset is adapted to nearly every form, and gives more general satisfaction than any other ever offered to American Ladies.

Beware of worthless imitations made of various kinds of Cord. None are genuine unless "Dr Warner's Coraline Corset" is printed on inside of steel cover.

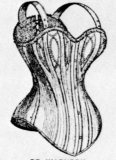

DR. WARNER'S CORALINE HEALTH CORSET.

THIS Corset is sure to give a lady an elegant form. Jerseys, which are so trying to most forms, fit perfectly over the Health Corset. The straps and skirt supporting pins can be used or discarded as each lady prefers. The flexible Coraline busts are a feature every lady admires, as they insure an elegant and graceful form, without the inconvenience and injurious effects of padding.

This Corset has now been before the public twelve years, with constantly increasing sales, and is to day the leading Corset in America. Every genuine Health Corset has "Dr. Warner's Coraline Health" printed on the inside of the steel cover.

DR. WARNER'S FLEXIBLE HIP CORSET.

THE Flexible Hip Corset is constructed after the analogy of the human body, the bones upon the sides passing like the ribs around the body. The front and back of the Corset is boned with Coraline. The combination of Coraline and bone secures the most comfortable and perfect Corset ever made. It is warranted not to break over the hips.

All genuine Corsets have "Dr Warner's Coraline Flexible Hip" printed on inside steel cover

DR. WARNER'S CORALINE ABDOMINAL CORSET.

THIS Corset is made with steels of the ordinary length, the Corset extending below the steel in front from two to three inches. Near the steel on each side an elastic gore is inserted, which combines the support of the Abdominal Corset with the comfort and freedom of movement of a Corset of the ordinary length. Ladies who cannot wear other Abdominal Corsets can wear this with ease, and those ladies desiring a long Corset will find this Corset highly satisfactory for either a stout or slight figure.

The genuine Corsets have "Dr. Warner's Coraline Abdominal Corsets" printed on inside steel cover.

Above: *Dr. I. DeVer Warner and his brother, Dr. Lucien C. Warner, developed the first fitted undergarments and the first A-B-C-D bra sizes. In 1912 the Warners opened the largest corset manufacturing plant in the world, occupying two city blocks in Bridgeport's South End. Authentic Warner corsets had "Dr. Warner's Coraline" printed inside the steel cover. This advertisement ran in 1883. Courtesy, Historical Collections, Bridgeport Public Library*

Facing page: *Founded in 1888, Harvey Hubbell's machine tool company at State and Bostwick Avenue developed many electrical conveniences still in use today. The building is still occupied today by Hubbell's company. Courtesy, Historical Collections, Bridgeport Public Library*

under the Bridgeport Brass Aer-A-Sol trademark.

Bridgeport's manufacturing prominence paved the way for another industry—machine tools. Edward P. Bullard, following a wave of industrial pioneers who left their home states for Bridgeport, realized that with all this growth, companies would need machines to make machines. He established the Bullard Company at Broad Street and Railroad Avenue in 1880 and produced tools for the manufacture of sewing machines, bicycles, textile machinery, and machines used in railroad repair shops and shipbuilding plants.

Harvey Hubbell founded a machine tool company at State Street and Bostwick Avenue in 1888 that became prominent for manufacturing wiring devices. Hubbell developed the rolled-thread screw, the electric pull-chain light fixture (which complemented Thomas Edison's light bulb), and the duplex interchangeable receptacle plug. Before Hubbell's creation, electrical wires were soldered into the wall outlet.

While Bridgeport served as the sewing machine capital of the world, it also became the world leader in corset manufacturing. Dr. I. DeVer Warner and his brother, Dr. Lucien C. Warner, based their Warner Brothers Company at 325 Lafayette Street in 1874, developing a long line of women's undergarments, including the two-way stretch girdle and the first line of bras utilizing the A-B-C-D sizing system. Warner's fitted corsets made the old tie-in style obsolete. As a result of the influx of out-of-state female workers, the Warners opened the Seaside Institute, an educational housing facility for women. First Lady Frances Folsom Cleveland attended the Seaside Institute dedication ceremonies on November 5, 1887. The facility later became the headquarters for the *Bridgeport Herald*. In 1912, Warners' became

"Unhampered by the Interstate Commerce Commission, immune from freight rate regulation, and undetected as yet by the Government." This was from an advertisement for the popular mechanical trains introduced by the Ives Manufacturing Company in 1901, which are still praised by collectors today. Ives employees posed for this portrait around 1910. Courtesy, Historical Collections, Bridgeport Public Library

the largest corset manufacturer in the world, expanding its plant to fill two city blocks in the South End, and employing 3,300 workers.

Companies such as the Warners' mirrored a period of ingenuity that included diverse inventors and risk takers. In 1871, William R. Frisbie baked five-cent pies from a house on Kossuth Street and delivered them by horse and wagon. In 1915 his son built a three-story bakery which produced more than 50,000 pies per day twenty years later. This bit of news might have been lost in city history had it not been for company employees flinging the heavy metal pie tins during lunch break (thousands found the bottom of the Pequonnock River) and Yale students skimming them on the New Haven Green. The Wham-0 Manufacturing Company spotted Yalies tossing the pie tins in the 1940s and developed their own plastic model (Frisbees), which have since soared through every yard, beach, and park in America.

Bridgeporter Charles F. Ritchel also soared— 200 feet over the Connecticut River in the world's first propeller-powered balloon flight on July 13, 1878. Ritchel controlled his hydrogen balloon through the action of foot pedals. He is also credited with inventing roller skates. His *Bridgeport Post* obituary reports he had 150 inventions, "all of them moneymakers," but his marketing inability failed to turn a profit. He died broke at age sixty in 1911.

The Ives Manufacturing Company, founded in 1868 on Water Street, instigated the wind-up toy craze, and steered the nation's railroad network into the home in 1901 by producing the first mechanical trains to run on tracks. "Unhampered by the Interstate Commerce Commission, immune from freight rate regulation, and undetected as yet by the Government," whistled the Ives advertisement for the miniature clockwork railroad system. The Ives Company closed in 1932, but its trains remain precious collector's items.

While the Ives Company invention relied on rails in 1901, that same year Gustave White-head relied on his propeller-driven aircraft in what was arguably the first airplane flight in history—two years before the first flight of Wilbur and Orville Wright at Kitty Hawk, North Carolina. Whitehead was a German immigrant who experimented with aircraft as early as 1897 in several East Coast cities before making his home on Pine Street in the West End where he built his aircraft. On August 14, 1901, as witnessed by a *Bridgeport Herald* reporter, Whitehead made four flights, ascending 200 feet and traveling about one mile. Six months later, Whitehead flew for about seven miles over Long Island Sound. Whitehead was apparently much too occupied with flying than promoting his accomplishment and when he really needed it had little documentation to support his air flights. Author Stella Randolph, who wrote two books on Whitehead, uncovered his feats in the 1930s. William O'Dwyer of Fairfield, whose more recent book, *History By Contract,* continues Randolph's research, and reports the Smithsonian Institution acknowledges the Wright brothers because their airplane could be obtained for display. Smithsonian officials and the Wright family signed a contract in 1948 agreeing that the plane must be returned should someone else be given credit for being the first to fly. As for Whitehead, he failed to market his aircraft and died penniless in 1927.

By air or land, Bridgeport labor produced many innovations. The Locomobile Company of America, which developed luxury cars that sold for more than $11,000 in 1922, proclaimed it produced the best-built car in America. The company policy emphasized comfort above all, and its objective was to build a limited number of exceedingly lavish Locomobile cars to perfection. Not more than four cars per day were assembled by hand to extend intimate attention to each car and owner. The company's limousine model had cut-glass side lamps, a tiffany shade covering the dome light, trim of sterling silver, an electric telephone allowing passengers

On the steps of Holy Rosary Church at East Washington and Harriet Street, the Frisbie Pie Company baseball team poses for this picture about 1935. In 1871 William R. Frisbie baked pies that sold for five cents and were delivered by horse and wagon. In 1915 his son built a three-story bakery on Kossuth Street and by 1924 nine tons of pies left Bridgeport every day. Before power became available on the East Side in 1905, Frisbie built his own powerplant in his basement. Photo by B. Brignolo, Brignolo Studios. Courtesy, Historical Collections, Bridgeport Public Library

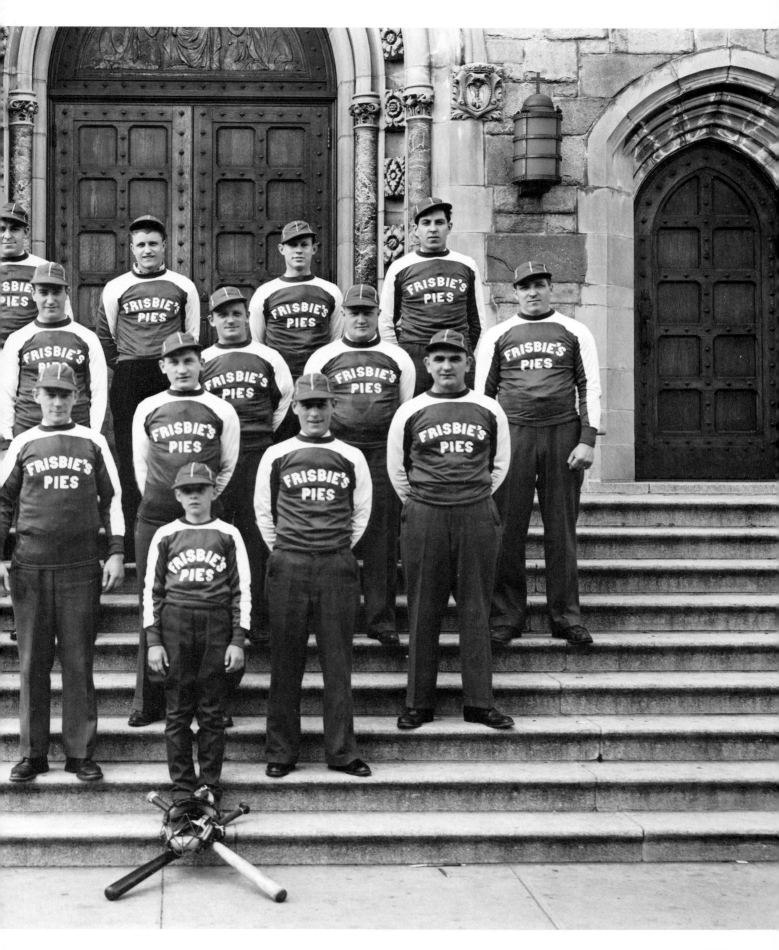

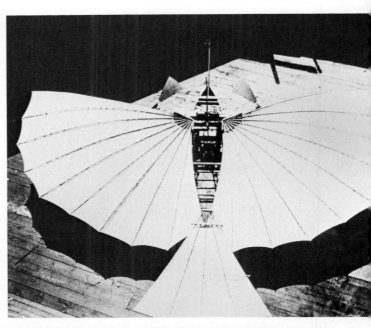

Right: *On August 14, 1901, Gustave Whitehead took his #21 aircraft for four flights, witnessed by a* Bridgeport Herald *reporter. Whitehead experimented with aircraft in several East Coast cities as early as 1897, but, unable to market his aircraft, he died penniless in 1927. Courtesy, Gustave Weisskoph Museum*

Below: *This January 1986 photo shows a modern reconstruction of Gustave Whitehead's 1901 plane, undertaken by engineers from Pratt and Whitney, Pitney Bowes, and workers from the SST project. Andy Kosch is the director of construction. Photo by Neil Swanson*

Left: *Whitehead posed in 1901 with his daughter, Rose, in the shade of his aircraft just months before his first flight. The craft's two propellers were carved from wood and were powered by an engine of Whitehead's own design. Courtesy, Gustave Weisskoph Museum*

Below: *Shown here without the propellers and with weighted wings to prevent an unplanned lift-off, the similarity of this 1986 reconstruction to Whitehead's original aircraft is striking. When completed, the craft will fly with wooden props and a steam engine, just as Whitehead's did eighty-five years ago. Photo by Neil Swanson*

Facing page: *This car, seen here in a 1948 photo, was the first American-built car to win the prestigious Vanderbilt Cup. The 1906 Locomobile set a speed record during the October 24, 1908, race, reaching a top speed of 64.38 MPH. At the time this photo was taken, the car belonged to Peter Helck. Courtesy, Historical Collections, Bridgeport Public Library*

Above: *In the late 1800s and early 1900s, the city expanded its water distribution system, especially for fighting fires. When P.T. Barnum became president of the Bridgeport Hydraulic Company some twenty years after its 1857 creation, the expansion of the water supply and the replacement of worn-out pipes began. Workers here are unloading the huge pipes to connect the city to the supply. Courtesy, Robert Clifford Collection*

Facing page: *This special 1917 Type Désobligéant Town Model was designed for Elsie Vanderbilt. In 1922, a Locomobile cost more than $11,000, a price only the rich could afford. Each car was hand-built with such conveniences as sterling silver trim, cut-glass side lamps, and even a telephone to speak to the driver. Courtesy, Historical Collections, Bridgeport Public Library*

Right: *The Carlson Brothers opened a carriage shop in 1909 and with the introduction of the automobile they began to produce metal truck bodies as early as 1912. Truck bodies like the Couplex Cab shown here circa 1920 were built to fit the chassis of many different manufacturers, such the White Model 60 shown. By 1936 the brothers had developed the Metro Truck, a cab that was ideal for many types of delivery purposes. Courtesy, Robert Clifford Collection*

to speak to the driver, and a concealed toilet case with a mirror. The company, which set up shop in Bridgeport in 1900, pioneered the development of steam, gasoline, and electric automobiles, but fell victim to the post-World War I depression. In 1922 it was taken over by General Motors founder William C. Durant, whose middle-priced models could not save the company from closing several years later.

R. Buckminster Fuller rented space in the old Locomobile plant and wasn't so successful with his Dymaxion invention, a three wheeled, cucumber-shaped vehicle that streaked 120 miles per hour. His urge for mass production received little interest from auto makers. Fuller went on to invent aluminum houses and the geodesic dome.

Two other Bridgeporters, William and Philip Carlson, took advantage of the growing automobile market. The Carlson brothers were Russian Jews who opened a carriage repair shop in 1909, produced metal cab bodies for trucks in 1912, and by 1936 developed the Metro Truck, a spacious cab used by dairies, bakeries, and the U.S. Postal Service.

The advancement of Bridgeport inventors and business leaders coincided with the progress of public utilities. Gas light came to Bridgeport in May 1849 when the state legislature chartered the Bridgeport Gas Light Company. Two years later the company, located on Housatonic Avenue, had seventy-six private customers and twenty-six public street lamps.

Bridgeporters greeted the coming of gas with opposition, insisting the night should be left alone because illumination would increase the most frequent crime—drunkenness. Electric power emerged in the early 1880s. In 1885 the city's two electric light companies—Thompson-Houston and Brush Electric Company—merged into the Bridgeport Electric Light Company on John Street. Bridgeport had more than 100 streetlights by 1890, and the fee was based on lamp size and number of hours in service before the installation of meters in 1894. On January 30, 1900, the Bridgeport Electric Light Company and New Haven Electric Light consolidated under the name United Illuminating. In 1908, the company operated twenty-four hours a day, marking around-the-clock electricity availability and significantly changing residents' habits of working until dark and going to bed shortly after.

Bridgeport had a limited public water supply during its first fifty years as a city. The city was dependent on several springs until 1853 when the need for an extensive supply, particularly to fight fires, was addressed. The Common Council named Nathaniel Greene to lay water pipes under principal streets so a full supply for the city could be furnished. Greene and others organized the Bridgeport Water Company which formed Bunnell's Pond in northern Bridgeport, filled by the water of the Pequonnock River.

In 1857, the Bridgeport Hydraulic Company was founded, but the city's wait for an adequate supply source, the replacment of worn-out pipes, and quality water main locations didn't end for twenty years, when P.T. Barnum became president of the company. Bunnell's Pond served as the city reservoir until Bridgeport Hydraulic expanded reservoirs in Easton, Fairfield, and Shelton.

Bridgeport's first telephone company—the Telephone Dispatch Company—opened on Main and Fairfield in July 1878, six months after New Haven became the first city in the world to have a commercial switchboard. Thomas B. Doolittle, who first suggested the use of hard

drawn copper for telephone lines, headed the Bridgeport phone company which numbered 100 subscribers, including Barnum. *The Story of Bridgeport,* written by Elsie Danenberg in 1936, credits Mrs. Augustine Gray as being the first woman exchange operator in the world. Southern New England Telephone Company was formed October 2, 1882, and moved about the city until settling into its present site at John and Courtland in 1930—the year Bridgeport service converted to dial operation.

*   *   *

Buoyed by the muscle of the immigrant groups, Bridgeport was building a solid industrial base while heading for its strongest period of growth in history during World War I. In the years just prior to the war, Connecticut was in the throes of an industrial slump with many factories working only three or four days per week. Bridgeport had become one of the most progressive cities in New England and although it suffered pains to employ and house the newcomers of the immigrant surge, it was prepared to meet the challenge.

In 1915, the English, French, and Russian armies placed heavy munitions orders with Remington Arms and the Union Metallic Company, the largest manufacturers of firearms and ammunitions in the allied countries. The Boston Avenue building was the marvel of its time—thirteen buildings a half-mile long covering eighty acres of floor space. The plant manufactured bayonets, guns of small and large caliber, and the Browning machine gun which fired a belt of 250 rounds of ammunition in about twenty seconds. At one point the company hired a new employee every twenty minutes and by 1916 it employed over 22,000 persons. The national troop-guarded zone known as "Remington City" became recognized as one of the most important and protected spots in the world.

Above: *The explosion of sixteen tons of gunpowder on May 14, 1906, virtually leveled "Success Hill." Not long after the accident, the area became known as the Remington Nature Preserve and many paintings of hunters with Remington arms were made for advertisements. Courtesy, Robert Clifford Collections*

Below: *Founded in 1867, the Union Metallic Cartridge Company became the Remington Arms Company in 1915. By the time the United States entered World War I, it was the nation's single largest factory, employing more than 22,000 workers. The plant produced seven million rounds of ammunition a week—two-thirds of American ammunition production. Courtesy, Historical Collections, Bridgeport Public Library*

The Bridgeport Chamber of Commerce, founded in 1915, organized the Bridgeport Housing Company which constructed war workers housing projects, including Seaside and Lakeview Villages and Black Rock Gardens.

Remington wasn't the only Bridgeport company that contributed greatly to the defense of the nation. The Locomobile Company manufactured Riker army trucks and Bridgeport Brass produced shell casings. The Lake Torpedo Boat Company, led by submarine designer Simon Lake, produced R-21 submarines that were launched at the foot of Seaview Avenue.

War contracts totaling in the millions catapulted Bridgeport as the leader in statewide prosperity. Bridgeport was called the Arsenal of Democracy and Mayor Clifford B. Wilson's progressive leadership spawned the "Essen of America." The *New York Times* maintained that "regardless of how the war is affecting others, it is demonstrating itself good business for Bridgeport and Bridgeport people."

But pains of growth accompanied Bridgeport's economic prosperity. Roughly 100 strikes marred the open-shop city in the summer of 1915 as Bridgeport became a main target of labor's drive for an eight-hour day. Bridgeport received international attention as national

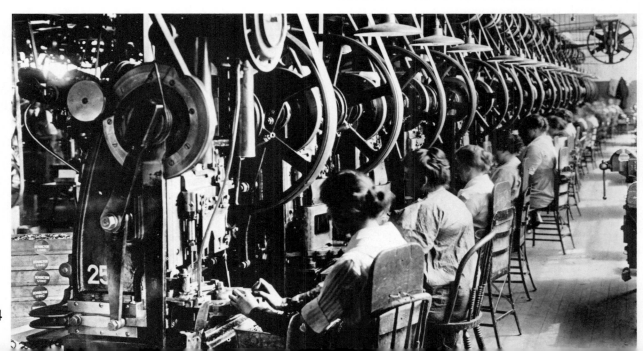

union leaders targeted Remington as the cornerstone of their labor fight. Strikes by building trades, iron workers, machinists, and others lit up the front pages. The walkouts generally included only small numbers of workers at any one time, and factories carried on without major interruption, but the persistent union agitation and the threat of Bridgeport factories being held up during the production of war munitions forced employers to grant concessions.

One of the standoff Remington strikes settled on July 23 left officials of the International Association of Machinists and the National Bridge and Structural Iron Workers claiming victory in securing an eight-hour workday. Company officials, however, maintained that strikes collapsed because they had planned for eight-hour workdays prior to the job action to prevent the city from being plunged into an industrial war. Either way, workers made strides for their eight-hour days and Bridgeport companies continued in their prosperity.

While more than 8,000 served in "the war to end war," thousands of skilled and unskilled workers flooded the city. As a result, rents rose by 50 percent, and Remington Arms and the federal government constructed hundreds of homes to fill the housing gap. The expanding trolley, police, fire, school, and street lighting services were financed by increased taxes and bond issues.

The national fear of radicalism generated during this period threatened order and stability in the state and spread into Bridgeport as well. In March 1919, Bridgeport Police raided the Industrial Workers of the World city headquarters and confiscated a truckload of Communist literature.

Nevertheless, by 1920 the city was the state's leader in industrial employment, and it emerged from World War I as the industrial center of the nation. But the end of the war caused the demand for products to fall, and Bridgeport faced some serious troubles within the emerging peacetime economic picture.

Simon Lake's Lake Torpedo Boat Company produced submarines as early as 1897, the year he submitted plans to the U.S. War Department. In 1918, he began building R-21 submarines for the government, along with O-series, N-series, and S-series submarines. Courtesy, Historical Collections, Bridgeport Public Library

Remington abandoned its huge Boston Avenue munitions plant for a Barnum Avenue location and the plant was occupied by General Electric, which commenced the manufacture of wiring devices. But the impact of the Depression forced a period of crisis for Bridgeport. Acute unemployment led Mayor Edward Buckingham to hire the jobless to perform municipal custodial chores for fifty cents an hour. In 1930 roughly 1,000 men each month repaired streets, painted buildings, and cleaned sidewalks; these tasks added some much-needed relief to the ranks of the unemployed that had swollen to more than twice the number from the previous year. But the worst was yet to come.

The city borrowed $500,000 in 1931, and in order to stretch the work relief funds, it slashed work hours and cut the hourly wage to thirty-five cents an hour, prompting Public Welfare Director Angus Thorne to lament "we can't give them much less." The city also gave to the needy direct payments called scrip—certificates given to merchants in exchange for food and clothing; the merchants were reimbursed by the city in cash.

But 1932 was the year of crisis. Mayor Buckingham desperately pulled out every trick possible to feed and cloth thousands of jobless, down-and-out citizens. The city turned vacant lots into gardens, and hundreds of aliens were dropped from the relief rolls so the city could care for its own destitute citizens. City employees contributed as much as 10 percent of their wages to help the needy, and thousands of dollars were cut from city departments, including $150,000 from the Board of Education.

Above: *With the lower peacetime demand for arms after WWI, Remington Arms no longer needed eighty acres of factory and moved to Barnum Avenue. General Electric has moved into Remington's huge Boston Avenue buildings and is the largest manufacturer in Bridgeport today. Photo by Neil Swanson*

Facing page: *Mayor Edward T. Buckingham's second term, during the Depression, led him to hire the jobless to perform municipal chores for just fifty cents an hour. As the economic crisis worsened, wages fell to thirty-five cents an hour, and in 1932 Buckingham asked city employees to accept a 20 percent cut in salary for two years. Courtesy, City of Bridgeport*

The work program was even eliminated in favor of food and clothing handouts, although thirty-two businesses jointly spent $750,000 on factory refurbishing to create jobs.

Conceding that Bridgeport was one million dollars in debt and could not meet its payroll, Buckingham made his most drastic—and politically dangerous—decision in asking all city employees to accept a 20 percent salary cut for the next two years. A group of prominent businessmen also urged a reduction of municipal expenses to the 1917 level, which launched angry protests from city employees who argued they shouldn't shoulder the burden of the Depression. To top that off, Buckingham's administration was criticized for overspending on repairs to the Stratford Avenue Bridge.

Waiting in the wings during the crisis was Socialist Jasper McLevy, who proclaimed that the answer to economic relief started with governmental reform and proper spending. The next year, 1933, McLevy captured city hall for the first of his twenty-four years in the mayor's office. It also marked the year Franklin Delano Roosevelt and the federal government took an active role in bailing out cities, as cash relief flowed from Washington. In 1934 the state Emergency Relief Commission, which supervised the spending of millions of federal dollars, launched numerous statewide building programs constructing hospitals, airports, roads, and town halls. All parts of the state benefited from the program, including Bridgeport, where Park Avenue was widened and extended to meet the Merritt Parkway.

Although a few labor unions had been formed sixty years earlier and had strengthened with the city's industrial growth, the labor movement enjoyed great progress and gathered clout as workers throughout the state joined the Connecticut Federation of Labor. Many union locals were formed in Bridgeport plants. Bridgeport was now working its way out of the Depression and had once again found economic prosperity as World War II approached. Led

Above: *With Igor Sikorsky at the controls, his VS-300 helicopter lifts inches off the ground in September 1939 during its first flight test. Courtesy, Sikorsky Aircraft*

Facing page: *Russian-born Igor Sikorsky is credited with being the father of the modern helicopter. Backed by United Aircraft in 1938, he was able to continue experiments begun in Russia around 1910. With the outbreak of World War II, Sikorsky Aircraft on South Avenue developed the world's first helicopter assembly line. Courtesy, United Technologies Corporation*

by skilled toolmakers, workers in this period established the era of the machine tool industry which made products for nations all over the world. This period also established the genius of Igor I. Sikorsky.

Worried by the German seizure of Czechoslovakia in 1939, France placed huge contract orders with the United Aircraft Corporation which then expanded the Chance-Vought Division, maker of Corsair fighter planes. A new plant was built by the Sikorsky Division in Stratford where half of the 11,000 Corsairs produced during World War II were manufactured. The gull-winged Corsair, first flown at the Bridgeport Municipal Airport in 1940, was the fastest shipboard fighter in the world, reaching speeds of more than 400 m.p.h.

119

Meanwhile, the Sikorsky Division in January 1941 had won a government contract for the R-4 model helicopter, which was used extensively in the war by American and British troops for rescue work. Russian immigrant Igor I. Sikorsky, the father of the modern helicopter, had won the backing of United Aircraft in 1938 for the development of the first practical helicopter. The war spawned the world's first helicopter assembly line at the Sikorsky Aircraft Bridgeport plant on South Avenue.

Bridgeport was once again a beehive of activity, a workingman's paradise where people could count on work when all else failed, where visitors and observers on passing trains could see the perpetual illumination of factories at work.

But Bridgeport once again learned that its dependence on war would come back to haunt it during the peacetime transition. Bridgeport's Chamber of Commerce Post-War Planning Council offered, through industrial site improvements, a solution for the false security offered by the demands of the war. The Connecticut Turnpike, which stormed through the edge of the downtown district, was touted as an urban renewal plan to eliminate dilapidated housing. And as unemployment slapped 15,000 residents, Bridgeport Brass Executive Herman Steinkraus' launching of the Barnum Festival in 1949 was perceived as more than a means to salute Barnum. It also served to take residents' minds off the post-war troubles by infusing civic pride. Chance-Vought departed for Dallas the same year, but its plant was occupied two years later by Avco, a builder of military turbine engines.

This model VS-300 helicopter was flown in a test flight over Stratford meadows in the early 1940s. Sikorsky's VS-300 was the first successful helicopter in the Western Hemisphere. Courtesy, Historical Collections, Bridgeport Public Library

Organized labor's reaction to mass layoffs forged strikes, including a 1946 work stoppage by the United Electrical Workers which briefly shut down General Electric. "Unions were recognizing that they were a potent force collectively," according to Michael J. Sorrentino, one of the emerging labor leaders of the period, and president of the Greater Bridgeport Labor Council since 1971. Sorrentino recalls this as a vibrant period for labor, when at UEW local 203 meetings, fights often broke out involving card-carrying Communists who wanted a larger say in union decisions. "I had to be a rough tough guy those days. I dished out my share of bloody noses." It got so tough that a Bridgeport Police Department car was stationed at Harding High School outside every local 203 meeting.

Bridgeport city employees, who had borne the burden of the Depression, demanded better conditions, and in one precedent-setting case the first municipal union was formed. The Fire Department-Bridgeport International Union of Firefighters slashed the firefighters' eighty-four-hour work week to seventy-seven in 1946 and down to forty-two hours by 1957. The fire union leaders also were successful in having an ordinance rescinded which forbade the formation of unions by city employees.

But like many industrial cities, something else was happening to the city. Bridgeport was getting old. Its rundown factories needed repair, its shabby downtown a facelift. More than that, the heyday of the machine tool industry in the 1950s was slowly losing its grip. Japan, which had been bombed into the ground, was forced into building modern facilities, and produced casting and aluminum which cut through the heart of Bridgeport's machine tool industry. The Japanese and its cheaper work force grabbed the basic market in cars and machine tools and eventually in the electronics industry. In order to cut shipping costs, Bridgeport companies moved closer to the Midwest where the car makers were located, others

A nationwide strike against General Electric in 1946 by the members of United Electrical Workers briefly shut down the company's Bridgeport factory. A police car was often parked outside local 203 meetings held at Harding High School to head off anticipated violence. Courtesy, Historical Collections, Bridgeport Public Library

Few things are still handmade these days, but until recently, Topstone Cigars were being rolled and packed by hand in Bridgeport, as this man did in 1950. The factory, located at 256 Middle Street, was the last cigar factory in the state. Photo by Fred Schulze. Courtesy, Historical Collections, Bridgeport Public Library

moved south for the luxury of cheaper labor, and parent companies closed antiquated Bridgeport plants. The post-World War II years saw Underwood, Singer, Columbia Records, Bridgeport Brass, Dictaphone, and others either relocate or shut down. The once-powerful Remington, which was purchased by the Du Pont Company in 1933, slowly moved departments to other plants in other cities. The industry void chipped away at the city's tax base.

The 1950s also saw many middle-class Bridgeporters, made prosperous by the war, leave the city for the status of the suburbs, in search of better homes, more property, and better schools. But census figures show that rushing to the suburbs wasn't as fashionable in Bridgeport as in Hartford and New Haven, which showed far greater population decreases. While the influx of blacks and Hispanics in the 1950s and 1960s filled housing units in the East Side, South End, and West Side, Bridgeport pulled north with a housing boom, and the North End provided a suburban atmosphere within the city limits.

People's Bank became the powerhouse financial institution in the city during this period, it's growth spurting when bank President Samuel Hawley mass marketed mortgages. The bank offered cheaper VA mortgages, and found ways for people to buy their own homes.

In recent years, Bridgeport has remained dependent on the military contracts secured by Sikorsky and Avco, which employ thousands and subcontract to the remaining skilled, but smaller machine trades. With much of the skilled labor force gone with the departing companies, Bridgeport has found itself in a state of transition. The Greater Bridgeport Labor Council, which has fifty-six affiliated locals and 15,000 working people, has stepped up its training programs in nursing assistance, high technology, and vocational exploration to prepare for Bridgeport's future.

The city has developed a growing professional status as accountants, physicians, and partic-

Fred Roberto (right), once the secretary treasurer of Local 191 United Brotherhood of Teamsters, was a very powerful union force. He was succeeded by Anthony Rossetti in 1985. Photo by Frank Decerbo. Courtesy, Post Publishing Company

ularly lawyers (who have located law firms near the city's two state courthouses and the Federal District Court), have been attracted by Bridgeport's cheaper rental space. Bridgeport business and industry faces a period of transition from being a heavy military and machine tool industrial complex to becoming perhaps a professional, retail, and service center. The past two years have seen developers taking a new interest in Bridgeport. A $24-million hotel and a $65-million headquarters for People's Bank are being built, and a number of older landmarks are being remodeled to create new office and commercial space. Some say it's Bridgeport resurgence—a "boom" period— while others less optimistic who have viewed a listless downtown, wait and see.

Beardsley Park circa 1930—as seen from what is now the site of Route 8. The Park was designed by Frederick Olmsted, who also designed Central Park in New York City. Swimming is no longer allowed at the park, though thousands still visit each year. The park is a favorite for baseball and softball fans, and, of course, frisbee throwers. Photo by B. Brignolo, Brignolo Studios. Courtesy Historical Collections, Bridgeport Public Library

CHAPTER VI

The

Park City

"When you're not on Broadway, everything is Bridgeport."
—Arthur "Bugs" Baer,
syndicated columnist

Every run-of-the-mill vaudeville comic harbors a debt of gratitude to Bridgeport. When all else failed, Arthur Baer's crack evoked enough laughter to keep loads of vaudevillians off the unemployment lines. Baer's 1915 remark was adapted by numerous show people, who added a twist of their own. George M. Cohan used to go around saying, "After New York, everything is Bridgeport." In fact, he used to say it so often that everyone gave him credit for coining the phrase. For many years Daddy Warbucks lectured Little Orphan Annie about Bridgeport in the musical *Annie,* and it provided the biggest laugh in the first act. Bridgeporters generally have considered the expression a rotten put-down, despite the vaudevillians' claim that the punch line would mean the same if connected to another city.

Entertainer quotes about Bridgeport were common over the years. From the 1920s through the war years, Bridgeport became known as a magnet for New York's theater and pageantry, a decent stop off between New York and Boston. It also garnered a reputation as something of a decent tryout town. If those fussy, working-class ethnics from Bridgeport liked it, so would just about anybody. Bridgeport's savage critics could flatten any turned-up actor's nose into mashed modesty. As a result, John Barrymore reportedly said, "If you think you're great . . . play Bridgeport."

Decades after Barrymore's barb, Paul Newman blurted out something else about the city. In 1973, after making a movie in Bridgeport, he called the city a "depressing little town." A resident of genteel Westport, Newman hasn't filmed a movie in Bridgeport since, and Bridgeporters aren't exactly getting down and beating the rug over it.

*   *   *

Bridgeport had little in the way of entertainment in the early days. Its introduction to show business was a few dramatic lectures. The first theatrical house was organized in the Gay Nineties by Lewis Christian Segee, who presented shows on the second floor of his Steamboat Hotel on State Street.

The emergence of Italian immigrant Sylvester Z. Poli, who established himself as a renowned sculptor in New York and then founded numerous theaters throughout the country, launched Bridgeport as a respectable theatrical community and beautified the downtown. Poli started a string of theaters that took his name with his purchase in 1902 of the Hawes' Opera House on Fairfield Avenue. He built his first show house in Bridgeport during the Christmas week of 1912, that would become known as the Globe Theater, on Main Street. Poli lured many of the bigger vaudeville headliners of the time, including Eddie Cantor and Al Jolson. In 1922 Poli opened Bridgeport's twin architectural beauties—the Palace and Majestic theaters. Roughly fifty Broadway stars, including Mae Murray and Johnny "Torchy" Hines, attended the theaters' openings on September 4. Previous to Poli's arrival, the city's theaters had benches or wooden chairs. Poli gave them comfort and beauty. The theatrical structures featured 6,000 seats, mirror and gold leaf decorations, plasterwork, marble and crystal chandeliers,

curved balconies, and stained-glass screens.

In the next ten years, several theaters, ballrooms, and eateries would fill Bridgeport's downtown. The city seemed to have something to meet every need: hotels, entertainment, dining, shopping. Bridgeporters would take in a show at the Palace, walk next door for a one-dollar pasta dinner at the Spaghetti Place, walk a block for a sundae at the Goodie Shop (which called itself "the best place in the city to get your candies and ice cream"), and then shop at Howlands or D.M. Read's.

By 1936, Bridgeport had more than twenty theaters, enough for every neighborhood. They were more than just places to watch a movie for ten cents. The Strand handed out dinner sets to families during the Depression, and its outside concession stand was popular with children—so popular in fact that inventory literally disappeared. The girls' bathroom window was located just in back of the concession stand, and children would make frequent trips to the bathroom, jump on each other's shoulders, reach out the window and quickly fill their pockets with candy behind the cashier's back. This practice, say those who remember filling their pockets, went on for years.

As the swing tunes and the jitterbugs jumped in Bridgeport dance halls such as the Ritz Ballroom during World War II, Columbia Records was the cornerstone of the city's entertainment industry. The forerunner of Columbia was the American Graphophone Company, the world's first manufacturer of talking machines. The company, founded in 1888 by Thomas H. MacDonald in a plant on Barnum Avenue, leased to the public the machines that were developed by Thomas Edison and refined by Alexander Graham Bell.

While many other factories made munitions and arms during the war, Columbia Records made music. In 1941, its 825 workers manufactured roughly 100 million records for such Columbia stars as Benny Goodman, Kay Kayser, Count Basie, Gene Autry, and Gene Krupa.

Sylvester Z. Poli, an Italian immigrant, received early recognition for his wax sculptures in New York. He went on to establish theaters throughout the U.S., and he opened Poli's Palace Theatre in Bridgeport seen here in the mid-1930s. Courtesy, Theatre Historical Society

Right: *In 1922 Poli's Majestic Theatre, and its twin, the Palace, opened on Main Street. Poli's first showhouse, the Globe, opened Christmas week in 1912 and attracted entertainers like Eddie Cantor and Al Jolson. Courtesy, Theatre Historical Society*

Below: *The chandeliers and fine metalwork of Poli's theater lobbies distinguished them from those built today. Note the posters advertising double features, something rare in modern theatres. Model airplanes hanging from the ceiling were also an interesting touch. Courtesy, Theatre Historical Society*

If you were lucky enough to attend the opening of Poli's Palace theatre on September 4, 1922, you and 3,600 other people would have seen what a "Palace" really was. Poli's Palace was truly beautiful, with gold leaf and mirror decorations, elegant plasterwork, and stained glass. Courtesy, Theatre Historical Society

Bridgeporter Edward Krolokowski, who gained stardom with his Polish polkas, made all his recordings with Columbia. Columbia assumed the leadership in the record-making industry and modernized factory equipment, presses, and machinery. It switched from cylinders to lateral-cut flat discs of hard rubber, introduced the double-faced disc, produced the first recorded complete symphony (Beethoven's Seventh), and introduced the 33-1/3 r.p.m. LP. Columbia designer Frank C. Kinley won the patent for the automatic stop, his invention for making phonographs stop when they played to the end of the record.

In February 1941, Columbia scurried to recall copies of an explanatory leaflet printed to accompany albums of Richard Strauss' *A Hero's Life* symphony. The leaflet explained that Strauss' work was among Adolf Hitler's favorites and offered a musical picture of Hitler's Nazi propaganda.

In 1964, despite pleadings from Mayor Samuel Tedesco and Connecticut Governor John Dempsey to stay, Columbia ended record production here, citing the high cost of operation and a large, outdated facility. The Columbia complex today is a professional office building known as Columbia Towers.

Numerous Columbia artists appeared at Bridgeport's favorite nighttime spots—the Lyric, the Pleasure Beach Ballroom, and in particular, the Ritz Ballroom. The Ritz came to Bridgeport through the efforts of two Bridgeport dancers, George S. McCormack and Joseph R. Barry, who moved their Brooklawn Dancing Pavillion, at Brooklawn and Capitol, to a larger,

Facing page: *Columbia took the lead in record-making technology with developments such as the flat disc, double-sided disc, and long-playing "microgroove" record. The "Magic Notes" seen on these U.S. and English pressings from the 1940s was a company trademark. Photo by Neil Swanson. Courtesy, Ruth Swanson*

Below: *As the forerunner of Columbia Records, the American Graphophone Company made music in more ways than one. Like most large industries at that time, the company fielded a marching band for local parades. Courtesy, Robert Clifford Collection*

trolley-accessible area on Fairfield Avenue in 1923. The Ritz was the most elegant dance palace in the city, with mural decorations, crystal chandeliers, a dance hall the size of an airport runway, and the biggest of the big bands—Louis Armstrong, Tommy and Jimmy Dorsey, Artie Shaw, Rudy Vallee, and Guy Lombardo (who set the all-time fan attendance mark, attracting 4,400 "Ritzites").

Just like every other theater in the city, the Ritz fell victim to the rage of post-World War II television. As the 1950s, 60s, and 70s passed, the Lyric, Strand, Globe, Ritz, Palace, and Majestic all closed. The day the music died in Bridgeport was New Year's Eve 1961, when couples danced at the Ritz for the last time.

Ritz owner Joseph Barry leased the old dance hall to a furniture company that year. A fire in June 1970 destroyed the old dance palace.

The Park City has been home to its share of famous entertainers. Robert Mitchum was born on Logan Street in the city's East End and as a child he was noted for his poetry while at McKinley School. Mitchum has had little or no contact with the city since his parents moved to Delaware during his youth. (But he did recently write a letter to the family now occupying his old house.)

Chuck Mitchell, who grew up on Pequonnock Street in the Hollow, has won fame late in his career as the red-neck saloon owner Porky Wallace in the 1982 box office smash *Porky's*. Mitchell returns frequently to Bridgeport to visit relatives on the Upper East Side.

Both Mitchum, who had the lead role, and Mitchell, a bit part, appeared in the television mini-series *Winds of War*, which was produced and directed in 1983 by Bridgeport native Dan Curtis.

Albert "Johnny" Altieri, the long-time page boy who was discovered by Philip Morris executives at the Stratfield Hotel, won fame as the "call for Philip Morris" voice in the tobacco firm's radio and television commercials. The seventy-one-year-old Altieri worked as the Philip Morris page boy from 1935 to 1960 and retired as a company sales representative in 1982. He remains today a Bridgeport resident.

Alfred Patricelli, a forty-year city resident, has promoted beauty pageants in Bridgeport and throughout the country for more than fifty years. From 1959 to 1977 Patricelli was the executive director of the Miss World-USA pageant, a stepping-stone for the careers of Lynda Carter, Marjorie Wallace, and Donna Dixon. Patricelli lost the prestige of the Miss World-USA directorship when a U.S. District Court judge stripped him of the title in a dispute with the pageant owners. The persistent Patricelli has struggled the last eight years in promoting his new pageant, Miss Venus USA,

which he annually stages at the Klein Memorial.

Novelist Maureen Howard, who was born in Bridgeport in 1930 and graduated from Central High School, has blended many of her Park City experiences into her award-winning books, including *The Facts of Life* and *Bridgeport Bus*. Howard has not lived in Bridgeport for about thirty years, but returns to the area to visit friends and relatives.

In 1969, Bridgeport-born songwriter Paul Leka was so uninspired by the opening words to a song scheduled to be the B-side on a 45 record that he tossed in the chant "Na, na, na, na, hey, hey, goodbye." Pretty soon, everybody around the world was singing it and it made Leka a lot of money and an established songwriter. *Na, Na, Hey (Kiss Him Goodbye)*, sung by a trio of Bridgeport boys called Steam, has since sold roughly three million records.

Leka has come a long way since his Tin Pan Alley song-peddling days in New York City. At twenty-four years old in 1964, he wrote songs for a publishing company owned by Bobby Darin before he discovered REO Speedwagon as a staff producer at CBS records. For the last fourteen years the Bassick High School graduate, who also wrote the hit songs *Green Tambourine* and *Rice is Nice*, has been a producer and arranger for many pop artists at his Connecticut Recording Studio on Main Street. Musicians such as Stevie Wonder, Rita Coolidge, Kris Kristofferson, and the late Harry Chapin have recorded music at Connecticut Recording.

But Bridgeport has had relatively little in the way of entertainment these recent years. The Greater Bridgeport Symphony attracts the largest crowds to the city's only full-fledged theatrical auditorium—the Klein Memorial Auditorium, opened in 1940 through money bequeathed from the estate of prominent city lawyer Jacob Klein. The Cabaret Theater, launched in 1977, has suffered several financial setbacks but continues to provide nostalgic shows and original revues by local talent, as does the Polka Dot Playhouse at Pleasure

Whether on the screen or at the wheel of Bob Sharp's Datsun 280ZX race car, Paul Newman is a force to be reckoned with. While filming in Bridgeport in the early 1970s, Newman made the comment that the city was "a depressing little town." Newman claimed that then-Mayor Nicholas Panuzio had called the city "the armpit of New England." Photo by Neil Swanson

Beach. And, through the promotion of Klein Memorial Director Dennis Dean, Kennedy Stadium has been the scene of popular concerts in recent years, including performances by the Beach Boys and Kenny Rogers.

Over the past fifteen years several movies have been shot in Bridgeport that have become storm signals for the city's image. When directors needed the presence of run-down housing or a smokestack, Bridgeport has fit the bill. O.J. Simpson and James Coburn filmed a bank robbery scene for the 1978 movie called *Firepower* in Bridgeport. The climactic scene for the 1983 film *Without A Trace,* starring Judd Hirsch, was filmed in the South End. In the film, Hirsch plays a cop who locates a missing New York City child among Bridgeport's decrepit housing. But the 1972 film that Paul Newman directed, *The Affect of Gamma Rays on Man-in-the-Moon Marigolds,* is the one for which every Bridgeporter has forever blamed Newman, for allegedly branding their city the "armpit of New England."

Newman didn't actually coin the phrase. He gave the credit to Mayor Nicholas Panuzio. In the November 1973 issue of *Cosmopolitan* magazine, Newman said, "I shot (the movie) in Bridgeport, you know, and I filmed what was there. It's a terribly depressing little town—the mayor calls it the armpit of New England."

Mayor Panuzio upheld his reputation as a polished orator with this response in the *Bridgeport Sunday Post:* "It's asinine to even have to deny that I would say such a thing about my hometown. And, as I said, I haven't been to the movies too much in the past few years so I don't have Mr. Newman's intricate knowledge of that part of the human body."

*   *   *

Bridgeport has been called the Park City for roughly a century. Ever since the mid-1880s, when the Park City Dye Works appeared in the city directory, dozens of businesses have incorporated the moniker into their names. Just where the name originated from may never have been officially recorded. No available mayoral addresses, Park Commission, Common Council, or Board of Trade (established before the Chamber of Commerce) minutes officially declare Bridgeport the Park City. It apparently established itself through word of mouth.

One account of how Bridgeport earned its pet name comes from a column written by James H. Sterling of the *Evening Times* in September 1922. Around 1880, as other Connecticut cities enjoyed nicknames, inquiries were sent throughout Bridgeport for a fitting name. Nothing clicked until *Morning News* reporter Arthur French proclaimed: "What's the matter with calling Bridgeport the 'Park City?'" So French seems as worthy as anyone to receive the credit.

Mayor Philo C. Calhoun was the first to actively lobby for the establishment of public parks in the Park City. In his mayoral message in 1857 he said, "It is to be regretted that provisions have not long since been made for the selection and purchase of ground for a public park. The want for such a place in our crowded limits for the free circulation of air and healthful exercise is seriously felt by our citizens, and universally remarked by visitors."

While William Noble and P.T. Barnum set aside Washington Park for public use in 1851 during the initial development stages of East Bridgeport, the five-acre tract was not officially transferred to the city until 1865. That year, Barnum, Captain John Brooks, Captain Burr Knapp, and George Bailey donated the initial thirty-five acres toward Seaside Park. Architects Frederick Olmsted (who designed Central Park in New York City) and Calvert Vaux designed the park site, and city land purchases and gifts from more than seventy donors added about 200 more acres by 1915—a breakthrough year for the beautification of Seaside.

Led by Mayor Clifford B. Wilson and city planner John Nolen, Bridgeport became one of the first cities in the nation to sponsor a Board of Recreation. The city built a bath house, developed sports facilities, and purchased swing sets and seesaws for Seaside Park, and built the Perry Memorial Arch (named for William Perry, who willed money for city improvements), which serves as the formal entrance to the park at the foot of Park Avenue. The arch was designed by Henry Bacon, who numbers among his works the Lincoln Memorial in Washington. The now 340-acre Seaside Park covers two and a half miles of waterfront.

Frederick Olmsted also designed Beardsley Park, whose initial forty-three acres was donated in 1878 by James Beardsley, a farmer who insisted that the land be used for no other purpose than as a public park. The city dedicated Beardsley's statue at the Noble Avenue entrance to the park in 1909.

Connecticut's only zoo has progressed rapidly from the two-bear exhibit that was first displayed in Beardsley Park in 1922. The 33-acre zoo now features hundreds of animals, from Siberian tigers to monkeys, and attracts roughly 100,000 visitors annually.

Pleasure Beach is perhaps the one park left that is a sad reminder of the demise of the premier summer resorts of New England dating from the Gay Nineties. Tourists from throughout the northeast traveled by trolley and ferry-

The Perry Memorial Arch is a familiar site to Bridgeport parkgoers. The arch stands at the entrance to the 340-acre Seaside Park, and was designed by Henry Bacon, the designer of the Lincoln Memorial in Washington. Photo by Neil Swanson

Facing page, top: *Beardsley Park and Zoo (the only zoo in the state) got its start in 1878 with forty-three acres donated by farmer James Beardsley. With 100,000 people visiting the park annually, it remains a favorite place to bring the family and kids for a day in the sun. Photo by Neil Swanson*

Bottom: *The Siberian tigers and the hundreds of other animals at the Beardsley Park Zoo attract kids and grown-ups on sunny days. Kids may ride ponies at the children's zoo. Photo by Neil Swanson*

boat to visit the original thirty-seven-acre area also known as the "Million Dollar Playground." J.H. McMahon and P.W Wren, two wholesale liquor dealers and land developers, turned the barren, sandy island into an amusement park in 1892. Three years later, a brochure of Pleasure Beach advertised a roller coaster, boardwalk, miniature railroad, skating rink, arcade, merry-go-round, a 5,000-seat colosseum, wooden horse rides on a rail (for which the park later took the name Steeple Chase Island before returning to its original name), and a track which was one of the prestigious stops on the bicycle racing circuit. It also boasted of the Pleasure Beach legend which alleges that the island was chosen by Captain Kidd for burying vast treasures.

"No exorbitant prices, an honest dollar's worth for all," was the motto. The Pleasure Beach Cafe served broiled lobster and soft shell crab for fifty cents, broiled blue fish for forty cents, and clams on the half shell (when local oyster beds were abundant) for twenty-five cents a dozen.

McMahon and Wren, as well as other private operators, ran into some financial troubles with the help of the fires that have cursed the island through the years; the first came on August 18, 1907, and destroyed the grandstand and weaving horse-rail ride. The Bridgeport Board of Park Commissioners bought the park

for $220,000 in 1919 and took over full operation in 1938, running the park during its most glorious days. Through the Depression it was a place to relax—on the glittery carousel, roller coaster, or in the big band ballroom. In its heyday, Pleasure Beach attracted hundreds of thousands each year. In the 1950s the amusement center began to falter through the city's willingness to allow it to deteriorate, and due to declining tourist revenues.

The park became a campaign issue in Samuel Tedesco's victory over Jasper McLevy in 1957. The Tedesco administration tried reviving the park through a massive public relations campaign, but the amusement center closed in 1960 and steadily sank into disrepair. The left-over buildings, ballroom, and rides fell victim to fires, vandals, and wrecker balls. Just about every year since, Pleasure Beach has been promoted as the ideal location for a jai alai fronton, dog racing track, gambling casino, college campus, jail, or resort center. Lots of talk and ideas, but little else. The fifty-three-acre peninsula (the U.S. Army Corps of Engineers used landfill dredge from Bridgeport Harbor to increase its size by sixteen acres and connect the island to Stratford in 1947) has resembled a ghost town except for the 600-foot T-shaped pier, the last relic of the former amusement center, which survives as a local fishing haven for snapper blue anglers. The pier sustained heavy damage when Hurricane Gloria swept the area in late 1985. However, the city is receiving federal assistance to restore the structure.

For the past twenty years, the seventy-six-year-old Pleasure Beach carousel, complete with organ and hand-carved chariots and galloping horses, has been the topic of numerous restoration proposals ranging in value up to $160,000.

Bridgeport has more than forty other parks, from the 320-acre Fairchild Wheeler Golf Course developed in 1930, to the .13-acre Wood Park acquired in 1880. Much of the

Left: *The "Million Dollar Playground," Steeple Chase Island, or Pleasure Beach, circa 1895. It had many names but they all described the thirty-seven-acre amusement park known to many as the place to be in the Gay-Nineties. The Dodge'em was among the many attractions offered by the park. Courtesy, Robert Clifford Collection*

Below: *Compare this 1985 photo to the earlier one and you see just how much things have changed at Pleasure Beach since its closure in the 1960s. Nearly every year, ideas for the land's usage surface, ranging from a dog-racing track to a casino to a jail. Today, police dogs are trained at the former amusement park. Photo by Neil Swanson*

This elite group of sixteen men served as lifeguards for the Pleasure Beach Park in 1927. Being young, tan, and blond wasn't considered a requirement to protect the hundreds of thousands of beachgoers that visited the park. Courtesy, Corbit's Studio

Facing page: *In 1907 a fire at Pleasure Beach destroyed the grandstands and consumed the large building at right. The Pleasure Beach Ballroom was again destroyed by fire in 1973. Today few of the original buildings remain. Courtesy, Robert Clifford Collection*

These before and after photos show the effect of the 1907 fire on the Steeple Chase horse ride. The ride was not rebuilt after the fire. Courtesy, Robert Clifford Collection

Above: *The once-great Pleasure Beach carousel now sits empty and boarded up in the huge vacant lot that was once packed with people. The carousel horses are now in a warehouse to prevent further loss. Photo by Neil Swanson*

Facing page, top: *September 27, 1985, meant "Gloria" to the state of Connecticut and much of the Northeast. Seaside Park was struck by 130 mph winds and tides twelve feet above normal. An estimated 185,000 United Illuminating customers were left without power. Photo by Neil Swanson*

Below: *Hurricane Gloria also damaged the pier at Pleasure Beach. Once 1,500 feet long, the pier is now about half that length. Photo by Neil Swanson*

There is something new at Pleasure Beach—these pilings are the start of bathhouses and a concession due to be completed by summer 1986. Also planned is a new boardwalk. The revitalization is estimated to cost about four and one-half million dollars. The radio towers in the background are for radio station WICC. Photo by Neil Swanson

parkland was either bought or donated after 1915 when city planner John Nolen proposed land acquisitions to beautify Bridgeport. Today Bridgeport boasts 1,374 park acres, one for about every 104 people—which is just about the figure the federal government has determined that cities need to accomodate residents.

* * *

Bridgeport parks have extended the perfect showcase for many of its sports stars, whether they be on a local or professional level. The city never has and probably never will be a major sports center, but it has had its share of local stars.

Louis Brock, a champion rope climber, was one of the first. Brock pulled his weight to the eastern rope climbing championship in 1881, with the hand-over-hand method. Bridgeporters (and Brock) crowed regularly about the 138-pound Brock's 16.5 inch biceps which measured larger than those of ex-bare knuckles champion John L. Sullivan, who made the downtown Tremont Hotel his home for a while.

In the Gay Nineties, Bridgeport boasted a champion roller team which won the Southern New England league title for three straight years. Led by center George "Dumpy" Williams, the team was a scrappy quintet on roller skates that played in a rink on Lumber Street.

Bridgeport also had a rather bizarre sense of sportsmanship as well, particularly at the turn of the century. Around 1905, Bridgeport could safely broadcast that it had the only true rattlesnake club in the country. One spring, a bunch of newspaper editors, including The Herald's Richard Howell, organized and manned a rattlesnake club. Armed with forked sticks, the scribes sojourned to the nearest place they could find rattlers—Kent Mountain in Kent, Connecticut—where an Indian named Big Chief Pan, head of the Schaghticoke Indians, helped them to find the timber rattlers. He also provided his sure-cure whiskey snakebite remedy which promised to save even the weakest man from the most poisonous snake attack. The trick was to scout out the snake, thrust the forked stick behind its head, and lean down and grab the snake and stuff it into a burlap bag. The unpardonable crime was to injure a snake in the catching; points were scored based on the handling of the timbers.

The popularity of these annual expeditions spread so rapidly that the head curator of reptiles at the American Museum of Natural History in New York joined the snake seekers, who generally exhibited their catch at Bridgeport gun and tobacco shops. The only accident involving both man and snake came when a rattler lodged its fangs into the hand of charter member Charles E. Wheeler, who was cured by a venom-sucking teammate and several instant gulps of Chief Pan's Sagwa remedy. The club died of natural causes with the commencement of Prohibition when the main ingredient of Pan's remedy—whiskey—became unavailable. It was probably the first sporting event in Bridgeport history that gave a bunch of newspaper people a good excuse to get out and drink.

But the rattlesnake club didn't have nearly as much fan support as the city's jam-packed wrestling matches at Eagle's Hall. Wrestling was probably Bridgeport's favorite early day spectator event; sports page play by local papers regularly drop-kicked the New York Yankees for wrestling and would banner screaming headlines as early as World War I. Such greats as "the huge" Polish grappler Larry Zybyszko and the "South African Boer" Peter Nogert would square off in Bridgeport arenas.

Bridgeport hasn't restricted itself to the offbeat sporting life. It has produced many local players who have performed in the professional ranks of the mass media-supported sporting events. James. H. O'Rourke, son of one of the first Irish families to settle in the city, played outfielder and catcher in major league baseball for twenty-one years in the late 1800s and was inducted into the Hall of Fame in 1945. At the turn of the century O'Rourke developed Newfield Park in the East End, which gave life to many baseball organizations including the Bridgeport Bears, an Eastern League professional franchise that folded in 1932. Newfield Park played host to many great baseball players. Lou Gehrig, who led Hartford's entry in the Eastern League before starring with the Yankees, played many games in Bridgeport, as did Babe Ruth, who made exhibition appearances while with the Bronx Bombers.

The first unassisted triple play in major league baseball was turned by a Bridgeporter. On July 19, 1909, while playing shortstop for Cleveland in the American League, Neal Ball snared a line drive, touched the runner off second base, and tagged the runner coming from first.

Bridgeport native George "Kiddo" Davis starred at Bridgeport High School before playing on the New York Giants World Series championship team in 1933. Davis, who compiled a lifetime average of .282, batted .368 in that World Series. Bridgeport's most recent entry into the majors is Kurt Kepshire, a star pitcher with Central High School, who chucked for the National League champion St. Louis Cardinals in 1985. Many of Bridgeport's baseball prospects have toiled in the Senior City League, a showcase of area talent for more than 100 years.

After returning home from World War II in 1947, Bob Sherwood's urge to play baseball was so great that he poured his last cent into building a sports stadium, founded the Bridgeport Bees minor league baseball team, and played centerfield for it. Sherwood and Carl Brunetto bought 6.5 acres in the North End and built Candlelite Stadium which included fields for baseball, football, and a one-fifth-of-a-mile track for stock car and midget auto racing. With the resurgence of minor league ball after the war, Sherwood entered the Bridgeport Bees, a farm team of the Washington Senators, into the Colonial League and later hired Hall

of Fame slugger Jimmy Foxx as manager. The team was noted for developing black and Cuban players just after Jackie Robinson broke baseball's color barrier. One of the star players, José Blanco, even had his wedding ceremony at home plate. Sherwood's team folded in 1953 as attendance declined with the emergence of television.

Certainly one of the greatest team dynasties in the history of organized sports was forged by the Brakettes, who in the last quarter century have won eighteen national softball titles, two world championships, and more than 1,500 games. Since Raybestos Division General Manager William S. Simpson organized and sponsored the team in 1947, the names of Bertha Tickey, Joan Joyce, Barbara Reinalda, and Kathy Arendsen have helped to make the Brakettes America's best women's softball squad. Bridgeport developer F. Francis "Hi-Ho" D'Addario, who died in a plane crash March 5, 1986, took over sponsorship of the team in 1985 after Raybestos, the long-time sponsor, ran into financial difficulties.

D'Addario also owned Bridgeport's Hi-Ho Jets professional football team from 1968 to 1973 which featured players such as John Dockery and Earl Christy, both of whom played on the New York Jets' 1969 championship team. The Bridgeport Jets, playing in the Atlantic Coast football league, initially drew large and enthusiastic crowds into Kennedy Stadium. Though the Jets never won a league title, their game in Orlando, Florida, probably did more to impact the women's movement than any other team or game anywhere. The Jets featured a 235-pound linebacker named Wally Florence, who hit anything in sight, and Orlando fielded a 5'2", 110-pound female extra-point kicker, who some thought brought to the team little more than a lot of attention. On one extra-point try, Florence lined up, barreled through the Orlando offensive line, and crunched the female kicker into the turf. Network television picked up footage of the locally filmed game, and the Jets were captured throughout the country. All the attention couldn't save the Jets from folding in 1973.

The biggest turf and court wars in Bridgeport high school sports have been waged between Harding and Central High, as each has recorded its dominant years in both football and basketball. Their Thanksgiving Day football clashes have often turned out more than 10,000 spectators. Central has graduated standout athletes such as Frank "Porky" Vieira and George "Kiddo" Davis while Harding boasts Charles Tisdale, one of the city's top high school quarterbacks, and Wes Mathews and John Bagley, both of whom currently play in the National Basketball Association. The two arch-rival coaches who have touched the lives

of many of the city athletes were Harding's Steve Miska and Central's Eddie Reilly, the first honored sportsman of the Greater Bridgeport Old Timers Association in 1958. Other influential coaches still active include Emmett Spillane, veteran sports editor of the *Bridgeport Post-Telegram* and Perry Pilotti, the founder of the Arctic Sports Shop, who has coached on a local level for four decades. In his position as the American representative of the Italian Baseball and Softball Federation, Pilotti has arranged for many Americans to play baseball in Italy, and he is liaison for Italian baseball in the Commissioner's Office of Major League Baseball, developing exchange programs and tours, and coaching Italians on baseball. He is also an advisor to the Italian Olympic Baseball Committee.

The man who has triggered the most attention on the Bridgeport sports scene recently is the 7'6" Sudanese, Manute Bol. University of Bridgeport (UB) hoop fans appropriately coined him "Basket Bol." For one year, Bol was a giant exclamation point for the UB program, scoring twenty points per game, rebounding, and swatting shots. Practically every major newspaper and sports magazine has profiled UB coach Bruce Webster's discovery. Citing financial problems, Bol left Bridgeport after one season in 1984-85 to play in a newly founded professional basketball league, and then jumped to the NBA's Washington Bullets who drafted him the league's second round in 1985.

Facing page: *Bridgeport has always had a great number of clubs, both ethnic and political. Here the 7th District Democratic Club poses for its team picture in front of the FDR club. Photo by B. Brignolo, Brignolo Studios. Courtesy, Historical Collections, Bridgeport Public Library*

Top left: *A popular Park City sporting event during the early 1900s was the one-mile hill climb sponsored by the Automobile Club of Bridgeport. On May 30, 1907, Harry D. Gates of the Fairfield Automobile Company drove a 16 HP Reo to the finish line in two minutes and sixteen seconds. Photo by Neil Swanson. Courtesy, Robert Clifford Collection*

Above: *You might say the 1984-85 basketball season was the year of "Basket Bol." Seven-foot-six-inch Manute Bol towers over other players considered tall in their own right. One newspaper story claimed Bol had chipped his teeth on the rim while still learning the game. Today Bol plays for the NBA's Washington Bullets. Photo by Barry Tenin. Courtesy,* People Magazine

A Jasper McLevy tradition: an evening victory motorcade on Main Street following the former roofer's 1941 mayoral election. A tireless soapbox campaigner, McLevy was respected as the workingman's friend who took patronage out of politics and cut Bridgeport's $16-million municipal debt in half during his twenty-four years in office. Courtesy, Historical Collections, Bridgeport Public Library

CHAPTER VII

Jasper

McLevy

"God put the snow there . . . let Him take it away."

—attributed to Jasper McLevy

I t's the spring of 1939 and Bridgeport's Public Works Director Pete Brewster is taking another needling about his tardy snow removal operations from reporters. The scene is Billy Prince's bar on State Street, where the truth or the near truth about city operations flowed freely for a good many years. "Napoleon," as Brewster's scribe friends called him, grew angrier with each sip of his beer and each jab from the probing reporters.

How, they repeatedly insisted, could Brewster allow so much time to elapse before firing up city snowplows to clear the streets? Brewster, of course, had been smarting since the previous November when *The Herald* had plowed him for "waiting 'till the sun shines" to clear the streets of snow. "Napoleon fails to fight storm, thousands suffer," the scandal sheet's headline declared. "Sole responsibility for the terrible condition of Bridgeport streets following last weekend's double snowstorm rests with Director of Public Works Peter P. 'Napoleon' Brewster," crowed the story's opening paragraph. And, for practically every week that winter, *The Herald* poked fun at Brewster's snow-plowing direction. After all, the city had initially appropriated only $300 in the budget to cover the cost of snow and ice clear-

This 1938 Bridgeport Herald *cartoon criticizes Peter P. "Napoleon" Brewster, director of public works, for his lack of speed in snow removal, but Socialist Mayor Jasper McLevy's penny-pinching city budget was the real culprit. Cartoon by Jess Benton. Courtesy, Historical Collections, Bridgeport Public Library*

ance that year.

So, with several months of persistent nagging catching up to him, Brewster picked this moment in Billy Prince's to break his long-standing silence. "Let the Guy who put the snow there take it away," he cut loose. Bridgeporters were never satisfied by the excuses given for the lack of snow removal, but this was the Depression, and although many vociferous complaints about mushing through the snow had piled up, residents had by then grown accustomed to their penny-pinching Socialist Mayor Jasper McLevy.

With each passing winter and with more taxpayers' complaints about the snow-covered streets, the story of how Jasper McLevy said "God put the snow there, let Him take it away," has been told countless times in front of fireplaces, in snow-stranded vehicles and, yes, in bars. Jasper McLevy, down through the

years, involuntarily received the credit for a line coined by his long-time and trusted employee. But for Bridgeport, it represented a sign of the times and the tight-spending of a reform mayor who helped lift Bridgeport out of bankruptcy and out of the dog days of the Depression.

Jasper McLevy was Bridgeport's mayor from 1933 to 1957, one of the longest tenures for a chief executive officer of a city of any size. That feat alone would be worth admiring, but for twelve straight municipal elections, Democrats, Republicans, and independent voters marched into voting booths to elect a Socialist as their mayor. Yet the Socialist affiliation was generally meaningless to those who supported him. They were loyal to a man who showed there could be honesty in government; someone who lived up to practically every campaign promise and kept taxes and spending to a minimum ... a man who would be known to them as just Jasper.

A few days after McLevy died in November 1962, William J. Walsh, the *Bridgeport Post* political reporter who covered McLevy for many of his twenty-four mayoral years, wrote: "To say that his death marks an end of an era is too trite, for this puts the emphasis on time rather than personality. Jasper McLevy was an era all by himself. His imprint on the city was the greatest since a distant predecessor in the mayor's chair—P.T. Barnum."

McLevy introduced the civil service system into Bridgeport to cut off the patronage that dominated political power in the past; convinced the state to maintain key city bridges and highways; made garbage collection a city function; revamped the sewage system with trunk sewers leading to disposal plants; supported slum clearance to pave the way for low-to-moderate-income housing units; and slashed in half the $16-million bonded indebtedness that he had inherited. Voter confidence in McLevy grew so strong that some even suggested that he could grow grass in the streets.

And in a way, he did that too—he built esplanades.

*   *   *

McLevy was born in Bridgeport on March 27, 1878, to two Scottish immigrants. The oldest of nine children, he left school in the eighth grade and went to work in local factories before joining his father's roofing trade, which he eventually took over years later when his father died from a fall off a roof. His inspiration to join the Socialist cause came from reading Edward Bellamy's *Looking Backward.*

McLevy was the last—and perhaps best—of the soapbox campaigners. Thirty years before he became mayor, he tirelessly campaigned on street corners and in front of factory gates for various elective city positions, with practically no success. A Scot with a weather-beaten face from his days as a roofer, he took to the streets with cracked hands and a battered felt hat. In those early days, McLevy didn't command much of an audience, so he'd plant a heckler in the crowd to trigger some give-and-take on the issues at hand. Often the heckler would shout,

"If you don't like it here why don't you get out." McLevy would reply, "I not only like it here, but I like it more than you because I want to improve it."

McLevy's first political success came in 1903. Although he lost his bid for the city clerk's position, voters soundly accepted his petition drive for a referendum to ask for the appropriation of free textbooks for elementary school children. McLevy modeled himself after the man re-elected as mayor that year, Denis Mulvihill, the Irish stoker. McLevy admired Mulvihill for becoming the city's first workingman's mayor—shattering the white-collar tradition of installing Yankee chief executive officers. In the following years, McLevy ran for a variety of municipal and state offices, including alderman, state representative, and state senator, receiving in some cases a few dozen votes in local races. Nevertheless, he continued to build his name recognition and attended nearly every Common Council meeting after 1900, building his knowledge of city affairs and parlaying his union activities into boosting a small electoral base. He had helped organize the Central Labor Union and was a leader in the Slate and Tile Roofer's Union, rising to become international president of the organization three times. And through his gritty union activities he learned to out-talk and out-pound the opposition with brilliant political rhetoric.

In 1911 McLevy took to his mayoral soapbox for the first time, maintaining that the only cure to the evils of patronage was civil service, an eight-hour work day, municipal ownership of utilities, and tighter spending—the Socialist platform he would continually espouse as he began building credibility with national Socialist Party leaders such as Norman Thomas, the long-time presidential nominee of the party. In McLevy's first mayoral race, the Socialist drew votes from elements disgusted with the political machine of Republican Town Chairman John T. King (perhaps the greatest

McLevy came right from the rooftop to become Bridgeport's mayor. The day after his 1933 victory, he first finished a roofing job before assuming office. Courtesy, Historical Collections, Bridgeport Public Library

political boss in city history), who nevertheless led Clifford B. Wilson to the first of five consecutive mayoral victories. McLevy, riding the fervor of the early labor movement, finished a respectable third, drawing 3,625 votes, 2,000 votes behind Wilson.

McLevy was up against the most charismatic politician of the times. King, a charming, calculating, brilliant strategist, had formed political clubs throughout the city for the sole function of doling out jobs in his patronage system. King had reversed the Democratic trend of Irish political leaders, building his power base in the Republican Party and becoming a national committeeman. He formed a political friendship with Allan F. Paige, a Yankee Republican in the shadow of the Mulvihill and Edward T. Buckingham mayoral years, and built a powerful patronage machine, a double machine. While King realized McLevy drew some anti-establishment votes from him, he also knew that the McLevy factor would siphon off more votes from the Democrats. All the things King stood for—power, patronage, political clubs—McLevy furiously fought against, but King wanted McLevy to run. And McLevy helped King's candidate become mayor.

McLevy often said that the Democrats were "spare tires" to the King machine and someday "when people get sick enough of this municipal circus we are liable to have a blowout that will affect all their tires." Still King became quite fond of McLevy as a politician and insisted he would make him mayor someday if only he turned Republican. Speculation centered on whether King financed McLevy's campaigns, since King spoke so highly of McLevy.

McLevy ran for mayor (and a variety of other offices) almost every election year after 1911, his vote generally unimpressive, but still a factor in the King-Wilson victories. McLevy, who married his childhood sweetheart Mary Flynn in 1911, preached the labor movement, and his voice was heard regularly in legislative halls in the battles to establish the Workman's Compensation Law and the Public Utilities Commission in 1913.

During the King-Wilson era, Bridgeport emerged as a major industrial city and as the country's arms and munitions center. Parks were beautified, dental programs instituted in schools, and dirt roads given a coating of expensive pavement. But much of the money spent on the city came from King's bonding policies. King strayed from the commonly known pay-as-you-go system to build up the city. It worked for quite some time, but King's machine became vulnerable as the city's bonded debt grew.

In 1921, Democratic Town Chairman John Cornell and his mayoral candidate Fred Atwater convinced voters the city needed spending re-

form, and King was dethroned, if only for one term. The two became embroiled in a fight for party control which King quickly exploited, and his precision figuring surfaced once again in the 1923 election. Realizing several hundred Germans were active in the Socialist Party and regularly supported McLevy, he nominated F. William Behrens, a German and local butcher, for mayor. King's strategy was to borrow just enough votes from McLevy for a victory over the Democrats. That election McLevy received 330 less votes than the previous one, precisely just enough votes for King's candidate to sneak past the Democrat.

During the 1920s, try as he might, McLevy could not convince the voters that both parties were no-good scoundrels and that the Socialist Party presented the only honest choice. McLevy's tireless love for the soapbox continued on street corners for biennial runs for mayor and governor. Although McLevy would not be elected mayor for another seven years, 1926 became a breakthrough year and resulted in the most radical change in Bridgeport's government. An investigation by State Tax Commissioner William H. Blodgett found that Bridgeport had not collected more than three million dollars in back taxes covering several years and three administrations. Blodgett said $38,000 in abatements had been granted on the night before the 1923 election, in what he described as "clean up night," and over the ensuing two-year period his investigation revealed abatements amounting to $400,000 for King's political friends. On top of that, the 1922 city tax book had suddenly disappeared. Blodgett cited sixty-seven cases of illegal abatements and charged the city with flagrant financial mismanagement.

"Bridgeport," said Blodgett, "is one of those towns that doesn't collect their taxes very well. That way of doing things came into vogue in Bridgeport years ago; it is ingrained there and people have become tempered to it."

As a result, the state legislature enacted the

Above: *Mayor McLevy and his second wife, Vida Stearns, celebrating their last mayoral victory on November 9, 1955. McLevy had married Stearns, an artist, in 1929, but kept the marriage a secret for five years until* The Herald *discovered the marriage certificate in the Office of Vital Statistics. His first wife, Mary Flynn, had died many years earlier. Courtesy, Historical Collections, Bridgeport Public Library*

Facing page: *Bridgeport Mayor Hugh Curran greets Vida McLevy Parsons at dedication ceremonies renaming the old City Hall as McLevy Hall on November 1, 1967. McLevy had suffered a stroke in 1960, forcing him into political retirement. He died on November 19, 1962. Courtesy, Historical Collections, Bridgeport Public Library*

"Ripper Bill," which ripped financial home rule away from Bridgeport. Under the bill, the governor appointed the tax collector, tax attorney, and the Board of Apportionment and Taxation, which set the city's millage rate. The Ripper Bill also cut into the political spoils of John T. King, who died in 1926, leaving no one to rally the Republican Party. McLevy actually denounced the Ripper Bill as "destroying the principle of home rule in Bridgeport," and he later used it as ammunition to forever blame the Republicans and Democrats.

Behrens managed to win the last of his three terms in 1927, which would be the last Republican victory in Bridgeport until 1971. Behrens' administration collapsed with the news of a bridge scandal involving the newly constructed Yellow Mill Bridge on the East Side. Charges of graft concerning the construction of the bridge surfaced and flushed out greater revelations. Members of the bridge commission which approved the construction contract had become secret members of a dummy corporation organized by the construction company. Essential bridge materials passed through the dummy corporation, some supplied by a contractor who was actually a bridge commission member. An investigating committee estimated the city made an overpayment of $183,000.

The Democrats seized the opportunity and brought back Edward T. Buckingham, a Yale graduate, who was beaten by the King machine in 1911. Buckingham promised voters no more "cost plus" contracts and won the scandal vote for a victory. While Buckingham banged away at the Republicans' bridge scandal, McLevy's chief charge against Behrens was that he increased the city bonded debt up to $14,828,000. In 1929, the 50-year-old McLevy polled only 1,968 votes, yet it was his highest mayoral vote since 1911, and he carried on, running for governor in 1930, gradually earning respect from the electorate through his effective workingman's political rhetoric. During his 1930 race for governor, he authored the fol-

lowing campaign letter to the live letter column of the *Bridgeport Post*:

I note by the evening papers that Dean Wilbur Cross declines to discuss with me the issues of the campaign and through his State Chairman P.B. Sullivan says 'It's bears, not chipmunks, we want' and further says that he hopes that I will not take any offense at the suggestion that during this campaign we are gunning for bear and can't waste any time or ammunition on chipmunks.

But really, are not my Democratic opponents starting out on a very ambitious hunting expedition, for hunters who haven't even shot a chipmunk for many years? Either the hunters have been poor or the ammunition faulty—or both! Many a good hunting trip has been ruined, however, by the squirrels nibbling holes in the bottom of the powder pouch.

There are more squirrels in Connecticut than bears, my kindly opponents, so why should I take offense at being labeled a little chipmunk? You will need a lot of little chipmunks, P.B., in this campaign to put your Dean across—so don't ride too high in your gilded chariot.

Great oaks from little acorns grow and great political parties from little chipmunks grow. A thought that is well to keep in mind, my worthy opponent.

Wilbur Cross was elected Govenor of Connecticut, but the patient McLevy would get more than even some eight years later.

*   *   *

Six months after Buckingham came into power on the crest of the Yellow Mill Bridge scandal, his administration allowed a contract for the repair of the Stratford Avenue Bridge at a cost of $33,000. After months of work, however, the repair costs had run beyond $150,000. Buckingham explained than an engineering contract mistake low-balled the repair figure at $33,000, and that bridge conditions were actually worse. But the public wasn't buying Buckingham's excuse. As it turned out, bridge repairs totaled roughly $280,000. Whether Buckingham was telling the truth or not, Bridgeporters had experienced their fill of bridge scams. It appeared that the question wasn't whether there would be a bridge scam this year, but which bridge would be involved.

Buckingham, meanwhile, had other problems—Bridgeport started feeling the stock market crash of 1929. The slowdown came harder and heavier with each passing month, and the worst was yet to come. Unemployment rose at record rates; the city borrowed millions to meet the welfare crisis. Charges of municipal corruption or the exposure of a political pork barrel may not have overjoyed voters in the past, but they could more easily swallow

the scams and forgive the elected officials during times of prosperity. In the eyes of the voters bearing the worst of times during the Depression, this practice grew too costly. With people out of work, they had time to listen to McLevy, who was now emerging as the 'I told you so' front-runner. He had warned before the disclosure of the bridge scandal that the city would overspend on the repairs, just as the Republicans had done years before. McLevy earned respect as the champion of the taxpayer. With his battered campaign hat and frayed shirt, his street corner crowds grew and intensified.

"They used to talk about the Socialists dividing up the wealth," McLevy told the crowds. "That makes the two old parties like the thief yelling 'Stop, thief' to detract attention from themselves."

McLevy also hammered Buckingham's exlusive use of a black limousine and two chauffeuring police officers during the economic crisis. Buckingham played into McLevy's hands by sneering at his shabby shirt, questioning this man who would be mayor. McLevy countered, "There are a lot of workmen's shirts in Bridgeport."

Still, McLevy was up against Democratic Town Chairman Cornell's powerful political machine, which had a campaign fund of roughly $60,000. Street money was everywhere for the Democrats, but McLevy had no campaign fund, no organization. He had but the nickels, dimes, and quarters of factory workers.

The 1931 poll results garnered Buckingham 17,889 votes, McLevy 15,084, and the Republicans showed a poor third. But McLevy had elected a slate of Socialists: an alderman, three sheriffs, and two selectmen. For McLevy, twenty years after he first trumpeted his cause on street corners, it was just a matter of time. People didn't care anymore that he was a Socialist. McLevy could now build a political organization based on his latest showing. He stepped up his push for civil service to eliminate the political spoils the two parties had ex-

On his sixtieth birthday, McLevy, his wife Vida, and their dog Lassie spend a quiet weekend at their country retreat in Washington, Connecticut. Courtesy, Historical Collections, Bridgeport Public Library

Mayor McLevy seemingly spent as much time discussing city issues at Van Dykes, his favorite spot for morning tea, as he did at City Hall. Here he is chatting with his longtime City Treasurer John Shenton. Photo by Fred Schulze. Courtesy, Historical Collections, Bridgeport Public Library

ploited, directing his calls to the blocs of ethnic voters.

The city's financial crisis deepened, albeit with some flashes of humor such as public debate over whether the monkeys at the zoo should continue to receive their bananas. But McLevy didn't find anything funny about the city's financial situation. Workdays were cut and scrip was handed out. The tax board discovered that $1,500 had been used to pay for the private phones of various city officials, including the mayor. On New Year's Eve 1932 it was announced that the city's cash had been exhausted and the payroll could not be met. City employees were paid two weeks late when Bridgeport Hydraulic, Bridgeport Gas Light Company, and Southern New England Telephone Company made advance payments of $340,000 on their tax bills. The Chamber of Commerce reached into the business community to form the Committee of 100 to determine ways to soften the burden of the Depression.

In the spring of 1933, only months from election time, Buckingham resigned as mayor for a workman's compensation commissionership, leaving James L. Dunn, president of the Common Council, as mayor. Voters were now clearly ready for a radical change and they registered their restlessness in the voting booth. McLevy received 22,445 votes, more than 6,000 votes ahead of Dunn. It was now official. Jasper McLevy had come into power on the sins of the Democrats and Republicans and he would attack the two parties unmercifully for the next twenty-four years.

The morning after McLevy celebrated his victory with friends and relatives, he stripped the political signs off his battered green truck, loaded his roofing materials into it, and drove off to finish a roofing job in Southport. Bridgeport citizens blacked in beards on McLevy photographs, comparing "Honest Jasper" with "Honest Abe" Lincoln, but McLevy told everyone he just wanted to be known as "the same old Jasper;" he held his inaugural luncheon in a diner a few blocks from City Hall. The first action he took as mayor was to discard the black limousine the Democratic mayors had used.

McLevy was not only a patient politician, he was a lucky one too. Eight days after his election, the federal government announced it would assume Bridgeport's largest Depression expense—1,000 persons on city relief rolls.

In the years ahead, McLevy became the most visible and predictable Bridgeport mayor ever. Never a desk mayor, he would stop in to his third floor office in the red brick City Hall on State Street for about an hour in the morning, then make on-the-job inspections at the Public Works garage or sanitation department, and lunch on corned beef and tea at Van Dykes

on Main Street. McLevy would often saucer his tea—transferring the hot liquid to his saucer, he'd then lean forward to sip. Some Bridgeporters would be absolutely horrified at the sight of their mayor saucering his tea, but they grew accustomed to it. After lunch Jasper would go back into the field until 4 p.m., return to City Hall for an hour or two, return home for dinner cooked by his sister Mabel, then go out to city meetings. Jasper had few friends outside of politics and inside he never groomed an heir. Three of his most trusted employees were City Attorney Harry Schwartz, Comptroller Perry Rodman, and City Clerk and Campaign Manager Fred Schwartzkopf.

McLevy clearly lived up to his workingman's promise. The five-foot-nine-inch mayor wore a wrinkled blue or grey suit, a shirt with frayed collars, sometimes a sweater over his vest, a battered hat, and a funny-looking tie. He never owned or rented a tuxedo and always preferred the corner setting of a diner to the banquets he loathed. McLevy rarely went to church except for funerals and retained the rigid marks of a strict Presbyterian upbringing: he never smoked or took a drink. His informal conversation was loaded with pungent curse words rivaling the speech of any blue-collar worker. He was a patriotic mayor, appearing at every parade waving an American flag. Indeed, he was a people's mayor.

He was also a strictly private man. His 1929 marriage to artist Vida Stearns remained a secret for five years, until the *Herald* dug up a copy of their marriage certificate from the Office of Vital Statistics. (McLevy's first wife had died many years before.) They maintained that they kept their marriage a mystery and lived in separate houses so Vida Stearns could care for her ailing father, Edmund Stearns. Some said that Edmund Stearns had a secret distaste of McLevy's desertion of Socialist principles, which also created dissension between McLevy and national Socialist leaders.

But McLevy clearly was elected as a reform

Above: *Whether it was at home in Bridgeport or at his week-end cottage in Washington, Connecticut, McLevy showed an unending affection for his dog, Lassie, a constant companion. Courtesy, Historical Collections, Bridgeport Public Library*

Facing page: *Jasper McLevy, Bridgeport's Socialist mayor, served the city for twelve terms, from 1933 to 1957. Local officeholders and city employees, as well as the Singer Sewing Machine Company Band, posed for this 1936 photo with the "Official Family." Courtesy, Historical Collections, Bridgeport Public Library*

mayor and not a Socialist. He repeatedly lectured people on honesty and morality, but did not often dip into Socialist principles such as the abolition of private wealth.

McLevy and his wife often took weekend holidays to their farm in the hills of Washington, Connecticut, with his collie "Lassie," who was the only living thing (including his wife) who ever received a public demonstration of affection from him.

Locally, McLevy built up layers and layers of trust and honesty, but he also became one of the giants on the state political scene. He continued running for governor many times after being elected mayor, and in 1934 he carried Bridgeport in the gubernational race, outpolling his old foe Governor Cross by 4,000 votes. He was largely responsible for the election of three Socialist state senators and two representatives, who comprised the city's entire legislative delegation at Hartford. With seventeen Democrats and fifteen Republicans in the Senate, McLevy skillfully secured the balance of power to win his legislative proposals by dealing with the Republicans, who in turn enacted McLevy's programs for the return of "home rule," state maintenance of key bridges and

highways, a centralized purchasing department, and civil service (the system that would hire prospective city workers based on tests results, eliminating much of the spoils that McLevy denounced so regularly).

The civil service regulations were compiled by City Attorney Harry Schwartz, one of McLevy's most trusted advisors. By living up to his word that politics would not control the city, McLevy became the guardian angel of civil service and actually created his own political machine by solidifying the devotion of all city employees whose positions were protected by the strong civil service system. In years past, City Hall would be just about cleaned out after an administration's defeat. But under civil service, city workers enjoyed the greatest job security, drawing the fire of post-McLevy era mayors and department heads, whose authority to transfer and terminate was limited by the regulations.

McLevy had now become a legitimate state power, but his greatest political triumph was ironically an election he didn't win. Continuing his biennial pursuance of the governor's seat, McLevy's ability to earn credibility through the scent of scandal peaked in 1938. The corner-

Above: *On December 14, 1938, McLevy chats with Governor Raymond Baldwin (right) and Wilbur Cross, who was defeated by McLevy's presence in that year's gubernatorial race. Courtesy, Historical Collections, Bridgeport Public Library*

Facing page: *McLevy prepares to pull the Socialist Party lever in the 1939 mayoral election. Courtesy, Historical Collections, Bridgeport Public Library*

stone of his gubernatorial campaign stemmed from the revolt against graft scandals involving the city of Waterbury and the Merritt Parkway. McLevy received an astonishing 166,000 votes on the Socialist ticket, roughly 64,000 votes behind the new governor, Raymond E. Baldwin, who would later serve as Chief Justice of the State Supreme Court. While the Waterbury and Merritt Parkway scandals tainted both of the major parties, McLevy's image of honesty siphoned enough votes from Governor Cross to swing the election to Baldwin with a 2,688 vote plurality. Politically, McLevy had gotten even with Cross who eight years earlier had labeled him a chipmunk.

* * *

In McLevy's first six years, federal relief spending in Bridgeport reached ten million dollars, yet McLevy seemed to grow more and more frugal on how it, and particularly city money, would be spent. For instance, in 1940 McLevy spent only $10 all year on office supplies and $89.44 on postage, telephone, and telegraph service. McLevy retained only one

secretary and his initial $7,500 mayoral salary was increased quite infrequently, reaching only $10,500 during his twenty-four years in office. His salary was far below the incomes of mayors running cities of comparable size. Often McLevy never spent unless it was absolutely necessary. For instance, the original snow and ice removal appropriation of 1939, the year complaints bombarded Public Work's Director Pete Brewster, was only $300. But the city ended up dipping into the general fund to spend $13,000 to plow the streets.

In 1939, McLevy shot down a proposal to pay $4,500 a year toward retaining a full-time school physician, even though federal money would have fully funded the first two years, paid for the physician's car, and would even have added assistance for many more years.

City health officials scoffed at McLevy's argument, insisting an additional $4,500 wouldn't affect the city budget and amounted to a mere seventeen cents per student.

When it came to federal money, McLevy said he couldn't be sure how long it would last. One of the expenditures he did allow was the installation of many miles of esplanades to enhance the city's beauty. They became known as "Jasplanades." He also spent money on the expansion of residential sewers that had initially emptied into Long Island Sound. Maintaining that the city needed a clean shorefront, he initiated the unglamorous sewage disposal project, laying trunk sewers that flowed uniformly to two disposal plants.

During his twenty-four years, four federal low-cost public housing projects creating 2,539 units were constructed, along with two state developments that added 1,280 moderately priced rental apartments. McLevy spoke often of slum clearance, but initial credit for constructing housing projects belongs to Father Stephen J. Panik. As many of the East Side's framed houses aged and fell victim to numerous fires, Father Panik proposed a predominantly federally funded housing project that would be affordable to the Depression-era citizens. McLevy initially opposed the project because the city's contribution would amount to 10 percent or roughly $650,000.

Father Panik took his proposal to the people with a public hearing. McLevy threatened to veto the proposal if the council approved it, and there he heard his first chorus of boos as mayor. The battle lines were drawn—Father Panik, a Czechoslovakian immigrant, had the city's liberal elements, McLevy had the Chamber of Commerce representing the interests of builders and landlords, who viewed public housing as a threat to their businesses. But most of the support grasped the hand of Father Panik. McLevy did an about-face on the issue and successfully appealed to the state to ease the city's financial contribution to the project.

Above: *In a rare photo, McLevy poses with Father Stephen J. Panik, who battled McLevy and subsequently won the mayor's support for slum clearance that led to the establishment of the Father Panik Village Housing Project. Courtesy, Historical Collections, Bridgeport Public Library*

Facing page: *The rains came in November 1949, but it didn't stop McLevy from his ninth victory motorcade. Courtesy, Historical Collections, Bridgeport Public Library*

By 1940, ground was broken on what McLevy called "the biggest event in the history of Bridgeport." McLevy often boasted that his socialist administration launched Bridgeport as a pioneer in the field of slum clearance when actually Father Panik was the force behind it.

McLevy also had some of his toughest battles with city employees, who agitated for better working conditions and more pay—the very things McLevy had fought for during his days as a union organizer. In 1945, the city's fire department was the first to break the ice with McLevy on the formation of a municipal union and it subsequently became the most active department in the city. In those days, firefighters earned about forty-three dollars for eighty-four hours of work per week. With the grueling hours taking their toll on department members, firefighters Joseph Shanahan, a lieutenant, and

Facing page: *The last of the soapbox campaigners stumps in front of a factory gate during his unsuccessful 1954 run for the governorship. McLevy's last term as mayor would begin the following year, as the Socialist began to outlive his support base. Courtesy, Historical Collections, Bridgeport Public Library*

Above: *McLevy cuts the cake on his seventy-first birthday, with his wife, Vida, and Lassie. McLevy gradually lost popularity among voters from 1949 until his defeat in 1957. In the 1951 election his 53 percent plurality was his lowest since his first victory in 1933. Photo by Fred Schulze. Courtesy, Historical Collections, Bridgeport Public Library*

Pat M. Sherwin, a private, enlisted the help of Joseph Cleary, a Teamster official with the American Federation of Labor. Reasoning that much of the city's private sector had been organized, and with the full backing of the *Bridgeport Herald*'s labor editor Jack Butler, they convinced McLevy to rescind a 1920 ordinance that forbade the formation of any municipal unions. But, a clause in their first union contract forbade the right to strike.

In 1946, firefighters' weekly hours were reduced to 77.5 hours and in 1948 fell to seventy-two. In 1949 the fire officials received overwhelming support on a referendum calling for a fifty-six hour work week, and firefighters' hours were reduced to forty-two in 1957, McLevy's last year in office. It wasn't until 1955 that a statewide act was passed requiring all municipalities to recognize unions as a bargaining unit.

In the years McLevy sought re-election, he received little competition from the other parties. In fact, Cornelius Mulvihill and Edward Sandula, the leaders of the Democratic and Republican parties, often threw in political unknowns as the biennial sacrificial lambs. Nevertheless, to save face, they had to run somebody, so they would generally pick out a local businessman, buy him a pair of new shoes and a suit and send him out for a licking. Any erosion in McLevy's popularity came painfully slow for the two parties. But some signs of hope came after World War II when several factors began to build up against McLevy.

In 1949, McLevy turned seventy-one years old and more than ever retained a frugal spending posture. During this period, Bridgeport experienced a housing boom as the city pushed northward. Along with their new homes, residents insisted on the same city services—police, fire, paved streets, sewers—as the rest of the city received. McLevy was criticized for not providing those services. Still others criticized him for not planning for redevelopment, for putting patches on top of patches as factories became antiquated and the city's downtown aged. McLevy's supporters maintained that no man could overcome the city's dependence on the war.

In 1951, McLevy's once-staggering vote percentages started to weaken. His 53 percent of the vote, although comfortably ahead of the other two parties, represented the lowest total since his 1933 victory. But more than anything else, the one factor catching up to McLevy was time. In his first mayoral victory, McLevy received support from various middle- and lower-income ethnic groups who remained faithful as long as they were able to vote. McLevy had outlived his vote base, and the newer, younger electorate didn't have the same allegiance to him. The Democrats meanwhile drew added strength from blacks and Puerto Ricans who moved into the low-income housing projects McLevy had helped to bring into the city.

In 1955, the Democrats nominated Samuel Tedesco, a forty-year-old lawyer who had not even been born when McLevy first ran for mayor. Democrats targeted as supporters Tedesco's numerous fellow Italian Americans and mainstream Democrats and the influx of minorities. Tedesco finished 5,300 votes behind McLevy. After that showing, Democratic leaders said it was just a matter of time, and in 1957, with enough voters believing the time was right for a younger man to lead the city, Tedesco defeated the seventy-nine-year-old McLevy by 161 votes. In a near-record city election turnout of 53,779 voters, the Democrats smashed the twenty-three-year-old Socialist control of the Common Council. In defeat, McLevy wryly cracked: "I suppose I could go back to the roofing business"—twenty-five years after he last did work on a roof. Promising that he would run for mayor as long as his health permitted, he lost to Tedesco by 15,000 votes in 1959, his last campaign for city office.

A stroke in 1960 forced McLevy into political retirement. One of his last public appearances came during the 1962 Barnum Festival,

Late in his career, McLevy was denounced for his penny-pinching tendencies. Photo by John Hayduk. Courtesy, Historical Collections, Bridgeport Public Library

which had always been one of his favorites. Jasper McLevy died November 19, 1962. More than 500 people attended the funeral of the man they called "Champ."

They paid tribute to the man's honesty when the city so desperately needed it, to his devotion to his city, to his frugal spending, low taxes, one cent parking meters. They hailed his open-door policy to the local grocer, political and labor leaders, a carpenter looking for a job, and even to a voter with a leaky roof.

A quarter of a century later McLevy is either denounced for being too cheap to redevelop the city and plow the streets, or he is revered as Bridgeport's greatest mayor.

As reported by the Bridgeport Post *on April 7, 1913, the mysterious explosion in the doorway of Kleinberg's Pawn Shop may have been the work of the "underworld," and the Secret Service investigated the blast. The damage, estimated at $18,000, blew out windows and destroyed much property for one whole block on both sides of the street. Three men were injured. Courtesy, Robert Clifford Collection*

CHAPTER VIII

Politics, Police, and Perpetrators

"Some towns play political softball, other towns play hardball . . . in Bridgeport they play hand grenades."

—Philip L. Smith, 1984

If Phil Smith had accomplished nothing more as chairman of Bridgeport's Charter Revision Commission, his assessment of Park City politics captured what most have tried to express but didn't quite know how. No truer words were ever spoken.

In his address to the commission, Smith had solid reason for delivering this flavor of real-world politics. In the previous decade alone Bridgeport's political pot of blood has featured car firebombings in front of Republican campaign headquarters and the home of one of its mayors, accusations of mayoral candidates accepting campaign donations from the mob, a conviction for taking illegal campaign donations, a mayor wearing a bullet proof vest, charges of mayoral corruption, double-dealing and racism, allegations of vote buying, stealing, and cheating, and absentee ballot scandals.

Say hello to Bridgeport politics—the favorite game in town.

* * *

John T. King emerged as Bridgeport's first political giant. The Yankees' control of the city remained powerful when he initiated his power base in the Republican Party through citywide political clubs which had one purpose: controlling votes through patronage. Splitting up the spoils was clearly a function of the Yankee politician, but King refined it, generating an earlier-day yuppie fraternity in these clubs. The number of jobs persons could hand out depended on the number of votes they could deliver. Patronage flourished in every city department, and from about 1911 to 1926 it was all handed out under the direction of one man—King. But it wasn't just the Republicans who wound up with the jobs, Democrats could win their fair share of positions. In the pre-King era, when a new administration was voted into office everybody got thrown out of work no matter what position they held. But the control of political clubs resulted in some longevity, stability, and King's double machine—when one leader controlled both political parties. In this way the Republicans found work, the Democrats found work, King remained king, and everybody was happy. It took a special politician to pull it off, and King electrified it.

King earned a high national recognition factor in Bridgeport as a Republican national committeeman whose high-roll dealings outside of Bridgeport caught up to him. He got linked to the Teapot Dome scandal in which some members of President Warren G. Harding's administration were tied to wrongdoing regarding the nation's oil reserves. King, who never faced criminal charges, died in 1926.

King set the standard for the city's greatest political bosses, but several years after his death, a man who had no money, no jobs to hand out, and few workers, stepped forward to rival and perhaps surpass King's political genius. While King built his strength and prestige with patronage, Jasper McLevy solidified his power through legislation that did away with the political spoils—he introduced the civil service system. In 1935, McLevy's shield of civil service cut through the heart of the patronage system, but, whether planned or coincidental, it actually built McLevy a triple machine, supplying job protection to a grateful voting bloc of city employees regardless of party affiliation. For years McLevy had shouted that the patronage system would be the ruination of

Riding the strength of Republican John T. King's machine, Clifford B. Wilson spent ten years in office and began Bridgeport's surge as the dominant industrial center in the nation. Courtesy, Historical Collections, Bridgeport Public Library

the city. Yet when McLevy dealt with state Republicans for the passage of civil service, he insured security for thousands of workers, and as a result, insured their indelible loyalty to him. They no longer had to worry about losing their jobs when a new administration came in.

McLevy's ultimate test of strength was challenged when the Republicans resurrected Clifford B. Wilson, the anchor of the old King-machine golden era, to face McLevy in 1935. It was a matchup of two of the greatest Bridgeport mayors, but Wilson represented the old-time politics and a threat to civil service while McLevy evoked job security.

Although McLevy dominated Bridgeport politics for twenty-four years, the Democrats and Republicans had strong party leadership during and after McLevy's era through several men, including Democrat Cornelius Mulvihill and Republican A. Edward Sandula. They were pragmatic politicians who could deal with

McLevy when they knew they couldn't beat him, grabbing any leftover spoils to feed their parties. Mulvihill engineered Samuel Tedesco's defeat of McLevy in 1957 and launched what would become fourteen consecutive years of Democratic mayoral control in Bridgeport. Shenanigans (or, it's not how you play the game, but winning that counts) have played a big factor in past Bridgeport elections, and one story has it that prior to the 6 a.m. poll-opening for the 1957 mayoral election, a leading Democratic figure slipped into a voting booth at Barnum School and rattled off a number of votes for Tedesco. Two hundred votes seems to be the figure old time politicians recall.

Right: *Many veteran political observers agree with McLevy's declaration that the 1957 election was stolen from him when a leading Democratic figure padded opponent Samuel Tedesco's tally by 200 votes. McLevy lost by 161 votes. Courtesy, Historical Collections, Bridgeport Public Library*

Below: *Democratic Town Chairman Cornelius "Connie" Mulvihill, here greeting John F. Kennedy in Bridgeport just days before Kennedy won the 1960 presidential election, dominated Democratic politics from the close of World War II until his death in 1963. Courtesy, Elizabeth Walsh*

Above: *On October 16, 1959, Republican mayoral candidate Edward Sandula (left) shared a torchlight rally with running mates Doris Mitchell and the fledgling James Stapleton. In 1969 the "happy family" broke up when Stapleton overthrew Sandula's grip on the party, to become a dominant city Republican force. Photo by Ed Brinsko. Courtesy, Post Publishing Company*

Facing page: *In 1978 Marie Scinto (left), a charter member of James Stapleton's upstart Republican Action League, became the first woman to serve as head of a Bridgeport political party. Courtesy, Post Publishing Company*

Tedesco defeated McLevy that year by 161 votes. While Mulvihill assumed a double machine, his friendly rival, Sandula, was more than willing to work with him to keep a firm grip on his Republican Party. Sandula tried to cultivate young, inexperienced people in the Republican Party who would look up to him and join his so-called strategy to build for the future, when actually the last thing he wanted was to have a Republican become mayor who could immediately undermine his stature in the party by challenging his leadership position. Sandula's downfall started when he lured a young attorney named James Stapleton to run on his mayoral ticket for city clerk in 1959.

The Republicans took another of their predictable biennial beatings that year, but Stapleton, writing his own political literature for campaign mailings, secured enough support to win a Board of Education seat in the next city election and build himself a small yet loyal following within the party. In 1968, Stapleton brought the house of cards tumbling down. Bridgeport's Charter Revision Commission placed several questions on the ballot, including a call for a four-year mayoral term and pay for aldermen. Stapleton was the only one who spoke out against the proposals during a Republican Town Committee meeting. Stapleton's boldness drew Sandula's wrath, who blasted his protege for deviating from the party's wishes. But Stapleton charged that the only thing Sandula cared for was sticking to a patronage deal cut with Democratic Mayor Hugh Curran, who supported the four-year term.

Stapleton had hit a nerve. Pressing his anti-charter revision issue, he won the editorial support of the *Bridgeport Post*. Stapleton and an insurgent following even placed ads in the paper denouncing the charter revision. Their efforts resulted in the proposed measures being shot down at the polls three to one. Incensed, Sandula vowed to finish Stapleton in the Re-

publican Party. But Stapleton, with the anti-charter group as a nucleus, formed a group to take over Bridgeport's Republican Party.

Stapleton could never beat the entrenched Sandula forces in a primary with the existing Republican voter registration list, so he decided to form a new party. Calling themselves the Republican Action League (RAL), Stapleton cultivated talented people who had not been given the opportunity to flourish under Sandula's regime. They included long-time Board of Education member Anita Vogel, Nicholas Panuzio, who headed the Student Center at the University of Bridgeport, and Marie Scinto, a homemaker who came from a political family and would later become the first woman in city history to serve as a town chairman. Using the battle cry "let's get rid of Sandula the boss dictator," and calling on voters to smash the double machine by restoring the two-party system, the RAL organized an army of notaries and marched door to door throughout the city; from the beginning of 1969 to the spring of 1970 roughly 5,000 Democrat and independent voters switched to the Republican Party, nearly doubling the total GOP voter registration. Stapleton then had a voter list that Sandula didn't control.

The RAL had its registration list, but when it needed a mayoral candidate, none of the Republican leaders stepped forward. Stapleton didn't want to be mayor. Neither did Anita Vogel. For that matter, neither did just about anyone else who was offered the opportunity. The eventual candidate was an unlikely one: Nicholas Panuzio, an affable, rotund administrator at the University of Bridgeport. But he was willing, and turned out to be a sleeper, pleasantly surprising his associates with enthusiastic oration and a nice feel for the blue-collar person of Bridgeport.

The RAL and Panuzio beat Sandula's endorsed candidate for mayor in the 1969 primary. The fact that Panuzio was beaten handily by Hugh Curran in the general election did

Above: *Some refer to State Comptroller J. Edward Caldwell as the "Chairman of the Board" of Bridgeport's Democratic Party. Caldwell served eight consecutive terms as a Bridgeport senator. Courtesy, Caldwell Family Library*

nothing to dampen spirits. Stapleton's next step was to challenge the Sandula-controlled town chairman George Ganim. No problem this time with fielding a candidate: Stapleton stepped forward. Before the actual town chairmanship election, Stapleton and Sandula calculated that they each had twenty-five of the fifty town committee votes. Strangely enough, on the night of the 1970 election, a committee member and Sandula supporter disappeared giving Stapleton a one-vote victory—and the town chairmanship.

For the first time in twenty-five years, the Republican Party had a new leader. In 1971 the party, invigorated by fresh leadership, again sent Panuzio to face Curran, who had adopted a surprise mini-tax to offset a city deficit. The Republicans seized the badly-timed mini-tax as the cornerstone of their campaign. In the closest mayoral election in Bridgeport history, Panuzio defeated Curran by nine votes, returning the Republicans to City Hall and the two-party system to Bridgeport for the first

Below: *No post-McLevy politician has sparked journalists' interest more than John Mandanici, Bridgeport mayor from 1975 to 1981. Whether it was defying corruption-seeking FBI agents or brashly pushing through a 50-percent pay increase for himself, "Mandy" always made a great story. Photo by Neil Swanson. Courtesy,* Fairfield County Advocate

time in more than forty years. And in a vintage display of Bridgeport political sportsmanship, on the night of Panuzio's victory a couple of Democrats dropped through the ceiling of the Town Clerk's office in City Hall to try and cast a few more absentee ballots to secure a victory for Curran. They were thwarted though, so the story goes, when they found the ballots were stored in a closet sealed with masking tape.

This was the beginning of two prosperous Republican years. In 1970 and 1971, the RAL helped to elect Sidney Dworkin as judge of probate, Stewart McKinney as 4th District congressman, Lowell Weicker as United States senator, Thomas Meskill as governor, and it assisted a state senator and five state representatives into office. Panuzio, who was reelected in 1973, abandoned his mayoral seat late in his second term for a presidential appointment in Washington, leaving President of the Common Council William Seres to finish out the last fifty-five days. The Democrats regained City Hall in 1975, behind the brash and colorful A&P store manager John Mandanici, who quickly built one of the most powerful political organizations in the state. Mandanici likened himself to the "Archie Bunker" voter. He kept taxes down while evoking a no-nonsense attitude that endeared him to many voters, but also made him enemies.

Mandanici's political fortune began to break apart in 1978, when he demanded a city pay raise package that provided him a 50 percent increase, raising his salary from $28,000 to $42,000. "Mandy," as he was called, maintained the move was necessary to attract a higher grade of candidate for the mayor's office. While few questioned the need to modernize the mayor's salary, Mandanici's insistence that the hike be made in one step started a wave of public criticism. Eventually, the Common Council approved his proposal, but the mayor was denounced by several aldermen, the Civil Service Commission, and the *Bridgeport*

Post's editoral chief Joseph Owens.

Mandanici was to face many more problems. A turning point in Bridgeport political history, and a contributing factor to Mandanici's defeat in 1981, came one year earlier with the election of Margaret Morton as state senator. Morton, a black funeral home director who had served eight years in the state house, defeated incumbent Salvatore DePiano by eight votes in a bitter, racially divided primary. Morton said Mandanici had consented to her succeeding DePiano upon his appointment as city tax attorney. When Mandanici and DePiano "double-dipped" (DePiano held both jobs at once), Morton went ahead with her primary challenge, noting that every city housing project was in her district.

"I felt I was a loyal Democrat," said Morton. "They had reneged on their promise that there would be no double-dipping. I wanted to make peace but they wanted to make war." Morton's victory infused hope into a black community which had experienced little involvement in

Margaret Morton's 1980 state senate election was a major victory for blacks in city politics. Photo by John Hayduk. Courtesy, Post Publishing Company

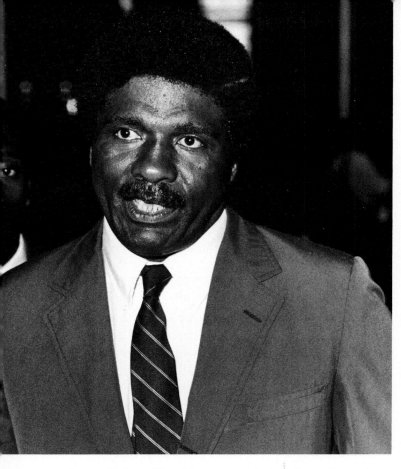

city politics. She had opened the door for other blacks such as Charles Tisdale, who served as an aide to President Jimmy Carter and earlier had served as director of the city's Action for Bridgeport Community Development program. In 1983, in fact, Tisdale parlayed his record and the increasing black political involvement to win the Democratic mayoral nomination, the first time in history either major party had endorsed a black candidate for mayor.

In 1981, Bridgeport endured its most vicious mayoral campaign ever, pitting Mandanici against Republican Leonard Paoletta, a former city tax attorney who capitalized on a series of federal indictments and party infighting that had splintered Mandanici's administration. Mandanici himself was told by federal authorities that he was a potential target of a federal grand jury investigation into the city's Comprehensive Employment Training Act operations, an investigation that spread into other aspects of his adminstration. The intensity of the campaign was heightened in August when the FBI employed a local car thief, Thomas E. Marra, Jr., to lure Bridgeport Police Superintendent Joseph Walsh, a target of a federal grand jury investigation, into a bribe. Walsh turned the tables on Marra and arrested him for attempted bribery. The botched sting attempt catapulted Bridgeport onto the front pages of national and international newspapers.

Mandanici made political hay of Paoletta's attorney relationship with Marra, claiming Paoletta helped to instigate the federal mission, and he also accused Paoletta of accepting campaign donations from two of Marra's associates linked to organized crime. Paoletta in turn hammered Mandanici for his indictment-filled administration and for further smearing an already seamy city image.

Two months after the sting attempt, Marra's car was firebombed outside of Paoletta's campaign headquarters, and a few weeks later, two cars parked in Mandanici's driveway were firebombed in the middle of the night. If that wasn't enough, Paoletta's house was burglarized. When the sparks settled, voters handed Paoletta a sixty-four-vote victory. The scars that were inflicted by the political hand grenades of the 1981 campaign were still raw more than two years later when Paoletta tried to fire Walsh from his civil service position on a number of allegations, which Walsh successfully defended in court.

MANDANICI   PAOLETTA   CINNAMO

Police Superintendent Joseph A. Walsh, hands raised, casts away two FBI agents trying to rescue informant Thomas E. Marra, Jr., following a federal bribery sting attempt against Walsh. Photo by Frank W. Decerbo. Courtesy, Post Publishing Company

Fights between politicians and police officers really aren't an unusual thing in Bridgeport. The position of superintendent of police was created in 1895 out of a political conflict between John Rylands, the police chief, and city leaders led by W.E. Grant, a police commissioner who wanted to get rid of Rylands. The Board of Police Commissioners (unlike during the Walsh affair more than eighty years later) were evenly split on Rylands' future. But city leaders opposing Rylands convinced the state legislature to abolish the office of chief of police. With Rylands out of a job, Eugene Birmingham, on April 23, 1895, was installed as Bridgeport's first superintendent of police.

The seed for Bridgeport's early day police force was planted with the founding of the borough of Bridgeport in 1800. As shops sprouted around the city and the potential for fire increased, a "public watch," comprised of volunteers who patrolled city streets, was formed. Roughly one year after Bridgeport's 1836 incorporation, twenty-five special constables were appointed to preserve the peace, and were granted the power to make arrests. Drunks caused most of the problems in Bridgeport's early days, and until a legislative act created a

Facing page, top: *Bridgeport police were mounted on bicycles in 1900, but by 1914 the mounted force had graduated to Indian motorcycles. Photo by Seeley. Courtesy, Historical Collections, Bridgeport Public Library*

Left: *The first chief of police in Bridgeport (front row, center) was Chief W.W. Wells, whose 1869 salary amounted to $100 per month. Standing next to Wells is Mayor J. Morford. Courtesy, Superintendent of Police Joseph Walsh*

In the early 1800s volunteers formed a public watch to patrol Bridgeport streets, looking out for criminal activity and protecting against fires. Soon after the borough's incorporation as a city, twenty-five constables were appointed, eventually forming independent police and fire departments. The horse-drawn steam pumper above was photographed circa 1912. Courtesy, Historical Collections, Bridgeport Public Library

city court in 1868, the mayor was also the local judge, a source of power many later mayors probably wish they could have utilized. A reorganization of the police department in 1869 created a chief of police (who earned $100 per month), a captain, two sergeants, and not more than twenty patrolmen. Bridgeport's mounted police force was created in the year 1900, although the city's finest rode bicycles instead of horses.

Through the years city police and firefighters have battled numerous elements of disaster and corruption, although most of the early disasters came from ferocious downtown fires or careless pedestrians and stray animals hit while crossing the nearby Water Street train tracks. The tracks were elevated in 1902 to everyone's relief. Mother Nature has thrown her share of curve balls at Bridgeport. The blizzard of March 1888 buried Bridgeport in drifts of snow as high as fourteen feet and some up to one mile long. The storm paralyzed the city for three days, ripped chimneys off roofs and roofs off shops; streets lamps and electric lights all went black and railroad trains stuck in the drifts were socked with more drifts no sooner had shovel brigades cleared the tracks. The Blizzard of 1888 was replayed in February 1934 when roughly twenty-eight inches of snow fell on the city, and again in February 1978 when Governor Ella T. Grasso closed down the state and ordered a ban on all non-essential traffic until work crews could clear away snow on the streets.

Perhaps the worst hurricane to hit Bridgeport arrived on September 21, 1938. The storm pounded Bridgeport's shoreline with menacing winds and violent waves, uprooted city trees, and heavily damaged the Black Rock Yacht Club and a major portion of the Pleasure Beach pier.

Several violent rainstorms created havoc in Bridgeport during the 1950s, including raging waves and jet winds on November 7, 1953, which destroyed nine cottages on Pleasure

Beach and flooded Seaside Park. Parking meters and cars were nearly submerged in the rain-swollen municipal parking lot at the rear of the Bridgeport Railroad Station.

Murders in the Park City's early days were infrequent, but on June 18, 1891, Jacob Scheele, a German national, was the last man to be publicly hanged in the city. Scheele shot to death a New Canaan, Connecticut, constable who was preparing to arrest Scheele, a saloon-keeper, at his home for violation of the town's dry laws. Just seconds before his execution at the Fairfield County Jail on North Avenue (which had been constructed twenty years earlier), the sixty-three-year-old Scheele announced to a crowd of police and selected city leaders: "Gentlemen, I am willing to die. I have changed my mind and now do not want to stay here. I wish you all goodbye and I hope the Lord Father in Heaven will pardon me." Hangings were transferred to the Wethersfield State Prison four years later.

On July 11, 1911, the wreck of the Federal Express in the West End killed fourteen people and injured forty-seven others when the train ran across a switch point at the Fairfield Avenue overpass at sixty miles per hour. The train jumped the tracks and plunged twenty feet into a roadway, destroying the locomotive and five cars. The impact turned the iron cars to scrap, rails were twisted and torn, and several headless bodies were found among the wreckage. The train was one hour late and was apparently speeding to make up time. Among the passengers were members of the St. Louis Cardinals baseball team, including manager Roger Bresnahan, a future hall-of-famer, who rescued many people injured in the wreck. The crash was the second most disastrous in the history of the New York, New Haven & Hartford Railroad Company, topped only by the loss of forty-four lives in 1853 when a train plunged from an open drawbridge in Norwalk, Connecticut.

One of the most intriguing hoaxes in Bridge-

On March 12 and 13, 1888, a blizzard blanketed Bridgeport with twenty-two inches of snow. Looking north from Gilbert Street toward the First Congregational Church, residents are seen digging out on Broad Street. Photo by Bronson's Photograph and Gallery. Courtesy, Historical Collections, Bridgeport Public Library

port history occurred in 1938, and as one *Bridgeport Post* account suggested on December 16, "nothing in local criminal history quite compares" to the McKesson and Robbins case. On December 16, Frank Donald Coster, the rich and respected president of the Fairfield-based McKesson and Robbins pharmaceutical company, shot himself in the head in his palatial Fairfield home. This would be front page news in any event, but just one day earlier Coster had been unmasked as the notorious New York swindler Philip Musica, whose lengthy bank-swindling activities earned him more than one million dollars a quarter of a century earlier. Musica had remarkably managed to put that behind him with a new name, new parents, and an impressive educational background that tranformed him into the financial-genius head of a major drug company and earned him a listing in "Who's Who in America." An investigation into the disappearance of some eighteen million dollars in company assets revealed that Coster had diverted cash to pay blackmail money to New Yorkers who knew him as Musica, the Italian immigrant swindler. All these revelations, however, didn't prevent McKesson and Robbins from prospering after Musica's death.

Bridgeport's Romanesque-style railroad station, vacant after the 1975 construction of a new railroad terminal, was destroyed by a fire on March 20, 1979, while the city's elite gathered at a St. Patrick's Day dinner in the Algonquin Club. The 203-foot long, 75-year-old building, of terrazzo and marble floors and red slate roof set with copper gargoyles on the tower, grew from the city's need for an elevated train system. The supervising architect was Bridgeporter Warren R. Briggs, who planned a station "pleasing to the eye and suitable to the surroundings." Police blamed the cause of the blaze on arsonists.

"The House of Happenings," a little, four-room house at 966 Lindley Street, produced one of the Park City's most bizarre stories. The

On July 11, 1911, the Federal Express train jumped the Fairfield Avenue overpass at sixty miles per hour, destroying the locomotive and five train cars. Among the passengers were members of the St. Louis baseball team, who survived the rail-twisting crash and posed for this photo (top of page) taken on top of an overturned Pullman. Both photos courtesy, Historical Collections, Bridgeport Public Library

house gained national attention in November 1974 when the owners claimed to have heard strange noises, curtains being ripped down, a television set being crashed to the floor, a refrigerator being lifted off the ground—a regular haunted house. Police, firefighters, and noted demonologists Ed and Lorraine Warren said they witnessed the strange occurrences. Thousands of curious onlookers lined Lindley Street, causing massive traffic tie-ups and forcing the police department to close the street to traffic. But Police Superintendent Joseph Walsh would have none of it. He maintained that the 10-year-old foster daughter of the family that owned the house admitted to staging the series of incidents. "There are no ghosts in Bridgeport," Walsh reassured.

*   *   *

Not all the city's perpetrators were ghostly or nameless; most that the city has known were those that could be seen, people more regularly identified as Dutch, Cigars, Tommy the Blond, or Fat Franny. In the last ten years, federal authorities have launched a massive crackdown on organized crime, gradually weeding out an element that had thrived when Bridgeport was thought of as one of the most wide-open mob cities in the country. Just how and why these men known as capos and soldiers operated so freely in the city has been open to speculation. The lack of manpower and resources has been the standard answer of the city police; federal authorities have claimed the only thing lacking was enthusiasm for the task. A clearer picture of the present-day Mafia element emerges by looking back to the Prohibition era.

Connecticut was one of two states that did not ratify the Eighteenth Amendment, which prohibited the manufacture, sale, or transportation of intoxicating liquors. State lawmakers cried that such a law was an infringement on the rights of citizens. Although the state was technically forced to abide by the federal law, Bridgeport law enforcement did little to enforce it. As a result, Bridgeport blossomed as a place where bootleggers could operate with little trouble. When Prohibition became law in 1919, the city had already earned its reputation as a hard-drinking, hard-fisted town. The patrons of the downtown speakeasies, many of them Irish, German, and Italian laborers, were not going to be deterred from their evening cocktail by lawmakers in Washington.

And for those who preferred privacy, there was always the option of making your own at home. It could be a messy chore, though, and ceilings splattered with home brew were not uncommon. The more fastidious moved their stills to outdoor locations. A wooded area in the North End developed into a noted haven and to this day retains the name "Whiskey Hill." Its remote stills were renowned for their quality, volume, and egalitarian sales practices. All customers, cops included, were welcome. But while the cops were customers, there were appearances to maintain. There were occasional raids.

It took the efforts of United States Treasury Department to put any noticeable dent in the local traffic. As a rule they did not inform local authorities of impending raids for fear a connected cop would alert a friendly still operator.

What wasn't being brewed locally was being smuggled. Whether by harbor or hearse, liquor flowed through the city. Close to New York,

but far enough away to provide some sanctuary, Bridgeport became attractive to men whose business practices occasionally drew the attention of law enforcement agencies. There were scores, but perhaps the most flamboyant and famous of them all was a man named Arthur Flegenheimer, better known as Dutch Schultz, the man U.S. District Attorney Thomas E. Dewey called the "biggest gangster" in New York City. Bridgeport's reputation as a wide-open town was an invitation for guys like Schultz, even after the repeal of Prohibition in 1933. Schultz spent substantial time in 1935 living at the Stratfield Hotel where he'd play cards with cops, lawyers, and heavyweight businessmen who thought of him as something of a celebrity. For Schultz, Bridgeport was a pleasant place to visit while avoiding the persistent inquiries of federal authorities. But if Bridgeport had a reputation, it was nothing compared to Schultz's.

"Dutch Schultz has given the Bridgeport Police Department 24 hours to get out of town," was the way *Bridgeport Herald* columnist Harry Neigher described the gangster's arrival here. But the last thing Schultz wanted in Bridgeport was trouble. He had plenty of that

An undertaker's wagon arrives to begin the removal of the fourteen people killed in the Federal Express wreck. Forty-seven others were injured. Courtesy, Robert Clifford Collection

In the only known posed photo granted to a photojournalist, Gus Curcio in March 1984 denied involvement in the 1981 mob-style execution of Frank Piccolo. Though acquitted of the Piccolo-related charges, Curcio was jailed on several other federal charges. Photo by Neil Swanson. Courtesy, Fairfield County Advocate

elsewhere. As it turned out, two days after Schultz got out of Bridgeport to watch the Max Baer-Joe Louis title fight in Yankee Stadium in September, federal authorites arrested him in New Jersey on tax evasion. About one month later Schultz was blasted to death in a Newark, New Jersey, restaurant.

Schultz was never a player in Bridgeport's underworld, just a visitor. The two men who ran the rackets with little trouble in the city during the 1930s and 1940s were Ernie and Frank Cozza, who built up quite a lucrative bootlegging, gambling, and prostitution operation. Later it would be men such as Thomas "Tommy the Blond" Vastano, Frank "Cigars" Piccolo, and Francis "Fat Franny" Curcio and his brother Gus, who would take over the action.

But it was only until the late 1970s that the wise guys had free rein in Bridgeport. Led by federal prosecutors Richard Gregorie and William Keefer, the U.S. Justice Department's Organized Crime and Racketeering Strike Force and the Federal Bureau of Investigation decided to move in earnest. Armed with court-authorized wiretaps, they started closing in on the local operations of the Vito Genovese and Carlo Gambino organized crime families. In some cases, they apparently didn't move fast enough. For example, someone eliminated the need to continue a federal grand jury investigation of Vastano, a Genovese soldier, by shooting him to death in his Stratford backyard.

Two shotgun blasts disconnected Piccolo in September of 1981 while he stood at a public phone booth on a Saturday afternoon on Main Street. Just months before, Piccolo had been indicted for allegedly extorting money from the king of the Las Vegas strip, entertainer Wayne Newton. Gus Curcio, who had operated in Piccolo's shadows in the rival Genovese operation, was arrested in connection with Piccolo's murder, but was eventually cleared. The Strike Force investigations culminated when the Curcio brothers and numerous other underworld figures were sentenced to double-figure jail terms.

Whether it was federal authorities or inter-mob rivals concerned with preventing leaks by colleagues in the secrecy of the grand jury room, the combined zeal of these two organizations put a serious crimp in organized crime activity in the early 1980s.

But while the feds had success in one area, they played Keystone Kops in another—the infamous sting attempt against Bridgeport's feared and revered lawman, Police Superintendent Joseph A. Walsh, on August 18, 1981. Two months earlier, federal authorities disclosed that both Walsh and his long-time associate, Inspector Anthony Fabrizi, were targets of a grand jury exploring possible violations of the Racketeer Influenced Corrupt Organization Act. In Walsh's forty years as a cop, he had earned praise as one of the department's finest officers, a detective who could figure out what phone number a person was dialing just by listening to the dial turn. His reputation was enhanced during the hot summers of the 1960s when Bridgeport avoided the kind of racial violence that plagued other cities during the civil rights movement. But where there is power like his, there is envy, and Walsh was rumored to have had a dark side, too.

"The Boss," as almost everyone who knew Walsh called him, fought with mayors and police boards for control of the department and with minority members of the force who claimed Walsh's department discriminated aginst minorities. Numerous charges of police brutality alleged that Walsh's management style encouraged the beatings. Whatever allegations surfaced, Walsh rose from the clouds of dust as the shrewdest, most powerful and charming politician in Bridgeport.

Federal authorities, however, had concluded that Walsh not only condoned corruption, but was corrupt himself. They employed a 28-year-old convicted car thief, Thomas E. Marra, Jr., whose family had known Walsh for decades, to bribe the superintendent to gain back the city's lucrative towing contract (which Walsh had revoked in May) for his uncle's garage. The federal investigation brought together the most powerful law enforcement officials in the country, including David Margolis, the chief of the national Strike Force operations, who ultimately authorized the mission.

As Marra, following lengthy discussions with Justice Department officials, headed to the downtown meeting spot with Walsh and wearing a concealed recorder, so too did the superintendent conceal a recorder, and he crooned the tune "Little Things Mean a Lot" on his way to the meeting. Federal officials hadn't counted on the fact that Walsh was prepared for a set up. While Walsh maintained "it didn't take a genius to figure out what was happening," Marra confessed later that the idea of stooging against a man he'd known all his life was too much for him, and he had gotten word to him.

Whatever the stories, it was clear the federal informant did everything strike force prosecutor Gregorie and FBI agents told him not to do: he brought up the subject of money, got

out of his car to talk to Walsh, and then made the bribe offer.

Walsh waited until Marra had handed him the envelope of cash, then arrested him for attempted bribery and called his men who were staked out in the old firehouse on Middle Street, for backup. Mass confusion and a tense stand off between two law enforcement agencies followed as FBI agents rushed to Marra's assistance and demanded that he be released. Walsh refused the agents' claims while his men dropped Marra's trousers to his ankles and removed the recording device and then took Marra into custody. (U.S. District Court Judge T.F. Gilroy Daly later dismissed the bribery charge against Marra, ruling that he was acting under the direction of the federal government and lacked criminal intent.) Photographs taken by *Bridgeport Post* photographer Frank Decerbo, who Walsh tipped off to be on the scene, appeared in international newspapers as the botched federal sting led newspaper, television, and radio reports. Walsh, for that episode, emerged as the righteous hero, and local government officials squeezed every drop of political opportunity out of the affair. An embarrassed U.S. Justice Department shuffled home. Marra, reverting to his old car thief habits, returned to jail on state and federal charges.

The "Bridgescam" affair proved at least one thing: in Bridgeport it's often difficult to separate the politics, the police, and the perpetrators.

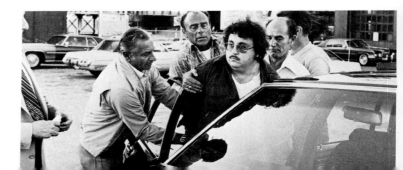

Bridgeport police arrest Thomas E. Marra, Jr., after Marra offered Police Superintendent Joseph Walsh a bribe. Marra was acting for the FBI in that agency's attempt to uncover corruption. The bribery charges against Marra were dropped. Photo by Frank Decerbo. Courtesy, Post Publishing Company

Francis "Hi-Ho" D'Addario was possibly the most important and influential businessman in Bridgeport. He controlled a construction company, an oil company, and a radio station in Bridgeport, and the Jai Alai Fronton in Milford. He is seen here at the site of the old Bridgeport Brass Company building, which he purchased in 1983. His most recent acquisition and "perhaps most challenging" was the old CrossRoads Mall (formerly Lafayette Plaza). Photo by Wayne Ratzenberger. Courtesy, Post Publishing Company

CHAPTER IX

Fighting the

Image

"Bridgeport . . . where the circus never left town."
                                        —*James G. Clark, writer*

Strange as it may seem, the ghost of Jasper McLevy still surrounds Bridgeport nearly thirty years after he left office. From 1933 to 1957 Bridgeport had one mayor—McLevy. Since then the city has had six and it is no less a tribute to McLevy's influence that the old-time Bridgeporter and the new have waged many a heated debate over his impact on the city.

The patience of the older voter who remembers and cherishes McLevy's reform and honesty expired relatively quickly against those men who succeeded the Socialist mayor. Yet the attitude of the newer, younger voter suggests that McLevy's failure to infuse the city with urban renewal forged the deterioration of neighborhoods, the loss of industry, a vacant downtown, and ultimately an ugly image.

For bad or good, Bridgeporters now live in the post-McLevy era—an era that has in some ways brought out the best and the worst in the city. It has seen a decrease in the white population as it joins the rush to the suburbs; it has seen a North End housing boom, redevelopment, new highways, sweeping social changes involving the minority community, the fall of the machine tool industry, the exodus of several major businesses, the collapse and rebirth

In 1957 Bridgeport elected Samuel Tedesco as its new mayor. Downtown redevelopment highlighted his eight years in City Hall and Tedesco said, "McLevy was a nice man, but he let the city crumble just so he could keep the taxes down." Photo by Ed Brinsko. Courtesy, Post Publishing Company

of neighborhoods, the transition from manufacturing to the service industry, and the hopeful vision of downtown revitalization.

Some of the post-McLevy mayors have universally agreed on approaches to these changes, while strongly disagreeing on other concepts and implementations for a progressive city. But clearly one standout and common issue each mayor has forcibly confronted is an albatross that has choked Bridgeport progress for more than a quarter century: the problem of a monotonous image.

And in some cases these mayors have been commonly accused of being a major contributor to the city's image problem.

*   *   *

Bridgeport is actually no different than any other northeast city victimized by a dependence on the temporary demands of wars. Antiquated business equipment and the urgent need for modern facilities has taken its toll. People have lost jobs because of corporate strategies to cut shipping and repair costs by moving closer to car makers; firms have headed south for cheaper labor costs or they have taken advantage of the cheaper Japanese work force, who have grabbed the basic market in the car, machine tool, and electronics industries—all of which Bridgeport has thrived on for years.

McLevy may have been frugal to a fault with city money by his refusal to raise taxes to support education and mend city streets and provide other services, but it wasn't his fault that the Singer Company left Bridgeport, that Columbia Records found it cheaper to move departments to New Jersey and New York, or that the technological advances of Japan left Bridgeport factory equipment antiquated.

Samuel Tedesco was the first mayor who inherited this fallout and a city desperately in need of a facelift. "When we took office the city was in bad shape," Tedesco recalled. "The roads were in bad shape, the schools were in terrible shape. McLevy was a nice man, but he let the city crumble just so he could keep the taxes down."

Less than two months after Tedesco took office in November 1957, the $464-million Connecticut Turnpike opened to traffic from Greenwich to New Haven. The planning and construction of this first major highway to race through Bridgeport had been many years in the works, and during the planning stages the route the interstate would take touched off much debate and discussion. McLevy persistently argued for State Highway Commissioner Albert Hill's southerly route, and disagreed with the Chicago engineering firm, H.W. Lochner Company, that suggested a north-central route through the newer section of the city. McLevy argued that such a northerly route would displace too many citizens. The southerly span, however, would overlook the West End, South End, and East End, as McLevy wanted, covering the deteriorating and gloomier sections of the city sprouting depressed housing and billowing industrial smokestacks; the most prominent of these was the United Illuminating Company's Harbor Station, finished in 1957 to complement the old Steel Point Plant across the harbor. This view of the old city, following a drive through an increasingly corporate Fairfield County, has done little to soften an outsider's view of Bridgeport. Tedesco embraced the turnpike route as maximizing accessibility to Bridgeport without massive displacement of city residents.

The cornerstone of Tedesco's eight years was urban renewal, and the lawyer fostered the biggest facelift in the city in forty years. He admittedly was willing politically to live and die by it. In his initial days as mayor in March 1958, he came under fire from picketing preservationists when he announced the upcoming demolition of the city's Gothic jewel, the Harral-Wheeler House, built in 1848 for Bridgeport mayor and saddlery entrepreneur Henry Harral and later purchased by sewing machine leader Nathaniel Wheeler. Candidate Tedesco had campaigned to save the building for a possible museum, but stated as mayor that money could not be raised to restore the home. Nathaniel Wheeler's son, Archer, left the house to the city for educational or park purposes, but nearly thirty years later Tedesco revealed "the Wheeler family was on my back to demolish the place because they felt it wasn't worth keeping up." The only artifacts left from the home are preserved at the Smithsonian Institution and in a first floor room of City Hall.

Demolition of almost any kind was frequent during the Tedesco years. In 1962, Tedesco launched the city's first urban renewal program—the fifty-two-acre State Street redevelopment project. While fifty-two acres may have seemed petty compared to Mayor Richard Lee's extensive renewal accomplishments in New Haven, for Bridgeport this project was indeed massive. Backed by federal money from the Kennedy administration, the project began in September 1962, with Tedesco sledge-hammering the first blow. The Chamber of Commerce's "Brand New Bridgeport" battle cry was raised by Redevelopment Chairman Arthur Clifford, and practically anything old in the State Street area—residential structures, churches, service stations—were bulldozed in favor of the Lafayette Plaza shopping mall, the new Route 25-8 connector (which rushed through the North End of the city), and the twelve-story People's Savings Bank, the first high-rise building construction in the city in nearly forty years.

Bridgeport's new commercial district was bounded by two highways and the Pequonnock River. All residences were removed from the redevelopment area, which contained no housing developments. Years later the lack of downtown housing became a major criticism of the State Street redevelopment project because no citizens were left in the immediate area to support the downtown businesses.

Other Tedesco projects included the construction of eight schools (including the new Central High School) and Kennedy Stadium, and the transfer of City Hall from State Street into the old Central High School facility on Lyon Terrace, which placed nearly all city departments under one roof for the first time.

While development progressed under Tedesco, the rigors of the mayor's office handed him a severe case of burnout. In addition, financial concerns led Tedesco not to seek a fifth term in 1965 and instead to accept a state judgeship.

Tedesco's city attorney Hugh Curran, a reserved, silver-haired Irish-American, followed Tedesco as a mayor who attempted to promote Bridgeport's resurgence through renovations of the Barnum Museum, the Bridgeport Public Library, and city parks. Curran also addressed the concerns of the black community by developing Model Cities, and the Action for Bridgeport Community Development program.

While Bridgeport had its share of isolated store firebombings, window smashings, and militant gangs due to the social turbulence of the late 1960s and early 1970s, the city did not suffer the racial hostilities that other cities did during that era. Curran credited a "rapport and dialogue with the black community," and praised Police Superintendent Joseph Walsh as a "fearless leader" whose meetings with minority groups defused tensions. Perhaps a more telling reason, however, is the location of the city housing projects, which are not concen-

trated into a single area and are removed from white neighborhoods. Most members of the predominantly low-income black community reside in separated city housing projects such as Father Panik Village, P.T. Barnum Apartments, and Beardsley Terrace Apartments, which are all something of communities unto themselves.

Although Bridgeport did not suffer the pains of violent racial tensions, racial discrimination lawsuits sought action against racial imbalances within the police and fire departments, and during the late 1970s and early 1980s these actions prevented hirings of any sort until the federal courts ordered sweeping changes. Before 1972 Bridgeport's Police Department had no black supervisors and only a handful of black officers, who were usually detailed to the least desirable sections of the city. Blaming the low numbers and poor job assignments on a steady flow of racial discrimination from Joseph

Walsh, the Civil Service Commission, and the mayor's office, Police Officer Ted Meekins formed a chapter of the Guardians, a national organization that specializes in protecting the civil rights of minority police officers.

Demanding that more minority police officers be hired and given equal job assignments as white police officers, the Guardians spent a hectic decade involved in court suits, investigations by federal agencies, and agreements worked out by federal judges. The first major victory for the Guardians came in 1972 when U.S. District Court Judge Jon Newman issued a ruling that the police department had discriminated against minorities and ordered the immediate hiring of minority officers.

Facing page and below: The Route 25-8 connector (seen here under construction), which offered greater accessibility to and from the suburbs, was evidence of downtown development during the 1960s. Photo Frank W. Decerbo. Courtesy, Post Publishing Company

Six years later U.S. District Court Judge T.F. Gilroy Daly determined that examinations for positions in the fire department discriminated against minorities. The court then ordered the city to pay millions of dollars to hundreds of minority applicants who had suffered from the discriminatory practices of the two departments. Judge Daly in 1982 found continued widespread discrimination and issued a remedy order that produced numerous police department changes, including the appointment of black and Hispanic officers to specialized divisions. A few months after Daly's ruling came an agreement worked out by lawyers for the Guardians and the city requiring that four Hispanics or blacks be hired for every five white police officers. This came after the Guardians' suit claimed that questions on the entry level test were discriminatory. Throughout the litigation, Superintendent Walsh argued that the Guardians' court action only served to tie up hirings and stall minority involvement. Yet in ten years, Meekins and the Guardians succeed-

ed in adding more than 100 minority police officers to the force.

* * *

As Bridgeport approached the mid-1970s, city officials hoped to land that one major development project that would infuse some life into the downtown. Pleasure Beach seemingly every year was mentioned as a site for a gambling casino or a race track. Mayor John Mandanici often spoke of constructing a downtown civic center, but the funding and interest from the state never materialized as arguments poured in from opponents who questioned whether people would support a civic center.

Bridgeport's Jai Alai Fronton was one of those development projects touted as the savior of the city. Sports entrepreneur David Friend, of Hollywood, Florida, and president of the Connecticut Sports Enterprises which promoted the facility, was awarded a state license to open the facility in 1974. Numerous civic groups opposed the construction, arguing that the East Side location on Kossuth Street could be better used for an industrial park or new housing. However, the 4,500 seat, $16-million fronton opened in June 1976 to packed audiences.

But Friend's involvement with Bridgeport Jai Alai triggered numerous controversies that kept the facility in the news for many years after its opening. Allegations of political payoffs, perjury, and improper bank loans dominated a series of Friend-linked scandals in Connecticut during the 1970s. Friend was acquitted of all charges, but the State Gaming Commission forced him to sell his interest in the fronton. It has proven to be a source of tax revenue to the city, but allegations surrounding Friend added to the growing skepticism about the personalities in Bridgeport's future.

Federal law enforcement officials claimed that a wiretap investigation revealed that Friend and Bridgeport mobster Frank Piccolo sought

Bridgeport Police Officer Ted Meekins has led the fight for increased minority representation in the city police department. In 1970 Meekins formed a chapter of the Guardians, a national organization that specializes in battling for minority police officers' civil rights. Photo by Neil Swanson. Courtesy, Fairfield County Advocate

Facing page: A decade of lawsuits charging racial discrimination brought greater minority representation to the Bridgeport Police Department. Here new recruits in 1983 commence training before hitting the streets. Photo by Neil Swanson. Courtesy, Fairfield County Advocate

197

Above: *With Tedesco's State Street Redevelopment Project came the Lafayette Plaza shopping mall and the garage, shown here in 1965. A source of criticism is the length of the parking garage, which gobbles up several blocks of downtown property. The shopping mall has been a failure, primarily due to the lack of downtown housing to increase the number of city shoppers, who have headed for malls in Trumbull and Stratford. Photo by Frank Decerbo. Courtesy, Post Publishing Company*

Facing page: *The floating Ferryboat Junction Restaurant moored in the Pequonnock River was touted by both the Mandanici and Paoletta administrations as the anchor of downtown entertainment. The boat's owner towed the boat out of the harbor in May 1983 as the restaurant's business bottomed out. In the background is the city's Jai Alai Fronton, another hopeful in the city's revitalization plan. Photo by Frank Decerbo. Courtesy, Post Publishing Company*

to purchase the *Leonardo da Vinci,* one of the largest passenger ships in the world, to transform it into a floating casino. The deal fell through in 1981, according to federal court documents, just weeks before Piccolo was murdered in Bridgeport, and as the ship burned off the coast of Italy.

If the incidents of 1980 and 1981 didn't plunge the city's image to rock bottom, they came close: Bridgeport Brass, long one of the city's anchoring industrial companies, announced that high operating expenses and an antiquated building would force its closing; police officer Gerald DiJoseph, checking on a motor vehicle parked in a garage on Jane Street, was shot to death; women were terrorized by a so-called "bumper rapist" who for several months hit the back ends of women's cars with his auto and then sexually assaulted them; a series of federal indictments socked Mandanici administration officials and uncovered corruption in several city-administered programs, including the city's Comprehensive Employment Training Act and the Rehabilitation Assistance Program, a housing assistance program for low-to-moderate income families. The Parking Authority was investigated for allegedly committing a variety of illegal practices, ranging from city employees receiving kickbacks to authorizing no-show jobs; the mayor himself was notified by federal officials

that he was a possible target of a grand jury investigation, but he was never charged; the manager of the city-owned Sikorsky Memorial Airport was convicted for lying to a federal grand jury regarding his relationship with mob boss Frank Piccolo.

Bridgeport had several other shocking developments in the summer of 1981 that made the city a reporter's dream, but also crippled the city's image. The sting attempt against Police Superintendent Joe Walsh in August and the shooting death of Frank Piccolo in September continued to put Bridgeport on the front pages of newspapers nationwide. Shortly after the Piccolo murder, Daniel Bifield, a member of the Hell's Angels motorcycle club who federal authorities had described as the "most dangerous man in Connecticut," escaped from the Bridgeport Correctional Center and led the FBI on a six-month manhunt before his capture in Denver, Colorado.

More fallout came with the 1981 mayoral election. Mandanici wore a bullet proof vest after death threats and car firebombings marred the general election campaign. Then one year later, Bridgeporters received the embarrassing news that the new $2.3 million firehouse completed on Central Avenue was actually constructed on private property. The city owned the building, but didn't own the land, and everybody wanted to know how the city could

manage to build a firehouse on private property. Mandanici and his city attorney placed the blame squarely on each other and the matter is still being resolved in the courts.

These kinds of stories contributed to the city becoming the butt of jokes and satire, such as Post Publishing Company writer Jim Clark's crack, "Bridgeport . . . where the circus never left town." It was mirrored in a controversial 1980 song called "Bridgeport," released by local rock group Uncle Chick:

The streets are dirty
and the weather's hot;
if you don't watch out
you're bound to get shot.
There must be some way
to get out of here;
cause you can't drink the water,
can't breathe the air.
Bridgeport, I don't wanna live in Bridgeport
I ain't going back there again.

The song's words were quite extreme from the upbeat 1915 tune, "Bridgeport I've a Longing for You," and the city's centennial song in 1936, "Bridgeport by the Sea." The Chamber of Commerce blasted the rock group for the 1980 song, and some radio stations refused to play the record, yet youthful audiences packed Fairfield County clubs to hear the group play the tune. The controversy and corruption of the Mandanici administration overshadowed the positive aspects of the Mandanici years. The three-term mayor prided himself on the industrial park that created jobs, and on the senior citizen housing projects that provided excellent living conditions for the city's seniors. But the indictments, Mandanici's brash manner, and fights with several Democratic leaders led to his downfall.

Addressing the city's tarnished image became a priority for Leonard Paoletta's 1981 administration. Immediately upon taking office, Paoletta pushed an image campaign called "Up On Bridgeport." The slogan boasted of the city's higher education institutions, health facilities, parks, recreation areas, ethnic diversity, and neighborhoods—all credible attributes for a city image campaign.

Bridgeport received a much-needed shot in the arm in December 1982 when the city pulled a moral victory from a disastrous fire. On December 7 an arsonist slipped into Beardsley Park and set fire to the Police Athletics League's Christmas Village, that for more than twenty-five years had been the site of a Christmas celebration for the city's impoverished children. But the reaction to the shocking fire sparked a massive five-day restoration mission that raised the village from ashes. It became more than a Bridgeport story, growing into one that brought out a collaborative crusade of pride, purpose, and generosity from people all over the world. More than 100 men and women tirelessly worked around the clock in a restoration effort that normally would have taken weeks. People donated thousands of dollars to construct a new building, masons and construction workers donated supplies and time, and others donated food for the workers. Toy companies rushed enough gifts to fill thousands of Santa's toy bags. Nearly 60,000 people visited the village in the days after its reopening. President Ronald Reagan proclaimed on national television, "Yes, Virginia, there is a Santa Claus." Christmas Village turned out to be the best kind of Christmas gift for Bridgeport's image.

Even with the mystique of Christmas Village, "Up On Bridgeport" failed and was dumped after two years because Bridgeport didn't have anything else new to boast about. Once-populated downtown buildings that featured stores, theaters, and industry had become increasingly vacant due to lack of housing to support downtown businesses and competition from suburban shopping centers. Bridgeport's gala downtown shopping days were over.

Toward the end of the "Up On Bridgeport" campaign, the Ferryboat Junction Restaurant,

BRIDGEPORT'S 150th ANNIVERSARY
1812 OVERTURE
NEW YORK
PHILHARMONIC
ZUBIN MEHTA, Conducting
An unprecedented event
A Free Outdoor Concert with Fireworks by Grucci
Seaside Park 8 p.m. Thursday August 29, 1985
Presented by:
The CITY OF BRIDGEPORT
and The BRIDGEPORT CONVENTION AND
VISITORS COMMISSION.
LEONARD S. PAOLETTA, Mayor
In conjunction with:
Southern New England Telephone,
WEZN 100 FM and
Post-Telegram Newspapers
SEAL OF THE CITY OF BRIDGEPORT
INCORPORATED 1836
For information, call 576-8494 (Rain date Friday, August 30th)
Courtesy of Sikorsky Aircraft. Copyright 1985 CoryType & Design.

Sport Hill Climbing Contest,
May 30th, 1908,
at Bridgeport, Conn.
Short Sleeve in Locomobile,
Time 1.25.

Above: *The ornate Ritz Ballroom (seen here circa 1925) was opened by Bridgeport dancers George S. McCormick and Joseph R. Barry. Courtesy, Robert Clifford Collection*

Right: *"Connecticut's Leading Night Club," Matt Lucey's Club Howard in the Howard Hotel, was one of many nightclubs and dance halls in Bridgeport several decades ago. Photo by Neil Swanson. Courtesy, Robert Clifford Collection*

Facing page, top: *The Automobile Club of Bridgeport once held a one-mile hill climb up Sport Hill Road. This 1908 postcard shows the winning car, a Locomobile, crossing the finish line. Courtesy, Robert Clifford Collection*

Facing page, right: *The size of the Remington Arms complex on Boston Avenue made this messenger boy on a bicycle a must. Courtesy, Robert Clifford Collection*

Facing page, left: *The small can of caps was produced by the Union Metallic Cartridge Company. Photo by Neil Swanson. Courtesy, Robert Clifford Collection*

Page 201: *As part of the celebration of the city's 150th birthday, citizens were treated to a fireworks display and an outdoor concert. Photo by Neil Swanson. Courtesy, The City of Bridgeport*

This truck, one of a fleet of 200, once delivered pies to thousands of people every day. In 1924, nine tons of pies would leave Bridgeport daily. The Frisbie Pie Company was established in 1872 by William R. Frisbie in a house on Bridgeport's Kossuth Street. Courtesy, Robert Clifford Collection

The Frisbie Pie Company,
Bridgeport, Conn.

What began as a small family-run bakery in 1872 grew into
the Frisbie Pie Company. This postcard from the early 1920s
shows the bakery that produced nine tons of pies each day.
Courtesy, Robert Clifford Collection

Above: *This folding fan was a giveaway with illustrations as well as the phone number and address of the funeral home. Photo by Neil Swanson. Courtesy, Robert Clifford Collection*

Facing page: *The Bridgeport Brass Company employed staff artists to paint views of the plant and its workers. The paintings appeared on calendars, magazines, and as large murals to highlight the plant and its products. Courtesy, Historical Collections, Bridgeport Public Library*

Above and facing page: *These postcards of Pleasure Beach Park best describe the once-great amusement park. The park featured a carousel, miniature train ride, Ferris wheel, roller coaster, and pool. Courtesy, Robert Clifford Collection*

The "Merry-Go-Round" at Steeplechase Isl'd., Bridgeport, Conn.

Dancing Pavilion,
Steeplechase Island, Bridgeport, Conn.

Facing page: *Boothe Memorial Park in Stratford.*

Above: *A 1950 painting by Ralph Boyer renders the heat of the electric furnace at the Bridgeport Brass Company. Courtesy, Museum of Arts, Science and Industry*

Above: *This worker pouring molten metal is typical of the scenes painted by Ralph Boyer for the Bridgeport Brass Company. Throughout the company's 115-year history, thousands of area workers produced an extensive range of metal goods, from hoopskirt rings to long-distance telephone wires. Courtesy, Museum of Arts, Science and Industry*

Facing page: *Bridgeport Brass Company staff artist Ralph Boyer worked for ten years at the brass mill, recording in oils the daily activities of the workers. Courtesy, Museum of Arts, Science and Industry*

Long Island Sound is well known to sailing enthusiasts along the Eastern and New England seaboard.

Above: The Circus is Coming to Town, 1885, *a reverse-glass painting by Milton Bond, appeared on the cover of* Venture Bridgeport, *a supplement to the January 20, 1985,* New York Times *and* Bridgeport Sunday Post. *The Bridgeport Chamber of Commerce commissioned this work from Bond, a native Bridgeporter and retired oyster boat owner. Courtesy, Bridgeport Chamber of Commerce*

Page 216: *The "Flying High" Kite Shop is one of many shops strung along the boardwalk at Captain's Cove Seaport. The shops offer original handcrafts, food, candy, and clothes. Photo by Neil Swanson*

a floating eatery moored in the Pequonnock River that was touted by both the Mandanici and Paoletta administrations as the anchor of the city's revitalization, was secretly towed out of the harbor by its owner, mortally wounding the city's image campaign. The ferryboat restaurant was about the size of a football field and featured a unique downtown dining style, but had difficulty meeting operating costs. The restaurant left Bridgeport with the owner owing the city roughly $18,000 in back taxes.

If anything, however, the failure of "Up on Bridgeport" seemed to feed Paoletta's will to accentuate the city's positive aspects. Paoletta and Chamber of Commerce Executive Director Neil Sherman effectively used Baldwin Plaza as a showcase for Christmas tree lighting ceremonies, for midday concerts, and as an end point for city parades, which added spirit into the city's character. Paoletta insisted that the burst of energy Bridgeport needed could be found in redevelopment of the central business district. During the past decade, Bridgeport had been bypassed by corporate giants while the rest of Fairfield County glowed like a shiny condominium on a beachfront. Bridgeport's lackluster image, poor test scores in its school system, and corporations' perception of a high crime rate in the area were some of the many reasons businesses stated for not relocating in Bridgeport.

In order to attract corporate offices Paoletta maintained that the city needed a hotel convention center. With the aid of federal money and banking institutions, the Paoletta administration worked closely with hotel developer Robert Schwartz on the nine-floor, $23-million Hilton Hotel, the first new building in the downtown area since the construction of the eighteen-story Park City Plaza in 1973. A strong economy and Bridgeport's cheaper real estate prices (ironically due to the city's poor image) have forged other renovation and construction projects since the hotel's completion, including the $8-million office building at 100 Fairfield Avenue and a planned $65-million twenty-story office tower for People's Bank. The Bridgeport Chamber of Commerce and the Neighborhood Housing Service last year launched the Gateway to the Sound project, a development program designed to beautify and upgrade the esplanades and sidewalks along Park Avenue from Fairfield Avenue south to the Perry Memorial Arch at the entrance to Seaside Park.

The standout development project in the city which has amazed Fairfield County skeptics stands alone in Black Rock Harbor—Captain's Cove Seaport. In 1982, Kaye Williams, a life-long Black Rocker who made his living lobstering in Island Sound, took over the city's marina which had been creeping into a state of disrepair. Williams was surrounded by a housing project, a garbage recycling plant, and the city dump known as Mount Trashmore (which was closed in 1985), but boldly risked $200,000 of his own money to revitalize the marina. He started by renovating damaged mooring slips, cleaning up a littered boat yard, and opening a commercial fish house. He attracted boat owners by charging cheaper rental prices, and fish house customers were attracted by the wide variety of fresh fish. In the past two years Williams has added a 400-seat restaurant, boardwalk shops, 400 mooring slips, party boat service, and he has anchored the *H.M.S. Rose,* a replica of the Revolutionary War ship, in the marina. He hopes to renovate the *Rose* in time to join the Tall Ships sailing for the 100th anniversary of the Statue of Liberty in July 1986.

The *Rose*'s renovation will be just one of many events honoring Bridgeport's 150 years as a city, and it is fitting that the ship is berthed at Black Rock Harbor, the port that launched Bridgeport as one of the major shipping areas of the world.

*   *   *

As Bridgeport enters its sesquicentennial year, Bridgeporters have reason to harbor a

Above: *The 400-seat restaurant at Captain's Cove Seaport serves fresh seafood indoors and out. The Seaport was leased by Kaye Williams in 1982 and features a commercial fish house, 400 boat slips, and party boat service. Photo by Neil Swanson*

Facing page: *The fire department never appreciates it, but few can blame these Bridgeport kids for cooling off in the spray on a scorching summer day in the city. Courtesy, Fairfield County Advocate*

In July 1971 this Corsair, one of 6,600 built in Stratford by the Chance Vought Aircraft Corporation, was shipped from El Salvador and presented to Bridgeport and Stratford as a memorial by the Chateau Thierry Detachment Marine Corps League. It rests at the entrance to the Igor Sikorsky Airport. Photo by Neil Swanson

hopeful vision of the future. The city kicked off its birthday bash in the summer of 1985 when the New York Philharmonic attracted some 20,000 fans for a concert and fireworks display at Seaside Park. The Bridgeport Chamber of Commerce, the Bridgeport Convention and Visitors Commission, and the mayor's office have earmarked 1986 as the year of Bridgeport's resurgence.

Bridgeport is even getting along with the town of Stratford these days, which is amazing considering that the two have been at odds ever since Stratford dumped Bridgeport from its ownership more than 150 years ago. Lately, the biggest battle between the two has centered on Bridgeport's ownership of the Sikorsky Memorial Airport which is located within the municipal boundaries of Stratford. The airport was founded in 1927 by Bridgeport businessmen aligned with the Chamber of Commerce, and Bridgeport's city government purchased the airport in 1937 for $115,000. Stratford opposed Bridgeport's unauthorized expansion of the airport in the 1960s and 1970s, and challenged Bridgeport's refusal to pay property taxes on the airport facilities. The two were locked in a court battle for many years but have apparently settled their differences: Stratford has withdrawn its cause of action for payment of property taxes in exchange for greater airport authority, including control of airport expansion.

Bridgeport is now a city in transition. Manufacturing jobs are declining while service-field jobs in the real estate, computer, and insurance industries are on the increase. But transitions aren't really so unique to this city. One hundred fifty years ago Bridgeport emerged as the small town that Stratford didn't want, and it strove to become a major city. The railroad, harbor, Yankee ingenuity, P.T. Barnum, industrial development, and Remington Arms represent just a few of the city's contributions to world progress. They are the things that could only have happened in Bridgeport.

Bridgeport is struggling greatly to recapture that progress; it is battling an image problem, suffering from the legacy of its dependence on the transient demands of wars, but it is fighting with a gritty determination to improve itself. If it doesn't get there tomorrow, it won't be for the lack of trying. After all, Bridgeport is the working person's town.

Just as Mayor Isaac Sherman, Jr., said 150 years before them, Bridgeporters today will have a lot to think about in the days ahead.

Democrat Thomas William Bucci and his wife, Karen, celebrate his November 5, 1985, victory over incumbent Mayor Leonard Paoletta. Photo by Ed Brinsko. Courtesy, Post Publishing Company

One of many Tedesco administration projects involved placing nearly all city departments under one roof. The former Central High School on Lyon Terrace became the new home for City Hall in the 1960s. City Hall was formerly on State Street. Photo by Corbit Studios. Courtesy, Historical Collections, Bridgeport Public Library

Epilogue

On November 6, 1985, the banner headline in *The Telegram* said it all: "It's Bucci in a romp." Thomas William Bucci accomplished what so many said couldn't be done. He united a severely splintered Democratic Party to become Bridgeport's forty-ninth chief executive, riding a 12,000-vote plurality.

Bucci's victory was indeed stunning considering that just three years ago, the labor lawyer had no political name recognition. Bucci's emergence goes back to early 1983. Unlike many politicians, Bucci was recruited to run for mayor that year by Democratic Town Chairman John T. Guman, Jr. Democratic Party leaders had suffered the pains of vicious infighting which helped Republican Leonard S. Paoletta squeeze past three-term Mayor John C. Mandanici in 1981. (Mandanici died in January 1986.)

Guman felt he no longer could deliver Mandanici back to the voters. Opting for a younger, fresher face who was untainted by the corruption of Mandanici's administration, Guman convinced Bucci, an assistant city attorney during the Mandanici years, to dive into Bridgeport politics. As *The Telegram*'s political columnist Jim Callahan persistently maintained both in newsroom and in city taverns: "John Guman reached down into the political swamp, and he pulled Tommy Bucci out of the muck and mud, setting him on firm ground. Guman then hosed him off, kicked him in the butt and announced to the world: 'Here's our boy!'"

Okay, so maybe it's not the nicest way to run for mayor, but Bridgeport politics aren't very nice.

Bucci lost in a four-way Democratic primary battle in 1983, but the loss seemed insignificant. He was being groomed for 1985, and he never stopped running for mayor after the loss. Where others failed, Bucci sat down with key party leaders and managed to secure their support for his next run. The party chiefs may not have liked each other, but they seemed to like Bucci's low-key, patient style which differed from the prevailing bombastic manner of past candidates. They also viewed Bucci as the only candidate who could defeat two-term Mayor Paoletta.

Along the way Bucci built name recognition by successfully battling Paoletta in court. He represented the Civil Service Commission in what a Superior Court judge ruled was Paoletta's illegal attempt to remove Police Superintendent Joseph Walsh, and the courts also sided with Bucci in a ruling stating that the mayor had issued several illegal contracts to consultants.

After Bucci won a four-way primary race, the general election didn't disappoint spectators who have grown accustomed to Bridgeport's circus-like political atmosphere.

Now it's Bucci, in the City of Bridgeport's 150th year, who has the honor of governing the fifth largest city in New England; sifting through the daily stacks of paperwork; trying to get the most out of department heads; addressing citizen complaints about the next door neighbor's dog; or dealing with the downed oak tree that the Public Works Department hasn't moved.

Oh, yes, and remembering the snow-covered streets that need plowing.

Cycling enthusiasts have a long history in Bridgeport. Clubs such as the Rambling Wheelmen rode the streets of Bridgeport in the late 1800s, and the streets and parks are full of bikes today during the spring and summer months. The track at Pleasure Beach was an important stop on the bicycle racing tour, as can be seen by the determined look on this young racer's face. Photo by Seeley and Warnock. Courtesy, Historical Collections, Bridgeport Public Library

CHAPTER X

Partners In Progress

The beginnings of Bridgeport's industrial community followed typical New England and Yankee patterns. Founded to supply the needs of local residents, the first industrial enterprises were linked to agriculture—gristmills, sawmills, tanneries, and shipping. Nevertheless, in the first half of the nineteenth century the stage was set for the city's future as a major New England industrial center.

Factory-made and store-bought products overtook local homespun and handcrafted items. The power of steam was quickly recognized. A multifaceted transportation network, an easily accessible location, and a steadily increasing population gave evidence of the business prominence to come.

Thousands of immigrants came to Bridgeport from many foreign nations, including Ireland, Poland, Italy, Germany, Hungary, and Russia. They became the area's work force and then a part of the American Dream. Many of these hardworking newcomers assumed a Yankee spirit and founded businesses that became the bedrock of the city's business community.

Throughout the years Bridgeport's business and industry became resilient to changing economic and social conditions. During the Depression no major industries closed, and all but two banks continued their financial services. And when the demands of World War II came to a sudden halt, the city's industry adjusted by following the chamber recommendations for the changeover from defense to consumer-oriented production. Although much of Bridgeport's industrial base is defense oriented to this day, it has an unusually diversified and flexible economy. Today Bridgeport, the seat of Fairfield County government, is the Northeast's fourth-largest banking center.

In this tradition of resiliency, Bridgeport now prepares for such future changes as a more service-oriented economy while recognizing the continued importance of high-technology production. Present-day entrepreneurs continue the spirit that kept the city successful over the past 150 years.

Throughout Bridgeport's history, however, the human element has been the guiding force. Individuals with the necessary imagination, foresight, and business acumen have helped to uphold the city's position as one of the strongest manufacturing and financial regions in New England. The pages that follow are a tribute to generations of vision, hard work, and dedication.

The organizations whose stories are detailed on the following pages have chosen to support Bridgeport's sesquicentennial celebration with this literary and civic project. They illustrate the variety of ways in which individuals and their businesses have contributed to the area's growth and development, and have made Bridgeport one of Connecticut's largest and most successful communities.

THE BUSINESS/INDUSTRY COUNCIL OF THE BRIDGEPORT ECONOMIC REGION

The Business/Industry Council is a private, voluntarily funded membership association of the regional business and professional community. It was established to achieve the long-term economic growth and prosperity of the Bridgeport economic region.

As a business organization, the council believes the accomplishment of a strong economy will enable the region to successfully develop every other cultural, social, and civic benefit that improves communities and the life-style of all who live in those communities.

This is neither a casual nor arbitrary mission. Business is the single greatest determinant of a community's future. Historically, no other force begins to approach the private business sector's ability to accomplish on behalf of its community. Business generates a vast array of resources that include great personal talent, systems, facilities, productivity, goals, wealth, energy, and vision. Recognizing this unique store of capabilities, business subscribes to a self-imposed obligation to do the job it is singularly qualified to do. That job is to achieve the long-term economic growth and prosperity that will generate the best possible future for the community.

This mission requires that business assemble, organize, and focus its massive resources. The Business/Industry Council was created for this purpose. It was established to be the forum by which the economic region takes command of its destiny.

While the organization enjoys a Bridgeport legacy of more than a century of service, it was only recently, in 1982, that it was greatly expanded to respond both to a new period of great economic opportunity and to the fact that the Bridgeport business community had in many ways become a single, large regional community comprised of numerous local neighborhoods and municipalities.

The council is deliberately structured to address issues and concerns of the overall region while simultaneously serving the particular needs and interests of local communities within the region. To accomplish this, it employs a heritage of continuity that transcends generations, a comprehensive system of volunteer committees that marshals the energies and expertise of business, and a structural system of operational efficiencies and marketability that enables programs and services to grow substantially faster than costs.

Through 1986 and the immediate future beyond, the ambitious mission of The Business/Industry Council will be pursued through five divisional councils: The Economic Development Council, The Government Relations Council, The Human Resources Council, The Local Affiliates Council, and The Membership Service & Development Council.

Few observers would dispute the opinion that the regional business community stands at the threshold of an era with enormous potential for long-term progress and prosperity. However, that development is not inevitable, nor is the opportunity infinite. To capture it will require more leadership, greater cooperation, higher investment, and faster action.

LOU KLEIN ASSOCIATES

In 1968 Lou Klein opened the doors of his recruitment and professional placement business. Since then, he has helped thousands of men and women seek meaningful employment and just as many companies find qualified employees. In fact, Lou is pleased to call himself "the old-timer" in the recruitment business.

"I've been at the same address at Commerce Park in the north end of Bridgeport since first starting Lou Klein Associates," the company's owner states. "This makes me the oldest in Park City, and I'm very proud of it."

Lou entered the professional placement business after twenty years in industry. He received a bachelor of science degree in mechanical engineering from Newark College of Engineering in New Jersey and a master of science degree in production management from Steven's Institute of Technology, also in New Jersey. He then worked for Johnson & Johnson, American Cyanamid, and Inland Steel Container.

Throughout the years Lou has stressed the importance of personalized service. He has kept his office small enough to make sure that each client receives the individual attention he or she needs. Today a staff of six handles a full range of professional areas: technical, administrative, financial, and engineering—for positions of $20,000 and up.

"Our business' credibility and success depend upon close associations," Lou explains. "Every person is totally unique and it's our responsibility to find the right fit between the employer's and the prospect's needs."

Because of his emphasis on individualized attention, Lou's motto has become: "We discriminate without prejudice." He says, "It is our role to determine who is the best person for the job, to carefully discriminate or select the right individual based on the candidate's credentials and our

Lou Klein proudly holds his Rotarian of the Year Award while (left to right) Bob Rogers, Bob Ware, Charlie Horsfall, and Joe McNamara extend their congratulations.

client's needs. All this must be accomplished, of course, without any prejudgment and with complete professional objectivity."

Performance has made Lou Klein Associates a much sought after service. According to Lou, just about every company in the greater Bridgeport area has filled a job opening through his efforts. Most new clients either come from referrals of those satisfied with Lou's services or from the personnel and employment managers of Fairfield County companies.

Lou Klein Associates is also one of the few Connecticut personnel agencies qualifying for membership in First International Personnel Consultants, Inc. (FIPC). This is a network of sixty-five professional recruitment placement consultants located in key areas throughout the United States. Each member is continually evaluated on professional competence and personal integrity.

Lou's list of community affiliations and activities is impressive. He is a member or a director of many area business and service organizations. On top of the list is the Bridgeport Rotary Club, which he was invited to join in 1973. The Rotary year 1979-

1980 he was the club's president, and in 1982 was the first recipient of its Rotarian of the Year Award. This honor recognized Lou for his help in ending the stalemate on the construction of a housing unit for 100 elderly residents.

This is the same concern for others that is seen at Lou Klein Associates, where "the client always comes first," says Lou. "The sign of the true professional in any business is the effort to place its customers' well-being first and foremost." This philosophy has helped make Lou successful over the past seventeen years—so successful, in fact, that he rarely advertises to elicit clients. They come to him by word-of-mouth recommendations.

Certified personnel consultants Lou Klein (center), his partners, Doug Renfrew and Linda Glover (seated), and their support staff, Phyllis Reiter, JoAnn McClellan, and Linda Martin (standing, left to right), fulfilling their goal of "discrimination without prejudice."

ST. VINCENT'S MEDICAL CENTER

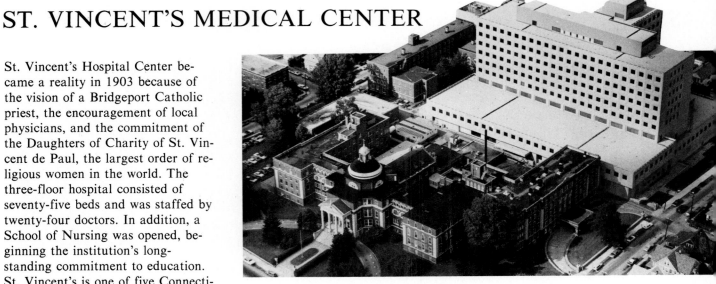

St. Vincent's Hospital Center became a reality in 1903 because of the vision of a Bridgeport Catholic priest, the encouragement of local physicians, and the commitment of the Daughters of Charity of St. Vincent de Paul, the largest order of religious women in the world. The three-floor hospital consisted of seventy-five beds and was staffed by twenty-four doctors. In addition, a School of Nursing was opened, beginning the institution's longstanding commitment to education. St. Vincent's is one of five Connecticut hospitals that retains its nursing program to this day.

Over the next three decades extensive additions were made to accommodate the consistently growing number of patients. At the same time, with the help of modern diagnostic and medical equipment, physicians successfully completed a number of life-saving surgeries, impossible only a few years earlier.

During St. Vincent's early days

staff physicians recommended the creation of a medical education program. Today St. Vincent's is affiliated with New York Medical College and the Yale University School of Medicine for teaching programs in surgery, internal medicine, and many other disciplines. Annually over sixty physicians in residency and fellowship programs are trained in numerous subspecialty fields at St. Vincent's, one of the 300 major affiliated teaching hospitals in the United States. The institution also provides training for radiology technicians as well as programs in medical, respiratory, and ultrasound technology and nuclear medicine.

Most hospitals add wings or floors as they grow. Instead, in 1976 St. Vincent's built a new, 440,000-square-foot building behind its original facility. This ten-story medical center accommodates 400 beds and a space age matrix of technology. The new facility's name was changed to St. Vincent's Medical Center in order to reflect the comprehensive services available to patients.

In the years that followed St. Vincent's became one of the first hospi-

Progress at St. Vincent's Medical Center is graphically portrayed in this 1976 photograph. In the foreground stands the original hospital complex. Rising behind it is the ultramodern St. Vincent's of today—one of very few complete replacement medical facilities in the nation. The original St. Vincent's has since been demolished to make way for parking.

tals in the state to utilize full-body CT scanning and also to develop a department of diagnostic radiology. It also became the regional open-heart center for Fairfield County. And, utilizing a tripartite approach of radiation therapy, surgery, and oncology (the area's first cancer unit), physicians have been able to do more than ever to help cancer patients.

A newly designed Short Stay Center accounts for over 40 percent of all surgeries performed at St. Vincent's. Expanded programs in cardiology, physical therapy, and neurosciences were typical of growth experienced in the early 1980s. New additions include a renovated Emergency Department and Psychiatric Day Treatment Center.

Those who dreamed of building a new hospital in Bridgeport in 1903 would not recognize today's modern facility, but they would be proud of the tradition of accomplishment that is part of St. Vincent's Medical Center's proud history.

Respect for life is a cornerstone of St. Vincent's Medical Center's philosophy. Here, a new father gets better acquainted with his child in the Family-Centered Maternity Unit.

ALLOY ENGINEERING COMPANY, INC.

"There's no other country but the United States where you can come in as an immigrant and build your own successful company." These are the words of Emmy Nowak, president and chief executive officer of Alloy Engineering Company, Inc. And she speaks from experience.

Hamburg, Germany, was Emmy's home until she was three years old. At that time she and her parents, Erwin and Elfriede Muller Stamm, immigrated to the "land of opportunity," settling in the east end of Bridgeport.

In time, all three members of the Stamm family were employed: Erwin as a tool and die maker earning eighty-eight dollars a month; Elfriede, washing clothes and cleaning homes; and Emmy, at fourteen years of age, waitressing at a Broad Street bakery.

However, nursing was Emmy's first actual occupation. Following graduation from Stratford High School, she received her R.N. from Bridgeport Hospital School of Nursing and became an assistant head nurse in the delivery room. She married Joseph E. Gorgens, who later became an engineer with a local manufacturing firm. She left nursing in 1956, but the role of housewife just didn't suit Emmy. "It doesn't offer enough of a challenge," Emmy recalls telling her husband. In response, he came up with an idea that changed Emmy's life. He suggested that they manufacture thermowells, because no one then, or now for that matter, specialized in producing this metal housing for temperature-sensing elements.

In 1958 the plan was put into action. Emmy would run the new business while her husband continued to work as an engineer. A $20,000 mortgage on their home enabled the couple to purchase surplus equipment dating from the 1940s. And the funds for a 7,000-square-foot brick building on Seaview Avenue came from Emmy's father. The industry was all new to Emmy, and she had a lot to learn; she now had her challenge.

After her marriage ended in divorce in 1961, Emmy decided to continue on her own. "My distributors and customers gave me the needed encouragement, and my employees, the necessary dedication," she recalls proudly.

The employees also helped Emmy when a fire in 1968 did $150,000 worth of damage to the plant. "The employees all said they would continue to work for nothing until we got things in order," she says. Instead, Emmy paid them minimum wage for a few weeks, giving her employees back pay a few months later.

Since then, Alloy Engineering has expanded into a 28,000-square-foot manufacturing plant, with the most recent addition being a 3,000-square-foot employee cafeteria and meeting hall. The firm has the latest equipment including automated systems. Gross sales of over four million dollars were reached in 1985—a broad jump from the $70,000 figure in 1958. Thermowells are sold to original-equipment manufacturers throughout the United States and Canada, with representatives also located in Europe.

Emmy Nowak, president of Alloy Engineering, enters her 28,000-square-foot manufacturing plant.

In 1966 Emmy married Bernard Joseph Nowak, who acts as purchasing agent and secretary of Alloy Engineering Company, Inc. Emmy's son, Richard Gorgens, has followed his mother's lead and has started his own company, Alloy Computer Products, in Massachusetts.

In 1982 Emmy Nowak was named a recipient of the YWCA of Greater Bridgeport's Salute to Women Award for her business acumen and community leadership—an honor she rightly deserves for meeting the challenges of the business world head on.

Emmy Nowak inspects the processing of thermowells.

KASPER ASSOCIATES, INC.

In 1920 eighteen-year-old Bridgeporter Joseph T. Kasper, Sr., was already active in the fields of surveying and engineering. He decided to take the next logical step—starting his own business. He saw Bridgeport's potential as well as a need in the private sector for an engineering and surveying firm.

Kasper's faith was rewarded. There were many improvements and much progress to be made in Bridgeport, and the firm grew along with the city. Kasper Associates has grown into a full-service, multidisciplined firm with a staff of 150, offering engineering, landscaping, architecture, and surveying services to public and private clients throughout Connecticut, New York, and New Jersey. The main office on Fairfield Avenue is supplemented by locations in Bethel, Vernon, and Wethersfield, Connecticut, and Wyckoff, New Jersey.

In 1984 Kasper Associates became part of the Kasper Group, Inc. In addition to Kasper Associates, the Kasper Group includes Design Collaborative Architects, P.C., specializing in architecture and interior design, and J&D Kasper & Associates, specializing in land and hydrographic surveying.

The services of Kasper Associates, under its separate landscape architecture, transportation, surveying, mechanical and electrical, civil/structural, environmental, and construction management divisions, are many and cover a broad spectrum. Services include designs for major

The new, 13,000-square-foot Bethel Kasper office building was totally designed by the Kasper Group.

corporations, renovations to private and public buildings and bridges, site-improvement design, designs for electrical and mechanical systems, master and site planning for private and public use, and designs for highway and transportation facilities.

Kasper Associates' project list is just as impressive. In Bridgeport alone, projects include a civic center study, urban-renewal projects, the Ox Brook flood-control project, the East Side Elementary School, YWCA and YMCA renovations, coastal plan for Bridgeport, renovation of the municipal parking garage and bus terminal, upgrading of the east side and west side wastewater treatment plants, and Waterfront Park on the Pequonnock River. Recently, the firm designed the Gateway to the Sound project, which includes esplanade improvements such as general landscaping, signage, and intersection renovations on Park Avenue from Fairfield Avenue to Long Island Sound.

Much of the firm's growth in the past several decades is due to Joseph T. Kasper, Jr., who joined his father in 1952 after graduating from Michigan State University. He became president in 1976 and is now chairman of the board of the Kasper Group.

Edward C. Leavy, who was appointed president in 1985, has an extensive background in engineering, both with private and public concerns. He joined Kasper Associates in 1982 as chief engineer, and the following year was appointed executive vice-president. Now president of Kasper Associates, Leavy will lead the firm in its continued pattern of growth.

WEST END MOVING AND STORAGE COMPANY

The year is 1928. John Kartovsky, Sr., an immigrant from Russia, is running his own coal-delivery business in Bridgeport. One day, as a favor, he uses his truck to help move a neighbor's belongings. At the end of the day he decides that he enjoys moving people instead of coal; it's much cleaner and he appreciates how people respond positively to his service.

Thus began West End Moving and Storage Company, with the first offices located in Kartovsky's house at 764 Howard Avenue.

The business grew quickly, and within a few years it had three trucks and three large garages built for storage. Even during the Depression, people had to move. West End provided the answer to their furniture moving and storage needs.

John Kartovsky's sons, Peter, William, John Jr., and James Collins (a half-brother), helped their father in the moving business as they grew up and took over management of the company upon his retirement.

During the 1950s and 1960s West End continued to grow, and in 1955 moved to its new headquarters at 706 Howard Avenue. The company developed an excellent reputation by handling corporate relocations and the moving of executives throughout the United States and worldwide.

One of the largest of all moves came in 1974, when West End relocated General Electric's entire corporate offices from Manhattan to the new world headquarters in Fairfield.

The corporate headquarters of West End Moving and Storage Company (below) is located at 241 Pine Street, Bridgeport.

Fifty-seven floors of furniture were moved in one weekend! The brothers proudly remember that the move started on Friday evening and was completed at 6 p.m. on Sunday so that General Electric could carry on business as usual on Monday morning.

By 1980 West End had outgrown its location on Howard Avenue. The firm moved to a new 4.5-acre site located at 241 Pine Street. The 57,000-square-foot building was "a fulfillment of our father's dream," says his son John, now president of West End. The other brothers are retired from the business and serve on the board of directors. The new partnership consists of John and vice-presidents Sheldon Levine and Leonard Toigo. Both men have long years of experience in the transportation industry and were able to provide the management transition by bringing their expertise to the company.

Today growth continues. The firm recently added a 16,000-square-foot warehouse annex, bringing the total

One of the firm's first major moves was the estate of Harold Gray, creator of the Dick Tracy *comic strip. John Kartovsky, Sr., is shown at right.*

building space to 73,000 square feet. West End is now a major New England moving company with some 110 trucks and vans and more than 150 employees. It also has locations in Danbury and Stamford. In addition, West End is the largest single agent for Global Van Lines, whose headquarters is in Orange, California.

According to its management team, the company plans to continue growth in the tri-state area and to expand corporate relocation and international services.

As John reviews the firm's history, he fondly remembers his father saying, "The harder you work, the luckier you get." John agrees. "Since our business started on the basis of a favor, it has grown into what we consider to be Connecticut's largest and finest moving company."

THE BODINE CORPORATION

During the Depression Alfred Van-Sant Bodine took a bold step: He purchased the bankrupt Anderson Die Machine Company. And thus, on July 5, 1933, The Bodine Corporation was born, a company that has proven to be a most successful family-owned and -operated machine tool business.

Bodine, known to many as "Bo," had the necessary background for such a venture. After receiving an engineering degree from Lehigh University, he held positions with Winchester Repeating Arms, Hunter Arms, Columbia Gramaphone, Dictaphone, and Raybestos.

Bodine had a litany of achievements. He and his wife, Ethel Phillips, reared four children: Alfred Jr., who died in World War II; Edward, now Bodine's chairman; Richard, president; and Betty Swain. Bodine was also devoted to higher education. He's remembered most for helping to transform Bridgeport Junior College into the University of Bridgeport. Today a residence building bears his name in appreciation of his efforts.

With Bodine's expertise and guidance, The Bodine Corporation grew extensively throughout the decades. At first machines were primarily produced for the electrical market, but Bodine later expanded into automotive and business machine industries. The firm also made enormous contributions to the war effort during World War II, producing machines for military fuses, aircraft fasteners, and optical gun sights, which earned The Bodine Corporation the Army-Navy "E" award.

In the 1940s both Edward and Richard Bodine graduated from Lehigh University and joined the company, working their way up from machinists to management positions. "Bo's training was far superior to any M.B.A.," remembers Richard.

After selling World War II-like machines during the Korean Con-

A typical Bodine Model 64, the product that marked the firm's entry into the synchronous in-line automatic assembly machine business.

flict, The Bodine Corporation joined other major companies in the ordnance business. For the first time the firm modified machines to suit the demands of purely assembly operations, with no chip making involved.

Following Bo Bodine's death in 1966, his sons took over management of the business and continued exploration into automatic assembly. Model 64 marked Bodine's entry into the synchronous in-line automatic assembly machine business. Many of these machines were used for assembling bomb fuses for Vietnam, confirming the company's reputation in automatic assembly.

Today Model 64 is used for GM automotive production by Delco Electronics and numerous other GM divisions. The Bodine Corporation's presence is still strong in the electrical industry with companies like Harvey Hubbell Incorporated, and in various hardware and electronic items used for millions of consumer devices.

Today the third generation of the Bodine family is active in the business, located on Mountain Grove Street. Richard's sons, Richard Jr. and Dave, and Edward's son William and daughter Carol are currently involved in company operations.

"It may be that the family-owned machine tool business is a vanishing species," admits Richard Bodine, Sr. "The company founded by A.V. Bodine, however, continues to battle the tide. We believe that a well-run corporation that accepts its civic responsibility is an asset to the community. We will continue to strive to be the best in the world at what we are doing."

COHEN AND WOLF, P.C.

Founded by the late Herbert L. Cohen and Austin K. Wolf in 1951, the law firm of Cohen and Wolf, P.C., has grown from its original two members to over thirty lawyers, maintaining offices in Danbury and Stamford as well as in Bridgeport. During those years members of the firm have played a vital role in almost all aspects of Bridgeport's legal and civic life.

Herbert Cohen epitomized in many ways the role the firm's attorneys have sought to achieve. In addition to being a highly regarded member of the bar, his life was devoted to many community activities as a representative in the Connecticut Legislature, chairman of the University of Bridgeport board of trustees and first chairman of its Law School Advisory Committee, president of Bridgeport's United Jewish Council, and chairman of the Connecticut Commission on the Arts. In 1981 Cohen and five other community leaders were honored as "master builders of Bridgeport" by The Business/Industry Council of the Bridgeport Economic Region.

Following his example, present members of Cohen and Wolf, P.C., have served as leaders of the Connecticut and Bridgeport bar associations and have also headed or served on the boards of many of Bridgeport's principal charitable, cultural, and civic organizations. Firm members have served as board members or presidents of the Park City Hospital, the United Way, the YMCA, the Greater Bridgeport Jewish Federation, the Bridgeport Area Foundation, the Chamber of Commerce, the YWCA, and three of the community's synagogues.

This ongoing commitment to

The firm purchased the United Illuminating building for its offices in 1981. The facility, erected in 1910 and gutted by fire in 1979, has been completely renovated and is on the National Register of Historic Places.

Bridgeport's growth took a significant turn in 1981, when the firm purchased the former United Illuminating building at 1115 Broad Street, which had been constructed in 1910 and was gutted by fire in 1979. "The building is a symbol of our commitment to Bridgeport in a very real sense," notes president Austin K. Wolf, referring to the extensive renovations the firm has made to this historic structure. The building has since received historic landmark designation and is on the National Register of Historic Places.

As Bridgeport's economy has grown and diversified, so too has the firm's practice. Attorneys at Cohen and Wolf, P.C., specialize in corporate law, litigation, taxation, estate planning, zoning, bankruptcy, labor law, education, real estate, and banking. In addition to these traditional areas of practice, the firm offers specialists in areas that were almost unheard of when it was founded, such as computer and environmental law.

As the firm moves into its second generation of providing legal services to the Bridgeport community, it welcomes the latest round of growth of the city. In this, its 35th year, Cohen and Wolf, P.C., congratulates Bridgeport on its 350th year.

Austin K. Wolf, president, looking at a portrait of the firm's co-founder, Herbert L. Cohen, who died on September 22, 1983.

UNITED ILLUMINATING

United Illuminating's old East Main Street station.

Picture Bridgeport at the close of the nineteenth century. As the sun sets over the city, a boiler foreman in a John Street power plant begins firing up the evening's streetlighting load. As darkness falls, the power switch is thrown and a few hundred street-lights glow until dawn.

The foreman is an employee of the Bridgeport Electric Co. which, on October 26, 1899, merged with the New Haven Electric Co. to form The United Illuminating Co.—a corporation that today serves nearly 300,000 customers in a seventeen-town area.

The major entrepreneur behind this Bridgeport electricity story was James English. Seeing the electric industry's great potential, he and six other New Haven businessmen took over the defunct New Haven Electric Light Co. in 1884. Just one year later he also obtained sizable interest in the Bridgeport Electric Co., serving as the firm's secretary/treasurer. In 1887 the growing concern received its first contract for streetlighting for the City of Bridgeport at fifty cents

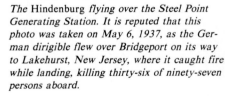

The *Hindenburg* *flying over the Steel Point Generating Station. It is reputed that this photo was taken on May 6, 1937, as the German dirigible flew over Bridgeport on its way to Lakehurst, New Jersey, where it caught fire while landing, killing thirty-six of ninety-seven persons aboard.*

per lamp per night.

By 1899, when English became the first president of the newly established United Illuminating, electricity had grown substantially in Bridgeport, being used for much more than just streetlights. D.M. Read Co. and Howland's Dry Goods were using electricity in their stores. Soon the Park City Theatre, with its huge 200-light marquee, the Moss and Kreiger's store and its 260-light sign, and the recently completed Atlantic Hotel were also glowing.

In a memorable event closing the nineteenth century, the Stratford Avenue Bridge became the first electrically operated drawbridge in the United States. P.T. Barnum brought

some of his elephants to stand on the bridge and add to the spectacle.

UI's business grew so quickly that a new power station was completed in 1910 on Congress Street, Fairfield Light and Power was acquired to expand the company's service area, and a new office building was opened at Broad and Cannon streets. English had also anticipated underground conduits. Thus, by the end of the first decade of the twentieth century, UI was also one of the earliest electric utilities with wires below ground.

Then came World War I and with it, an unprecedented demand for electricity. In 1918 UI generated 100

234

A 1912 electric service truck.

million kilowatt-hours of electricity, versus 19 million in 1913. After the war the increase of electric appliances continued this great demand. During the 1920s UI built and quickly expanded upon the Steel Point Station in Bridgeport. The firm also opened a new service building on East Main Street.

In 1939 UI decided it was necessary to build a new substation, feeders,

and distribution lines. A generator—double the size of the largest units then on the system—was installed at the Steel Point plant; more significant, a transmission line was constructed from New Haven to Bridgeport along the New Haven Railroad.

By the mid-1950s UI customers used fifteen times as much electricity as they did forty years earlier. In response, the firm had already constructed sixty-eight substations to distribute the electricity from three power plants.

In 1958 UI's new Bridgeport Harbor Station power plant became the first generating facility built under a statewide capacity coordinating plan with power interchange features designed to effect greater efficiencies in operation and power production. Three years later the Bridgeport Harbor Station was expanded to meet increased demand. By the late 1960s UI customers used thirty-five times as much electricity as they had fifty years earlier, and the utility had 105 substations and four power plants to meet the increased need. The company had $280 million invested in plant equipment, including a 400,000-kilowatt generator at Bridgeport Harbor Station. In addition, since 1934 UI had applied pollution-prevention technology and invested millions of dollars to ensure that all operations had minimal effect on the environment.

Today UI stands ready to meet the future electric needs of its more than a quarter-million customers in the greater Bridgeport and New Haven areas. It is striving to meet a number of goals aimed at helping the utility fulfill its primary corporate mission to provide customers with an adequate and reliable supply of electricity at a reasonable rate. At the same time UI will continue to be a good corporate neighbor involved with the community and protecting the environment from unreasonable impacts as the result of its operations.

The reduction in UI's dependence on imported oil as a generation source is among the stated goals. The firm aims to reduce oil dependency that was in excess of 90 percent before 1985, so that this fuel source will not contribute more than 30 percent of the electricity generation required to meet customer needs in 1990. Likewise, UI wishes to achieve a flexible energy mix so that no more than 50 percent of its required capacity is restricted to any one energy source by 1990 and beyond.

By 1990 the company projects an energy mix that will include coal, nuclear, oil, gas, refuse, hydroelectricity, and a combination of cogeneration, conservation, and load management. While much production will come from highly efficient fossil units, UI's involvement in three nuclear units is equally important. The success of UI's coal reconversion project at Bridgeport Harbor Station's Unit 3 since January 1985 has already substantially reduced oil dependence.

United Illuminating views the future with a strong sense of commitment to servicing its customers. It is an opportunity to meet the challenge of providing the best possible service to nearly one-fourth of Connecticut's population, and to assure a supply of energy that has become so increasingly vital to the health of the area's economy.

One of the firm's new modern facilities, the Western Service Center.

BRYANT ELECTRIC, A DIVISION OF WESTINGHOUSE ELECTRIC CORPORATION

In the 1880s the world was preparing for a whole new age: the age of electricity. Ideas, innovations, inventions, and industries were the order of the day. It was an ideal time for young, creative men like Waldo Calvin Bryant to pursue their visions and make their profound impact on peoples' lives at work, at home, and at play.

Bryant was born in 1863 in Winchendon, Massachusetts. After receiving a bachelor's degree from Worcester Polytechnic Institute in 1884, he began his employment with Thomson-Houston Electric Co. in Lynn. A year later he was assigned to the Waterbury, Connecticut, Electric Light Co.

From this exposure Bryant learned about wiring systems and the practical applications of electricity. He soon realized that wiring methods were crude and often makeshift. Exposed knob and tube wiring controlled by knife switches were commonplace and very dangerous.

Bryant's inventive mind, bent on perfection, could not accept such electrical hazards. In the summer of 1888 he set up shop in a loft on John Street in Bridgeport to work on his ideas full time. The answers came quickly. By October he had already patented the push-pull switch. The innovation was an overnight success because it was totally enclosed, more attractive, safer, and a convenient means of controlling electricity.

Bryant and his then eight employees quickly outgrew their first business quarters and in 1890 moved to the corner of State and Organ streets into an old schoolhouse owned by the enterprising P.T. Barnum, of circus fame.

In addition to manufacturing the invention, Bryant Electric Company also repaired electric clocks and installed arc lighting in saloons and

Waldo Calvin Bryant, founder, Bryant Electric Company.

door bells on houses. The firm continued its rapid growth, and the schoolhouse was purchased and razed in 1892 to make way for the company's first brick building, several thousand square feet in size.

To meet the growing demand for wiring devices, Bryant purchased the Perkins Electric Switch Co. in Hartford in 1900, moving the entire operation to the Bridgeport facility. Another joining of forces came a year later when Bryant Electric be-

came a wholly owned subsidiary of Westinghouse Electric Corporation. In 1986 Westinghouse and the Bryant Division joined in celebration of the 100th anniversary of the parent company. Both Waldo Bryant and George Westinghouse were advocates of the safe use of electrical energy and played a vital role in expanding electricity's popularity and widespread use from coast to coast. Because of Bryant's reputation and name in the industry, Westinghouse kept the original name of the company intact.

In the years that followed Bryant obtained over 500 patents for new wiring devices to meet the growing applications for controlling energy. During World War I he was asked by the War Department to serve as chief of the Bridgeport Ordnance District of the State of Connecticut and four western Massachusetts counties.

In 1928 Hemco Plastics Division Company was acquired to supply much-needed plastic parts used in insulating. During World War II this division manufactured materials crucial to the war effort such as parts for radio and radar installations. The

Bryant Electric's State Street manufacturing facility.

Wiring Device Division was also active in the war effort, producing devices for combat ships and torpedo mechanisms. Army-Navy "E" flags were awarded to both divisions for their efforts.

Bryant died in 1930, but he is well remembered for his excellent products, which were referred to as "superior wiring devices." He is also recognized for his exemplary working conditions. Bryant practiced the mottoes "a friend to the working man," and "fair dealing with all employees," insisting upon a clean and attractive work environment. His employees received retirement benefits long before social security was even considered, and the company sponsored group insurance, savings through payroll deductions, and social activities for employees and their families.

Through the years the Waldo Bryant tradition has been followed, and the firm has continued its pioneering efforts. In 1960 Bryant Electric originated the use of nylon as a wiring device material. Impact resistant, arc resistant, and extremely durable, nylon represented a significant advancement in electrical safety. Other introductions followed, including circuit breakers in 1961, the first complete line of NEMA-configurated nylon devices in 1965, and the self-grounding feature for receptacles in 1971.

The current Bridgeport plant, still at its original location, exceeds 500,000 square feet with more than twelve acres of floor space. In 1981, after an expanded product line and restructured organization, Bryant's management staff expanded into new quarters in the Sylvan Executive Center, also in Bridgeport. The firm also supports the community by working actively with, and financially

George R. Dunbar, general manager, Bryant Electric.

supporting, social and civic organizations and their activities.

Today, under the direction of general manager George R. Dunbar, the division manufactures over 3,800 products and markets many other Westinghouse commodity-type products as well. Some fourteen million wiring devices are produced each year. Tech-Spec® (Technology beyond Specification Grade), a whole new line of plugs, connectors, receptacles, and switches, first introduced in 1980, symbolizes Bryant Electric's continuing emphasis on innovation and quality.

All management policies at Bryant Electric are aimed at increasing quality and productivity. All employees are committed to producing top-quality products and providing premier customer service. They are making sure that the customers get the very best; Waldo Bryant would be proud!

In 1981 the firm's management staff moved into new quarters in the Sylvan Executive Center.

LINDQUIST SUPPLY COMPANY

Charles G. Lindquist came to Bridgeport from Sweden in 1892 at the age of nineteen. For the next twenty-seven years he was an employee and then an officer at a local hardware company. With this background, he organized the Lindquist Boerum Company in 1919, soon changing the name to the Lindquist Hardware Company.

Through the years many other Lindquist family members came into the business; George, the founder's nephew, joined the firm in 1926 and served as president and treasurer from 1949 through 1972 and then served as chairman of the board until April 1985. Leonard, George's brother, joined the firm in 1932 and retired in 1983 as executive vice-president and secretary; Robert, George's son, became president in 1985; and Kenneth, Leonard's son, is currently the corporate secretary.

William E. Weaver, who has been with Lindquist Supply since 1960 and is now chairman of the board and treasurer, says the company has made many changes over its nearly seven decades. The business began with four employees in a twenty-foot store at 383 Fairfield Avenue. Through the years it expanded at this location and by 1945 there were fifty employees operating out of 15,000 square feet of floor space. During World War II Lindquist received publicity when Norman Rock-

well used the store's window as a prop for a *Saturday Evening Post* cover.

In the 1960s the firm continued to change. "We adopted the new name of Lindquist Supply Company to emphasize our selling to industry," explains George Lindquist. "We also acquired a Danbury branch."

From its start Lindquist Supply has always been greatly involved with the Bridgeport community, with most of its officers represented on local service, civic, and religious boards. In 1973 then-chairman George Lindquist received the Senior Builder Award from the Bridgeport Area Chamber of Commerce "for his exceptional community support."

A southern view of the Lindquist Supply Company prior to the City of Bridgeport's urban-redevelopment project twenty years ago. The firm's Builder's Hardware Division is on the left. Photo circa 1956

Today the Lindquist Supply Company is one of the largest industrial supply businesses in Connecticut. Its 115 employees sell industrial supplies and builder's hardware to Connecticut industry, contractors, utilities, and government organizations. The firm stocks more than 30,000 different industrial items and over 15,000 builder's hardware items in its 60,000 square feet of warehouse space still at its original location on Fairfield Avenue. A recent addition is a 5,700-square-foot warehouse in Hartford.

Customer service still remains a top priority at Lindquist Supply. Through its computerized inventory control and system contracting, the company accomplishes its goal. In 1985 it was named in the top fifty on a list of America's best distributors compiled through an exclusive survey of manufacturing suppliers. Lindquist Supply distinguished itself through outstanding service, market penetration, and growth. The award says, "What these firms have in common is loyalty to suppliers, a dedication to serving customers, and an intense pride in what they do."

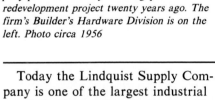

Lindquist Supply has undergone many changes in its history. This is the present-day facility on Fairfield Avenue.

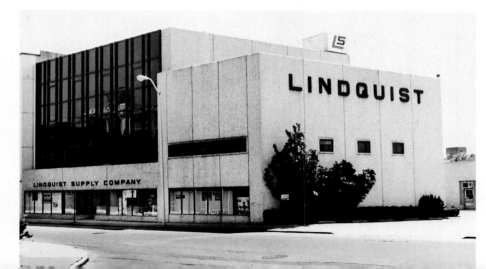

THE CONNECTICUT BANK AND TRUST COMPANY

The Connecticut Bank and Trust Company's earliest presence in Bridgeport dates back to July 21, 1926, when the doors of the Black Rock Bank and Trust Company first opened for business at 2834 Fairfield Avenue. From its modest beginnings in a remodeled store, the bank rapidly began to prosper. Within one year and eight months the bank had set a Bridgeport record by exceeding one million dollars in assets in such a short time. By 1929 the bank's business had expanded to the point that additional space was required. Without a single break in banking operations, the original wooden structure was jacked up and moved north on Brewster Street. The new building on the original site was opened on November 20, 1930, by Bridgeport's Mayor E.T. Buckingham, who made the first deposit. In 1960, after three decades of continuous growth, the Black Rock Bank and Trust Company merged into the National Bank & Trust Company of Fairfield County, which was renamed The State National Bank of Connecticut two years later. In 1982 The State National Bank of Connecticut merged into The Connecticut Bank and Trust Company (CBT) under the charter of the former bank, which represents the oldest continuing national bank charter in the United States. Prior to the bank's merger with The State National Bank of Connecticut, CBT had gained a presence in Bridgeport through the 1971 merger of Columbus Industrial Bank, located at 171 State Street.

Today CBT's presence in the greater Bridgeport area includes thirteen branch offices, a bank card center, data-processing center, and regional headquarters representing the bank's corporate, commercial, international, and private banking divisions.

CBT merged with the Bank of New England Corporation, headquartered in Boston, in 1985. Through subsequent mergers with Maine National Bank of Portland, Maine, and Old Colony Bank of Providence, Rhode Island, Bank of New England Corporation assets have grown to more than seventeen billion dollars. As a member company of Bank of New England Corporation, CBT retains its preeminent position in Connecticut, with 155 offices throughout the state, its own management team and directors, and some 5,400 employees.

CBT continues to complement its long history in Bridgeport through active involvement in community affairs.

The Connecticut Bank and Trust Company's Bridgeport executive offices at 10 Middle Street.

HARVEY HUBBELL INCORPORATED

Harvey Hubbell, founder.

The saying, "Necessity is the mother of invention," surely applies to inventor Harvey Hubbell. When Thomas Edison invented electric illumination, oil lamps did not disappear overnight. It took many other talented inventors and their numerous discoveries to form the electrical industry as we know and appreciate it today. Harvey Hubbell was one of those industry giants, and his innovations set industry standards.

Hubbell and his family moved to Bridgeport in 1863, when he was just six years old. He attended the Easton Academy for his primary education and Eastman's Business College in New York. Later, when he enrolled in Cooper Institute in New York City, his inventive mind was already developing product ideas.

After working in the printing industry for a time, he decided to open his own manufacturing facility in Bridgeport. Although he created several early products, including the first tapping machine, it was the pull-chain light bulb socket that made him a recognized figure in the electrical industry. In 1901 the pull-chain light bulb socket comprised the entire Hubbell product line, with sixty-three sockets and their variations in the first twelve-page catalog—a catalog that today is nearly 400 pages long!

The Harvey Hubbell Machinery & Tools plant in 1899.

At that same time Hubbell was in New York City and happened to pause with interest at a penny arcade that had some electrically operated equipment. An exasperated workman was detaching electrical wires from binding post terminals on the wall in order to move the equipment and clean the floor. "Why couldn't the wires be attached to a 'plug' and just 'plugged' in and out of the machine or wall?" questioned Harvey. Thus came his patent for another industry first: a separable plug and connector.

Harvey Hubbell Incorporated has moved several times because of its continued growth. In 1911 the doors were opened to the new U-shaped building on State Street and Bost-wick Avenue where the firm operates today. It was the first reinforced concrete building in New England.

Both the electrical industry and the Hubbell factory were booming in the 1920s. An advertisement from that time boasted "over fifty million Hubbell receptacles already installed." New Hubbell products were also developed at a considerable pace and included new styles of pull sockets, plugs, and receptacles; 32-volt plugs and connectors for farmers without city power; the Loxin lamp bulb, able to withstand the vibrations of trolley cars; and switches for the newly invented radio.

In 1927 Harvey Hubbell, Jr., became president of the company following the death of his father. Sharing his father's inventive spirit, Harvey Jr. expanded the twist-lock line of connectors and developed the "Hubbellock" line of quality wiring devices.

During World War II the demand for Hubbell products grew tremendously as the firm developed products especially for military needs. Such devices included large pin and sleeve connectors for recharging aircraft batteries and panel jacks for radio transmitters. Everyone had one goal in mind—to win the war—and Hubbell certainly did its share.

The period between 1946 and 1960 was a time for readjustment, moving from wartime to a peaceful economy and catching up with the needs of industrial customers and the building contractor market. And the company accomplished that both on land and at sea. In 1952 the oceanliner *United States* was completely fitted with Hubbell wiring devices made for its narrow stateroom partitions. In 1957 a four-story addition was made to the firm's Bridgeport facility. Nine years later the technical center and parking garage were added.

Of course, some new products were also brought into the market. The Hubbell line of corrosion-resistant devices was conceived by the president, an ardent boater. This new product line, originally designed for pleasure craft, has also found many industrial applications in areas where a corrosive atmosphere poses problems for standard wiring devices.

The readjustments made during the preceding decades proved successful. Harvey Hubbell Incorporated experienced a tremendous period of growth during the 1960s. In fact, annual sales increased sixfold. The firm also embarked on a period of acquisition, now with thirteen divisions and subsidiaries in twenty-five manufacturing locations throughout the United States, Canada, and the United Kingdom.

Today the Wiring Device Division of Harvey Hubbell Incorporated in Bridgeport continues to break new

Upon the death of his father in 1927, Harvey Hubbell, Jr., assumed the presidency.

ground and set new quality standards. It offers 4,000 different catalog items to meet its customers' growing needs. There are more than 200 million active Hubbell wiring devices at work in the United States, each reflecting the technical advances and creative engineering achieved by the Wiring Device Division.

The combination of all these factors—technological innovation; Hubbell quality in management, manufacturing, and products; and orientation to customers' current and future needs—forged the exceptional growth of Harvey Hubbell Incorporated throughout the past eight decades. And these capabilities will continue to extend the firm's leadership into the future.

The Wiring Device Division of Harvey Hubbell Incorporated in Bridgeport, the firm's first major facility.

CUMMINGS & LOCKWOOD

Cummings & Lockwood, one of New England's largest law firms, opened its Bridgeport office in 1963 to serve area businesses, industries, and individuals. As Bridgeport and Fairfield County have grown in importance—a growth matched by few other regions in the United States—Cummings & Lockwood has evolved into a firm with a wide-ranging practice and a strong corporate and individual client roster.

Today the firm represents the Bridgeport Board of Education and two of the city's three hospitals in addition to local businesses and industries. From time to time it has also represented the City of Bridgeport in selected matters. Although the firm's Bridgeport practice has primarily consisted of labor matters, Cummings & Lockwood's partners and associates are becoming increasingly active in the area of corporate law, litigation, real estate, and individual client matters.

It was many years ago, however, that a sensational murder trial first brought the courtroom skills of Homer Cummings, a co-founder of the firm, to the attention of the people in Bridgeport. Cummings was prosecutor for the State of Connecticut in the trial of Harold Israel, an unemployed drifter accused of murdering the Reverend Hubert Dahme, a pastor of St. Joseph's Church in Bridgeport.

After months of studying every piece of evidence, the testimony, and the confession that the police had obtained from Israel, Cummings brilliantly presented the matter to a Superior Court jury. In summation he said, "It is just as important for a state's attorney to use the great powers of his office to protect the innocent as it is to convict the guilty." He then moved, despite public pressure, that Israel be set free on the basis of his assertion that the accused person could not have, in fact,

committed the murder.

His handling of the Israel case is to this day cited as a landmark, and for many years his statement was required reading for all U.S. attorneys.

Cummings & Lockwood got its start in Stamford seventy-six years ago on September 1, 1909, as Homer Cummings and Judge Charles Lockwood scurried around that city buying pencils—the word processors of the day—and other supplies, checking out library books, and addressing the announcements of their new law firm.

Today Cummings & Lockwood has 62 partners and 73 associates. These are served by a staff of over 200, including 30 paraprofessionals. In addition to its Bridgeport and Stamford offices, it has offices in Greenwich and Hartford. In Florida, the firm has offices in Palm Beach and Naples.

Cummings & Lockwood's clients range from individuals seeking counsel with respect to trusts and estates or matrimonial law to large multinational corporations involved in complex leasing and financing arrangements. The firm's practice falls mainly into eight broad areas: corporate and other business entities, litigation, tax, real estate, labor, energy, the environment, and a broad spectrum of services to individuals including financial, tax, and estate planning; trust and estate administration; and resolution of family difficulties.

E. Terry Durant is the partner

The staff of Cummings & Lockwood's Bridgeport office consists of (left to right) Austin F. Reed, Gregory B. Nokes, Misty Pilz, Janet Sia, Doris Rosenthal, Pamela Boston, Barbara Hanson, Donald F. Houston, Kathleen Canavan, Peter E. Gillespie, Margaret M. Sheahan, Sandra Oberg, Joyce Orgera, Idalia Lopez, Nicky Taraian, Colette Poxson, Jay E. Bovilsky, and E. Terry Durant. Not present are John A. Sabanosh and George N. Nichols.

in charge of the Bridgeport office. Other resident partners include John Sabanosh, George Nichols, and Donald Houston.

Partners and associates in the firm believe in Bridgeport and in its potential for growth and have supported this belief by their involvement in local and civic affairs. Durant, in addition to being a member of the board of associates of the University of Bridgeport, is past president of the Bridgeport Area Chamber of Commerce, while Jay Bovilsky is a member of the group's Crime Reduction Task Force, and Austin Reed serves on its membership committee. Cummings & Lockwood also contributes to the chamber's Summer Job Youth Program for disadvantaged youth. Other partners and associates are involved in civic affairs in neighboring communities.

While Cummings & Lockwood has experienced extraordinary growth since the days of its founders, the firm's philosophy has never changed. Quality service to its clients and to the community has remained the firm's most important goal.

FLETCHER THOMPSON

Award-winning design citations, computer-aided design capability, as well as major master-planning efforts, including the 300-acre Dow Corning Center in Midland, Michigan, characterize the long and fruitful history of Fletcher Thompson.

Bridgeport-based and one of New England's largest architectural and engineering companies, the firm was founded in 1910, when E. Leslie Fletcher started Fletcher Engineering in a building on State Street. After Charles L. Thompson joined Fletcher, the corporate name was officially changed to Fletcher Thompson.

The firm's first contract was for the structural design of the Hudson, New York, post office. Unlike today, in its earlier years Fletcher Thompson acted as a general contractor in addition to providing architectural and engineering design services.

During the next decade the business grew steadily. A branch office was opened in New York City, and Fletcher Thompson obtained licenses to work in New York and New Jersey. At the time one of the company's major customers was Bridgeport Brass.

In 1916 J. Gerald Phelan, a graduate of the Pratt Institute School of Art, joined the organization, becoming the first trained architect on staff. Introducing new services and substantially furthering the firm's growth, Phelan was subsequently named president and chairman of the board. Today his son, John G. Phelan, is president and chief executive officer of Fletcher Thompson.

By World War II the corporation employed a staff of twenty-five and was one of the largest engineering and architectural firms in the state. Bridgeport was growing, and Fletcher Thompson was involved in extensive building programs for Bridgeport Brass, Bullard Company, and Bassick Company.

When the Depression struck the

The McDermott Chevrolet building on the corner of West Avenue and State Street was originally designed by Fletcher Thompson in 1929. In those days the building served as the showroom for Ford.

staff diminished. The first "break" came in 1932, when the firm was awarded the contract for the West Haven Armory. Business steadily improved thereafter.

In 1934 Phelan moved the focus of the company from engineering specialties to a more active architectural practice, designing churches, hospitals, and schools as well as industrial facilities. Buildings such as the north wing of St. Vincent's Hospital, the St. James Church auditorium, and Holy Name Church in Stratford were commissioned.

In 1952 the International Concrete Construction Corporation of Lynn, Massachusetts, and Fletcher Thompson joined forces to utilize large, precast concrete panels tilted up to form structural walls. This tilt-up system, previously used only on the West Coast, was pioneered in the East by the firm.

Through the 1960s Fletcher Thompson's contracts continued to grow in number and included Fairfield Hills Hospital in Newtown, Harvey Hubbell Incorporated, Bridgeport Lycoming, Sprague Meter, Sikorsky Aircraft, Fairfield University, General Electric, and D.M. Read Company.

St. Vincent's Medical Center on Main Street was designed by Fletcher Thompson in 1976. The ten-story, $31-million modern medical facility contains 440,000 square feet of floor space.

Under the direction of John Phelan, Fletcher Thompson continues to expand. Departments for contract administration, interior design, equipment planning, cost estimating, project management, business development, and architectural research have been added, supplementing the structural, electrical, heating, ventilating, air conditioning, and fire protection engineering services on which the firm's early reputation was built.

BRIDGEPORT HYDRAULIC COMPANY

P.T. Barnum served as president of Bridgeport Hydraulic Company for nine years.

Bridgeport has been known for high-quality water since pre-colonial days, when the Pequonnock Indians drank from the pure waters of its natural springs. By the late 1700s Bridgeport was an important stop for sailing ships, which replenished their water supplies with casks hauled overland from nearby lakes and springs.

The Reverend Elijah Waterman had a better idea. In 1818 he gave Bridgeport its first water distribution system—hollow log pipes and an open trough through which water flowed to the harbor from springs at the top of Golden Hill.

But the need for an improved water supply became clear when the Great Fire of 1845 broke out in George Wells' Oyster Bar and engulfed the city's business district. The tide was low, and firefighters pumping water from the harbor could not maintain sufficient flow. Forty-nine buildings were destroyed.

Bridgeport's first distribution reservoir was actually this masonry tank.

The Bridgeport Water Company was founded in 1853 to provide water service, but failed in just two years. In 1857 a new investor-owned water utility led by Joseph Richardson was chartered to continue and expand service. Thus Bridgeport Hydraulic Company (BHC) was born. Although deterred from major projects by the Civil War, BHC expanded the rudimentary water supply system it had inherited.

Enter P.T. Barnum, stage left. The famous showman had been waiting in the wings to influence BHC's fortunes. As mayor of Bridgeport in 1875, he had challenged BHC to improve its service. He got his chance in 1877 as another major fire underscored the need for an expanded water supply and Barnum was elected president of BHC. During his nine-year tenure BHC built additional reservoirs at higher elevations to increase water pressure and improve the city's firefighting capability.

BHC continued to grow by acquiring small water systems. By 1900 Bridgeport's population was 70,000 and industry was expanding rapidly. Although BHC had storage capacity of nearly three billion gallons, company planners saw the need for even more capacity to support future growth. One such visionary, Samuel P. Senior—who served as chief executive for thirty-five of his sixty-one

years with BHC—developed a plan for vast expansion. Under his leadership the 2.3-billion-gallon Trap Falls Reservoir was completed in 1905, the first of BHC's four great reservoirs—all planned by Senior and continuing today as the backbone of the region's water supply.

As World War I began, the demand for water was eight billion gallons a year. With Bridgeport manufacturers contributing heavily to the war effort and the area's population burgeoning, annual usage by war's end in 1918 had surged to thirteen billion gallons. But Senior's planning, including construction of the 3.8-billion-gallon Aspetuck-Hemlocks Supply System, allowed BHC to meet these demands.

During the 1920s the 5.8-billion-gallon Easton Lake Reservoir was completed, and BHC acquired land for a giant new reservoir in the Saugatuck River Valley. But construction was delayed by the Great Depression, and BHC shortly found itself in a race against time to provide for increased water needs resulting from World War II and Bridgeport's resumption of its role as the "Arsenal of America." BHC pushed forward with the massive project, which involved pouring 80,000 yards of concrete, building new bridges and miles of new roads, and installing a pipeline link to the Aspetuck-Hemlocks Supply System. The 11.9-billion-gallon Saugatuck Reservoir was completed in 1942, doubling BHC's supply capacity, and Bridgeport's major role in the war effort continued unimpeded.

In the decades that followed BHC focused on meeting the needs of suburban expansion, installing many miles of new water mains and tapping groundwater sources, most notably with development of the vast Housatonic Well Field in Shelton. By its 100th anniversary in 1957, the firm was delivering forty-five million gallons of water a day to a population of 270,000. In the early 1960s BHC expanded its service area to include eight communities in New Haven and Litchfield counties.

From 1962 to 1966 the region suffered the worst drought in its history. During this and subsequent periods of low rainfall, BHC supplies have proved ample to fully meet customers' needs and also to help nearby water utilities. Dedicated to water quality as well as quantity, BHC in 1981 completed an $18-million, state-of-the-art filtration plant at Trap Falls Reservoir, demonstrating its commitment to upgrade water treatment processes as new water quality considerations emerge and

The bucolic peace of Bunnell's Lower Reservoir at the turn of the century.

A water quality test procedure at BHC's main quality-control laboratory in Bridgeport.

new technology to address them becomes available.

BHC has won widespread recognition for its leadership position in the water supply industry. It has earned several national citations for innovative management, and was named "Connecticut Conservationist of the Year" in 1981.

Under the direction of president and chief executive officer William S. Warner, BHC today is the largest operating entity of The Hydraulic Company, a New York Stock Exchange-listed firm that also is engaged in forest products and real estate development businesses. Among the ten largest investor-owned water companies in the nation, BHC provides public water supply and fire protection service to a population of 370,000 in seventeen Connecticut communities. It has reservoir capacity of 24.8 billion gallons, supplemented by substantial well fields, and sells some 59 million gallons a day from its 78.2-million-gallon-per-day total capability.

Significant expansion was achieved in 1984 with the acquisition of Stamford Water Company, which serves a population of 82,000. And in 1985 BHC completed the first section of a regional pipeline that will enable it to sell water initially in New Canaan and ultimately in Stamford, Darien, and Greenwich.

As it moves into the future, Bridgeport Hydraulic Company remains committed to providing its customers with an abundant supply of quality water and to continuing the high level of service that has characterized its remarkable past.

Electric pumps at the Donald W. Loiselle Water Treatment Plant at the Trap Falls Reservoir transfer water from clearwells to a 10-million-gallon storage tank.

THE E&F CONSTRUCTION COMPANY

The Bridgeport Post Building was an E&F Construction Company project in the 1920s.

E&F built many of the local high schools in the 1920s and 1930s.

Good friends Fred Frassinelli and Philip Epifano both immigrated to the United States in the early 1900s to provide new opportunities for themselves and their families. In 1922, after successfully working for construction firms, the two men decided to team up in work as well as in friendship. They thought that their commitment to hard work and integrity would be an excellent foundation for the formation of their own Bridgeport concern—The E&F Construction Company. Thus began a two-family partnership that lasted for more than sixty years.

Both Frassinelli and Epifano believed that individual attention to detail, the continuing development of new techniques, and a personal pride in seeing a project through to its successful completion were tantamount to the operation of their new construction firm. From the first major contract in 1925 for a $90,000 clothing store in Bridgeport to the thousands of assignments that have followed through the years, E&F has operated as an independent, high-integrity, quality-conscious business.

The E&F Construction Company,

first located at 94 Wells Street, grew rapidly because of the owners' integrity and construction know-how. And, as the company grew, so did the size and scope of contracts throughout the greater Bridgeport area. For example, World War II saw E&F active in the construction of large wartime housing projects such as the P.T. Barnum Project and the high-rise Beardsley Terrace Apartments.

After the war the two E&F owners were joined by their sons, Fred Jr. and Philip Jr. Fred Jr. is presently chairman of The E&F Construction Company. Before joining the firm, he attended Dartmouth College, hoping to become an architect. Upon joining his father in the family business, however, his direction changed and he's been with the firm ever since. Now that Philip Jr. has retired, Fred Jr. and his family are sole owners of The E&F Construction Company. Fred and his wife, Sarah (Ann Wheeler), have two sons, Fred and David, who are carrying on the fami-

ly tradition at E&F, and two daughters, Sarah (Keenan), who is with an architectural firm in New York City, and Hannah, a college student.

Founder Fred Frassinelli died in 1950. His friend and partner, Philip Epifano, still lives in Bridgeport.

The founders' sons have kept alive their fathers' values. From World War II to the present, E&F has maintained a high-quality profile in office, educational, and health care construction. The type of service it provides has been altered, however, reflecting changes within the construction industry. Originally, the firm was a lump-sum bid contractor, but now E&F has followed the trend

246

in construction management. "Our innovative staff is able to develop a total package, including build to suit, turnkey, and lease backs, where we service all needs from site analysis and financing to final interior planning," says Fred Frassinelli, Jr. "We are also one of the first contractors in the area to develop an in-house computerized cost system for monitoring all projects—of any size."

E&F is the 46th-largest construction manager in the nation as rated by the *Engineering News Record.* This achievement is partially due to the firm's ability to perform most of the project with its own work force, allowing the company to meet the challenging schedule requirements in "fast-track" projects. At the Yale campus renovations in 1976, E&F performed over five million dollars of work in fifty-nine days by maintaining a crew of 500 men working two shifts, six days a week.

This ability to meet clients' needs has brought an impressive volume of work to E&F, including sixty major contracts for hospital construction in sixty years as well as major contracts for construction of some of the larg-

The firm serves a wide area around Bridgeport from its headquarters at 505 Sylvan Avenue.

est office buildings in Connecticut. In the industrial area, E&F has built large manufacturing facilities such as the one-million-square-foot Sikorsky Aircraft plant. In the commercial field, the firm's prestigious client list includes ITT, Combustion Engineering, and Bridgeport's jai alai facility. E&F's first contract with Bridgeport Hospital was in 1929. Since then it has undertaken many projects for the facility, including a two-story addition of 169 beds and an emergency wing.

Presently the firm is constructing the Metro Center in Hartford, a $25-million office tower; General Reinsurance, the largest building in Stamford; and Whitney Grove, a $22-million project that is the largest such development in New Haven in the past fifteen years.

In 1984 E&F formed the Sylvan Group, Ltd., a holding company including The E&F Construction Company, The E&F Development Company, The E&F Leasing Company, and E&F Properties.

"The future will be quite excellent for us," forecasts Fred Frassinelli, Jr. "We plan to further our work in Connecticut but also spread out into a larger part of New England, primarily in our specialty area of hospitals and medical centers."

Over the years The E&F Construction Company has met the needs of a diverse list of clients with a full range of services. "Excellence in construction emerges from a complete understanding of a client's needs, and a corporate ability to commit to meeting them," says Fred Jr., who follows his father's earlier commitments. "Our experience in the complete construction process has enabled us to provide that excellence."

The Richardson Corporation facility in Shelton reflects E&F's tradition of excellence.

POST PUBLISHING COMPANY

Early on the cold morning of February 7, 1883, a 22-year-old printer named George Washington Hills set out to fight Bridgeport's newspaper establishment. Armed with less than $100 and an old foot-powered Universal press capable of printing 150 copies of a four-page, four-column newspaper, he was ready to launch his dream: *The Daily Post*—a one-cent newspaper affordable for local residents in this working-class city.

Although Bridgeport's population of nearly 50,000 supported four daily newspapers and a number of weeklies before the *Post* was born, none were destined for a long life. Hills' newspaper would be different. It would be independent in politics and "defend the interest of the working man against those of monopolists and capitalists, and its opinions will be fearlessly given," wrote Hills in the *Post*'s premiere edition.

Following some early hard times the *Post* quickly increased both its

circulation and its advertising revenue. By 1886 it was described in Orcutt's *History of Bridgeport* as "a handsomely printed daily, exactly the same size as *The New York Sun*." Claiming 40,000 readers, every evening edition sold as many papers as the combined circulation of its two remaining competitors.

In 1891 Hills founded the Post Publishing Company and began construction of a new building to house all production facilities. By the turn of the century the newspaper was being printed with hot lead type in essentially the same manner it would be for many decades to come.

During the mid-1890s Hills established another newspaper, *The Bridgeport Morning Telegram,* to compete with the only other morning paper, *The Morning Union*. The *Telegram* emphasized national and international news; the *Post* focused on local news. It even used color on the front page, an oddity before the turn of the century. In 1901 the Post Publishing Company bought *The Morning Union* and merged it with the *Telegram*.

Under Raymond Flicker's guidance, Post Publishing Company flourished and expanded. Pictured is the newsroom in 1955.

The *Bridgeport Sunday Post* was launched in 1913. That same year Hills sold his interest to Kenneth and Archibald McNeil; his mission of serving the working class with a newspaper was accomplished.

Four years later Walter B. Lashar, president of American Chain and Cable Co., purchased the three Post newspapers. Apparently he disliked the life of a newspaper mogul, and in a matter of months put the publications up for sale. His offer was accepted by Edward Flicker of Cincinnati, who had been general manager of *The Cincinnati Enquirer*.

One of Flicker's first directives was to sell the Post Building at 49 Cannon Street and move the company to 140 Middle Street. It remained there until 1929, when another site was considered preferable. At that time a four-story, brick-and-steel building was constructed at 410 State Street, which still houses the main offices of the Post Publishing Company.

Flicker died in 1939 and was suc-

In 1929 Edward Flicker constructed a new four-story building to house Post Publishing Company.

Post Publishing Company president Elizabeth Pfriem has completely remodeled the building's interior. Shown is the state-of-the-art newsroom.

newspapers' advertising base; and the major conversion of the presses that accommodate the Standard Advertising Unit measurement used by the majority of newspapers nationwide.

Hills' promise to defend working-class interests has been maintained over the past century through the papers' editorial pages. In recent years the *Post* had alerted voters to flaws in a proposed new city charter that was ultimately defeated in referendum, has helped bring about the repeal of a hastily passed state income tax bill in the General Assembly, and has initiated legislation to name the state police complex in Meriden after the late commissioner and Bridgeporter, Leo J. Mulcahy.

ceeded as president by George C. Waldo, Jr. Following Waldo's death in 1956, Flicker's son, W. Raymond, became president.

Under Raymond Flicker, the corporation expanded considerably. In 1966 a two-story addition was completed. A one-story printing plant, housing new high-speed presses, was built at 600 State Street in 1970.

Flicker died in 1971 and was succeeded by John E. Pfriem, the son of the late Alma Flicker Pfriem, who had served as secretary and assistant treasurer of the company. In 1977 the newspapers experienced a complete change in production methods and appearance, moving from lead type and casting mats from metal to photo offset printing. Stories are now written and edited on video display terminals and are printed by computer onto photographic paper.

Expansion continued into the 1980s with a new warehouse building at 585 John Street and the addition of a fourth newspaper, *Saturday*—a combination of the Saturday editions

Still at its same location, the Post Publishing Company building of today displays a modern facade and contemporary addition.

of the *Telegram* and *The Bridgeport Post*.

When Pfriem died in 1983, his wife, Elizabeth, became president and treasurer of the Post Publishing Company. Under her direction the newsroom's major renovations were completed and include a new state-of-the-art computer system for editorial application; the Harris inserter, a machine capable of handling a half-million pieces of advertising inserts per hour, considerably increasing the

The Post Publishing Company's newspapers have stood the test of time by adapting to meet the needs of a changing community and remaining resolutely supportive of that community. In the future they will continue to inform and serve southwestern Connecticut residents.

DELOITTE HASKINS & SELLS

The accounting firm of Deloitte Haskins & Sells has a unique English and American tradition. William Welch Deloitte set up practice as a public accountant in London in 1845 at the age of twenty-seven. His company expanded, and in 1890 Deloitte & Co. established an office in New York City.

A few years later, in another part of New York, Charles Waldo Haskins and Elijah Watt Sells founded their own accounting firm while the American accounting profession was still in its early stages. While most accounting firms had their roots in England, Haskins and Sells was one of the first to be established in the United States. In 1918 Haskins and Sells opened its first New England office in Boston. In 1952, after decades of substantial growth, the two practices merged to form what is known today as Deloitte Haskins & Sells.

Deloitte Haskins & Sells is now a "Big Eight" multiservice accounting firm, employing more than 26,000 in over 100 offices in the United States and 430 locations worldwide. Each office is responsible for maintaining a high quality of service to its clients.

The state of Connecticut was first served by DH&S in 1956 with the opening of the New Haven office. In 1970 Hartford was added. Seven years later the Fairfield County office in Stamford, which now acts as the central office for the entire area, was established. William G. Parrett is the partner responsible for this area, which includes over 200 professionals, many of whom were recruited from Connecticut schools such as Fairfield University, the University of Connecticut, the University of Bridgeport, the University of New Haven, Albertus Magnus College, and Quinnipiac College.

The firm's clients include multinational corporations, government agencies, small businesses, and entre-

William G. Parrett, partner-in-charge, Connecticut area.

preneurs. In addition to the more familiar services of accounting, auditing, and tax planning and compliance, Deloitte Haskins & Sells has a Management Advisory Service that brings together teams of professionals to carry out specialized consulting services that provide clients with objective management advice and technical assistance.

The firm also has an Emerging Business Service through which DH&S specialists provide new and growing businesses with the same full range of services available to larger corporations.

A number of times each year DH&S holds topical seminars, which are tailored to address timely subjects of interest to both clients and the community at large. Informational pamphlets and a biweekly publication, the *DH&S Review,* are mailed to selected individuals, providing the latest information on significant legislation and current trends in the accounting field.

DH&S professionals are involved in all aspects of community life as well. Individuals from all areas of the firm contribute significant amounts of time and talent to organizations such as the United Way, the March of Dimes, chambers of commerce, professional and alumni associations, and local civic, cultural, and health-

related organizations. It is through this kind of social responsibility that the firm makes a continuing effort to serve not only its clients but the community.

Deloitte Haskins & Sells has been a leader in the accounting profession throughout its history. The firm's Connecticut practice has anticipated the area's rapid rate of growth and increased its service capability accordingly. Its long-range planning mandates a continuation of the highest-quality professional service to all of its clients in the Connecticut region.

Fairfield County office partners (from left to right): Michael W. Bowman, Edward W. Graycar, James V. Schnurr, William G. Parrett, and Harold J. Tinkler. Not pictured: Stephen B. Bauer, David Christie, and Chester A. Hobert, Jr.

COMMUNITY HEALTH CARE PLAN

In September 1985 the state's first two health maintenance organizations, Community Health Care Plan of New Haven, founded in 1971, and Connecticut Health Plan of Bridgeport, established in 1977, joined to form a special health care system. The result is the CHCP Health Network, providing a highly accessible program of prepaid health care covering much of central and southern Connecticut.

The beginning of Connecticut Health Plan (CHP), one of the new network's partners, dates back to 1973. Under the auspices of the Higher Education Center for Urban Studies, Connecticut Health Plan was established in order to provide a means of delivering quality health care services, while at the same time controlling the increasing cost of medical care. With start-up funds from the Department of Health, Education and Welfare, the Bridgeport Health Center was opened in 1977 at its present location at 4000 Park Avenue.

Since 1985 the Bridgeport Health Center was one of eight such facilities in the CHCP Health Network. All centers, including those in Branford, Hamden, New Haven, Shelton,

Stamford, Wallingford, and Waterbury (opening in September 1986), offer members everything they need for complete, prepaid medical care including visits to the doctor, X-ray facilities, laboratory, pharmacy services, and minor surgery.

All CHCP members select a primary physician who not only takes care of the patient's health care needs, but coordinates all the health care services the network offers. This doctor also handles referrals to specialists and arranges for outside services and hospitalization. A total 55,000 statewide members have become affiliated with the network through CHCP's contractual agreements with over 1,500 businesses in the state.

In the Bridgeport Health Center alone, 10,000 members benefit from the medical care of six internists and four pediatricians. There are also specialists in allergy; cardiology; dermatology; ear, nose, and throat; gastroenterology; psychiatry; obstetrics/gynecology; ophthalmology; ortho-

Since 1977 Community Health Care Plan has provided medical care to its members in the Bridgeport Health Center at 4000 Park Avenue.

CHCP emphasizes the importance of keeping people in good health by providing preventive medical care such as pediatric checkups.

pedics; radiology; surgery; and urology. The physicians and specialists are affiliated with all three Bridgeport hospitals.

One of the ways that CHCP is able to hold down health care costs is by stressing preventive medicine and early diagnosis. A variety of health-related programs are offered to members throughout the year, including stress management, freedom from smoking, babysitter training, and effective parenting. There are also support groups for patients suffering from alcoholism, epilepsy, and diabetes.

The Community Health Care Plan has always been, and plans on remaining, a nonprofit health maintenance organization. All surplus funds are directed toward minimizing premium increases, improving the delivery of health services, expanding benefits, and purchasing equipment. Thus, such action will guarantee compliance with CHCP's mission statement: "to provide its members with comprehensive, high-quality medical care, on a prepaid, group-practice basis, and at a predictable and reasonable cost." As president John Nelson states: "Our main concern has always been, and will always be, how can we best serve our members?"

WICC 60 "THE RADIO TRADITION"

In the 1960s Fairfield County commuters were entertained by WICC's satellite studio.

When radio broadcasting first began in the 1920s, a whole new form of entertainment was created. Vaudeville singers and comedians, concert singers and instrumental soloists, lecturers, dramatic shows, and news programs were listened to and enjoyed by millions of people in their homes across the United States.

The first radio station to be licensed by the FCC in Connecticut was the W "Industrial Capital of Connecticut," or WICC Radio in Bridgeport. In 1926 this station became part of the Old Yankee Network, an NBC-affiliated radio chain located throughout New England and hooked together by the telephone system.

"Although WICC carried the network programs—Jack Benny, Charlie McCarthy, Red Sox games—from the very beginning it stressed service to the community, making sure that all programming reflected the needs of its audience," states Ray Gardella, current vice-president and general manager of the station.

Throughout the next several decades WICC continued broadcasting a mixture of community and NBC national programming. With the advent of television, WICC put an even greater emphasis on local news and programming and broke off from the network. In the 1960s and early 1970s WICC became known as "Service Six," producing local programs about the community. Many of these programs originated from varying places in the area and were aired live from its mobile studio.

In the late 1960s the Tribune Company added WICC to its other media companies—*Chicago Tribune, New York Daily News,* WPIX-TV (Channel 11), WPIX-FM, and the Independent News Network—and committed to continue WICC's tradition of service to the community.

The promise has been kept. "Even when the FCC reduced its demands on radio for local programming, we did not relax our efforts." For example, in the mid-1970s Morgan Kaolian became the station's exclusive airborne traffic reporter. Likewise, everyone wants to hear what Walt Devanas has to say about the local weather. This staff meteorologist has been with WICC for over twenty years, and has become a household name throughout the station's broadcast area. WICC maintains the largest news staff in the area to provide constant coverage of local events. It is the "information station."

A favorite radio station throughout southern Connecticut, WICC sees its popularity verified year after year by the rating services. Seven out of every ten adults who live in the area listen to the station during the course of each month. Of the 9,600 radio stations licensed in the United States today, in relation to population size WICC ranks within the top ten nationwide for the number of listeners. At prime time—morning commute— it holds third place.

The station serves the community in many ways. Every month it airs approximately 1,400 public service announcements for civic and charitable organizations and activities, which add up to a donation of air time of almost $100,000.

WICC supports a wide range of local endeavors. During the past fourteen years, for instance, the Holiday Fund has raised money for needy children in the community. Almost $50,000 will be disbursed this year to hospital pediatric wards, daycare centers, and similar organizations. WICC finds many opportunities throughout the year to serve its neighbors.

Noting its slogan as WICC 60— "The Radio Tradition," the station is just that, continuing a tradition of sixty years of service to the greater Bridgeport area. Truly, WICC mirrors the community.

CONNECTICUT NATIONAL BANK

The granite, limestone, and glazed brick building at the corner of Main and State streets served as Connecticut National Bank's Bridgeport headquarters from 1915 until earlier this year, when it was razed to permit construction of Bridgeport Center, a 450,000-square-foot office complex scheduled for completion in 1988. The Barnum Museum, which will adjoin Bridgeport Center, can be seen in the distance at right.

Today's Connecticut National Bank is the result of almost 200 years of banking expertise, dating back to the years just after the American Revolution.

In 1792 Revolutionary War hero Jeremiah Wadsworth called together a group of prominent Hartford business and professional men to petition the Connecticut Legislature for permission to charter Hartford Bank. For twenty-two years Hartford Bank was the only financial institution in the city. After the Civil War the bank became part of the new national financial system, and its name was changed to Hartford National Bank. The years that followed brought many economic trials, but Hartford National Bank maintained sound financial practices and continued to grow and prosper.

In the post-World War II years Hartford National Bank continued to expand statewide through mergers and consolidations. In 1969 a parent bank holding company was created called Hartford National Corpora-

tion. In 1982 final approvals were obtained for the merger with Connecticut National Bank, another long-standing state financial institution.

Connecticut National Bank got its start as Bridgeport Bank in 1806 on Main Street. The views of the institution's first president, Dr. Isaac Bronson, were ahead of his time. An example was his insistence that no loans be made for more than sixty days and that no additional credit be granted until the original loan was repaid. Such policies helped Bridgeport Bank weather the financial storms and panics that frequently occurred during the nineteenth century.

In the twentieth century the institution, which was then called the Bridgeport National Bank, also experienced a series of consolidations including one with Connecticut Bank. In 1955 its name was changed to Connecticut National Bank.

In 1982, when Hartford National Corporation acquired Connecticut National Bank, the newly merged institution was called Connecticut National Bank because of its statewide connotation. Hartford-based Connecticut National Bank now has approximately twenty branch offices serving the greater Bridgeport area.

In 1985 Connecticut National and People's Bank announced that they would be participating jointly in the

development of the Bridgeport Center. A 450,000-square-foot complex with a proposed eighteen to twenty stories, the Bridgeport Center is an integral part of the renewal efforts of downtown Bridgeport. Scheduled to open in 1988, it will encompass the entire three-block area bounded by Main, State, and Water streets and the Connecticut Turnpike. Located one block from Bridgeport Harbor, it will adjoin the historic Barnum Museum.

Connecticut National Bank, with its two centuries of tradition, has a proud record of growth and achievement through exciting, challenging, and often turbulent times. Its achievements are a tribute to the leaders of the bank, who through the years have established strong principles of integrity, sound judgment, and meeting and anticipating the needs of its customers. Those principles remain a guide for the continued growth of the institution. With assets of $7.1 billion on December 31, 1985, Connecticut National Bank has the largest banking network in the state and is the only institution operating in all six of the state's major metropolitan areas.

Connecticut National's new regional offices at Bridgeport Center will feature a two-story atrium visible through the building's entrance, as shown in this model. Bridgeport Center is a new office complex designed by Richard Meier and Partner, Architects, New York. The firm won the Pritzker Architecture Prize in 1984.

HAWLEY INDUSTRIAL SUPPLIES INCORPORATED

In 1915 The Hawley Hardware Co. on Main Street was stocked full of any and all necessary gadgets.

The early twentieth century produced many notable industry pioneers in Bridgeport—such as Hubbell, Sikorsky, Bullard, Moore, and Wahlstrom—who are still very much recognized today through their past achievements or present operations. One of the established Bridgeport businesses that these men often frequented, in their quest for gadgets to develop new ideas or expand upon the tried and true, was Hawley Hardware. Although this firm has kept a low profile since its early beginning in 1888, today's Hawley Industrial Supplies Incorporated has

serviced every major manufacturer in the greater Bridgeport area.

The roots of the corporation were planted in 1876, when Hanford Plumb and 21-year-old Charles Hawley founded Plumb and Hawley, a hardware enterprise on Main Street. In 1881 another young man, Joseph Stagg, came to work for the partners. It wasn't long before Plumb and Hawley had a falling out. As a result, during the Blizzard of 1888, Hawley and Stagg crossed the street and founded The Hawley Hardware Co.—the store thus named because the former had the financial backing.

While Plumb's business died out in 1902, Hawley Hardware grew. At the turn of the century it was in both retail and wholesale supplies, selling mostly to blacksmiths and country stores; there were just a few indus-

Top row, from left: Joseph Henry Stagg, president, 1905-1927, and Joseph Henry Stagg, Jr., president, 1929-1969. Bottom row: Dwight Elliot Stagg, president, 1969-1977, and Joseph Henry Stagg III, president since 1977.

trial accounts at first. Stagg—the first, and for a long time only, salesman—traveled by bicycle and train to see his customers. Later, after proving his worth to Hawley, he was allowed to travel on the more costly horse and buggy. Great strides were made when the store was the first to use an automobile for a delivery truck—a "Locomobile" manufactured in Bridgeport.

Joseph Stagg passed away in 1927, and a few years later his sons, Joseph Jr. and Dwight, purchased the operation from Hawley.

Under the brothers' direction, the business grew substantially, from a retail hardware store to a major industrial supply house with customers throughout Connecticut. They also had the assistance of Bill Kurtz, who joined the organization in 1947 as a

salesman. Today he is executive vice-president, "linking the company to the past but helping in the direction of the future," he relates.

In 1958 Hawley moved to its present 37,000-square-foot location on Fairfield Avenue, doubling its space and greatly expanding its inventory. This was just the beginning of future expansions: branches in Waterbury, New Haven, and Hartford. The corporation also changed its name to Hawley Industrial Supplies to better describe its business specialty.

Joseph "Jerry" Stagg III is president of the firm, which is the largest industrial supply house in the state.

In 1958 the firm moved to its current head-quarters location, a 37,000-square-foot facility on Fairfield Avenue.

"We are also 'nip and tuck' for first in New England," he notes. The company is well known for the largest assorted inventory on the Eastern Seaboard, and for its excellent service.

The owner thanks Bridgeport for allowing three generations to prosper. "I owe the city, and now it's time for me to give something back," he states. And indeed he has made his contributions. Jerry Stagg serves on the board of many fine Bridgeport institutions, and is also very much involved with several revitalization organizations.

Although much has changed in the Hawley story since that snowy winter of 1888, one thing remains the same. Just as the industry leaders turned to Hawley Hardware then, they turn to Hawley Industrial Supplies today.

DRESSER INDUSTRIES, INC.

In 1852 Edward H. Ashcroft of Lynn, Massachusetts, acquired the American rights to produce the Bourdon tube, patented in France by Eugene Bourdon. This device led to what has become the industry standard in pressure gauges—the Ashcroft gauge.

In the 1850s the economic climate was ripe for a manufacturer of industrial products designed for steam-generating equipment. Population growth was outpacing existing power sources. While American industry saw a future in this form of energy, the pressurized water vapor caused explosions and was costly to generate. Thus a challenge was presented to inventors.

Edward H. Ashcroft of Lynn, Massachusetts, was very aware of the opportunities for anyone improving the control of steam. With this in mind, in 1852 he acquired the American rights to produce the Bourdon tube, patented in France by Eugene Bourdon. This device led to what has become the industry standard in pressure gauges—the Ashcroft gauge.

In order to devote more time toward making these products, in 1867 the entrepreneur hired Charles Moore to handle the sales responsibilities of the Ashcroft Company. He then founded the Consolidated Safety Valve Company and developed a successful safety valve for steam use.

By 1880 the 61-year-old Ashcroft was credited with about sixty inventions, and had withdrawn more and more from everyday operations to concentrate on his efforts in product development. Moore, no longer content as a salesman, joined with industrialists Henry Manning and Eugene Maxwell and purchased the Ashcroft Company.

The railroad industry was expanding daily, a growth that was significant to the newly formed operation of Manning, Maxwell and Moore. To meet the growing demand for its products, the organization moved to enlarged facilities in Bridgeport.

One of the most interesting and advantageous associates of Manning, Maxwell and Moore was tycoon "Diamond Jim" Brady, who first was a company salesman, subsequently was named a board member, and in 1912 became vice-president. His contacts with railroad and industry leaders surely added to the firm's profitability.

In 1928 the corporation added a complete line of industrial instruments by acquiring the American Schaefer and Budenberg Company. Several other firms were also purchased, including Shaw Crane, Hayden and Derby, and Fitchburg Lathe.

Manning, Maxwell and Moore continued to grow and in the late 1940s and early 1950s moved its operations to a new headquarters in Stratford.

Plants were constructed in Berea,

Kentucky, in 1961 to manufacture gauges and in Alexandria, Louisiana, to produce Consolidated and Hancock valves. In addition, the company achieved sales in varied industries such as atomic energy, aircraft, power, chemical, and industrial.

Dresser Industries, Inc., of Dallas recognized the importance of Manning, Maxwell and Moore in American industry and obtained all of its assets in 1964. The new name became Dresser Industrial Valve and Instrument Division.

Today the Stratford operation, located on twenty-three acres on East Main Street, houses the division headquarters and produces millions of precision parts for gauges and instruments to the highest military and nuclear specifications. A computer-processing system keeps track of the over 50,000 different items manufactured for more than 100,000 customer orders each year.

The Berea plant, which manufactures a variety of commercial gauges for OEMs, continues to expand. It currently has over 400 employees working in a 93,000-square-foot plant.

In 1973 Dresser Industrial Valve and Instrument Division purchased the Heise Bourdon Tube Company in Newtown. Once an engineer with Manning, Maxwell and Moore, the founder, Otto Heise, is credited by the Bourdon Company as making the only significant change to the Bourdon tube design since its invention. The Heise facility now houses complete engineering laboratories, combining modern technology and state-of-the-art electronics.

To complement its fine line of industrial and precision instruments, in 1981 Dresser acquired Datametrics, Inc., a manufacturer of a highly diversified line of measurement and control electronic products. The firm is located in Massachusetts, in a 35,000-square-foot plant with 130 employees.

Decades of research, development

Dresser Industries has kept pace with the needs of its clients from the Ashcroft gauge in the first railroad to newly designed mechanical systems and electronic pressure indicators and transducers.

and marketing, and sales of Ashcroft pressure and temperature switches and gauges have led to a burgeoning business for Dresser. This necessitated a move in 1984 for the Ashcroft Control Instrument Operations. The new facility in Milford, Connecticut, houses the manufacturing, engineering, and marketing organizations for switch products.

It can safely be said that no power plant in America is without an Ashcroft instrument. Practically no process plant—food, chemical, or refinery—lacks an Ashcroft product. The products of the Ashcroft Company, Manning, Maxwell and Moore, and now Dresser Industries have spanned the history of industry in the United States. The first railroad had an Ashcroft gauge; the *Spirit of St. Louis* had a Manning, Maxwell and Moore gauge and altimeter; the Nautilus atomic submarine carried an Ashcroft gauge and thermometer; and the Viking spacecraft to Mars was tested with Heise gauges.

And as future advancements are realized, Dresser Industries will continue to be there.

BRIDGEPORT HOSPITAL

When Bridgeport resident George F. Lewis came home after completing Yale Medical School and serving as a military cadet in a Civil War hospital, he strongly believed that his city needed a hospital. Providing care in people's homes or at makeshift quarters in the police department basement surely was inadequate. It took a lot of convincing, and the devotion, financial support, and time of many concerned Bridgeport citizens including P.T. Barnum, but Bridgeport Hospital was finally founded in 1878 and opened in 1884.

Since then the institution has evolved from its original capacity of forty-seven patients to a 650-bed facility. The largest hospital in Fairfield County and the fourth largest in Connecticut, Bridgeport Hospital has 500 physicians working with a staff of 2,000 highly skilled full- and part-time professionals, and technical and support personnel, assisted by over 500 volunteers.

Bridgeport Hospital's commitment to providing the finest health care for Fairfield County residents is exemplified through its unique services. Each year in the fifteen operating rooms more than 13,000 surgeries are performed. The open-heart surgery team performs over 300 operations each year. The Center for Cardiovascular Care carries out cardiac catheterization and coronary angioplasty—a nonsurgical alternative to the bypass—with state-of-the-art sophistication.

The Andrew J. Panettieri, M.D., Burn Unit is the only such facility between New York and Boston. Severely burned victims are referred to the unit from all over Connecticut.

Expectant mothers receive care from conception through delivery. The genetics clinic offers individual counseling for parents as well as screening and testing for genetic disorders. Doctors on staff specialize in high-risk pregnancies. Following delivery, the hospital provides the only level-three newborn intensive care unit in Fairfield County. Seriously ill or premature newborns are brought to the hospital from all over southern Connecticut.

Each day more than 130 people receive expert help from the emergency department's trauma, cardiology, burn, orthopedic, pediatric, and hand injury teams. SURGEASE, a one-day surgery service with its own preoperative areas, operating rooms, and recovery areas, offers many services on an outpatient basis.

Bridgeport Hospital's concern for its patients goes beyond physical care. Counseling to individuals and families, support groups, specialized clinics, blood pressure screening, and a 24-hour poison center are only some of the community services it offers.

Tertiary health care is often associated with the foreboding environment of computerized diagnostic tests and remote, white-coated specialists. Bridgeport Hospital believes that the business of health care is much more than the cold, mechanical application of technology to human disease. As a result, the high-quality health care that it provides combines compassion and caring with scientific advances for the health and benefit of all patients.

"Bridgeport Hospital has set the standard of medical excellence in Bridgeport since 1878," says president Michael E. Schrader. "As the greater Bridgeport region has changed and expanded, so has the hospital. We look forward to the transformation of our role in the next 150 years."

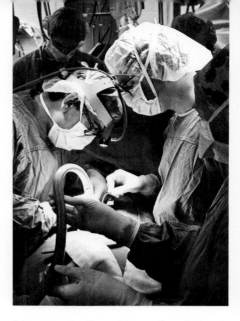

Neurosurgery, along with neurology, is the core of the Bridgeport Hospital Neurosciences Unit, the first in Connecticut. The unit is served by a team including physicians, nurses, radiologists, therapists, and social workers. Photo by Mauro Marinelli

The diagnosis of heart disease, dissolution of blood clots, and opening of blocked arteries all take place in the Bridgeport Hospital Center for Cardiovascular Care. The electronic sophistication of its catheterization laboratory is unequaled east of the Mississippi River. Photo by Mark Coelho

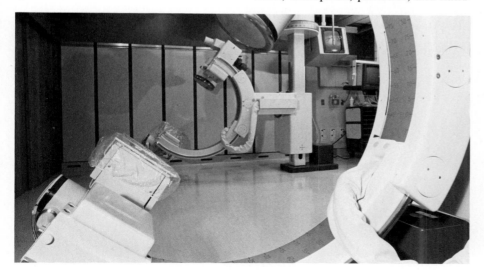

LEAKE & NELSON
"IRON MEN SINCE 1915"

For over seven decades Leake & Nelson Co. has been a major steel fabricator and erector for the construction industry. In fact, it is the largest fabricator and erector in southern Connecticut, involved in some of the area's most recognizable projects from throughway bridges to commercial office buildings. However, all this would not have been possible without a fortunate chain of events that occurred in the early 1900s.

In 1915 Arthur G. Leake and William Henderson founded the A.G. Leake Erecting Co. in Bridgeport. Meanwhile, Chris Nelson was a foreman in the ironworking business in New York. Originally from Denmark, Nelson had come to New York several years earlier.

As foreman, Nelson was contracted to work on the Poli Theater in Bridgeport. As fate would have it, he fell in love with Bridgeporter Pauline Brock and decided to stay in the Park City and start his own erecting business.

In 1926 Nelson joined Leake and Henderson to form the Leake & Nelson Co. Leake left the firm, and later the two remaining partners ran the business until the early 1960s, when Chris Nelson passed away and Bill Henderson retired. Today Chris' son, William, and his grandsons, Terry and Michael, run this highly successful erection and steel fabrication firm.

Since its founding in 1915, Leake & Nelson has been a pioneer in erection procedures and techniques and holds several patents in field welding and truck cranes. The firm also fabricates its own steel to ensure a high-quality standard.

Prior to World War II Leake &

Terry L. Nelson, vice-president/treasurer; William E. Nelson, president; and Michael L. Nelson, vice-president, at the main entrance to the firm's corporate office in the manufacturing facility at 555 Bostwick Avenue, Bridgeport.

Nelson began the steel fabrication business it is known for today. European craftsmen and blacksmiths completed fine ornamental ironworks for clients such as Connecticut National Bank and the Broad Street Library. This slowly led to structural steel work for buildings. The company also erected close to 100 bridges on I-95 from Greenwich to New Haven during the 1950s.

Throughout the 1950s and 1960s Leake & Nelson's fabrication and erection business was growing and included projects such as the Fairfield University field house, additional floors for Bloomingdale's in Stamford and SNET Company in Hartford, and the Connelly Boulevard Bridge on the Wilbur Cross Parkway. In 1973 the firm used its fabrication and erecting expertise in the construction of its own facility on Bostwick Avenue, becoming one of the first companies to support the west end redevelopment of Bridgeport.

Recently Leake & Nelson has been involved with major projects at the Crown Plaza Holiday Inn in

Stamford, the Stamford Plaza Hotel, the seventeen-story Long Wharf Maritime Center, and the Avco-Lycoming Company, where helicopters were used to install rooftop framing. The firm has also entered into the industrial fabrication industry with air cargo containerized freight-handling and -shipping systems for use in Saudi Arabia and Europe and by the U.S. military.

Terry and Michael Nelson plan to continue the Leake & Nelson Co. tradition of a successfully growing enterprise. "We have a solid reputation in our field," states vice-president Terry Nelson. "There isn't a town in Connecticut we can't go into without holding our heads up high—proud of our heritage, good will, and tradition."

The Leake & Nelson Co. used the first truck cranes in Connecticut on December 29, 1929, to erect long-span steel trusses. The firm pioneered steel erection techniques such as the largest field-welded structure, the Hall of Records in New Haven, in 1911.

GENERAL ELECTRIC COMPANY

Left:
GE operations have been located in Bridgeport since the early 1920s. Over the years a wide variety of businesses have adapted office and manufacturing space to meet changes in product markets and business needs.

Below:
In May 1915 thousands of workers labored around the clock to construct the world's largest factory. A building this size was needed to fill Czar Nicholas II's order for one million rifles and 100 million rounds of ammunition for the Imperial Russian Army.

The General Electric facility on Bridgeport's Boston Avenue is unlike any other manufacturing plant in the world. Nearly a half-mile in length, the structure boasts a rich history, many unique design elements, and an uncommonly immense size—two million square feet located on eighty-two acres of land.

While GE owns and occupies the plant today, the building was originally built for far different purposes. When Germany invaded Russia at the beginning of World War I, the United States remained neutral but vowed to support its allies—Russia included—with munitions and food supplies. As a result, Czar Nicholas II commissioned Remington Arms to produce one million rifles and 100 million rounds of ammunition for the Imperial Russian Army. Since no existing factory could handle such a vast order, work began on a new manufacturing facility—one that would eventually produce 5,000 rifles and 25,000 bayonets each day.

From late 1914 to early 1916, thousands of laborers worked day and night to build the new facility. In the course of just over a year, the largest factory ever constructed rose from Bridgeport soil. The main structure included thirteen individual five-story buildings encompassing 130 wings—all under one roof.

Since the plant had its genesis in the production of potentially explosive munitions, many special safety provisions were incorporated in the facility's design. Brick walls sixteen inches thick, reinforced concrete, wooden floors ten inches thick, and separate work areas were features important to the buildings' intended use. Narrow entrances and hallways connected thirteen individual buildings constructed with large windows for light and ventilation. These fea-

tures still shape the buildings' character and influence the use of the facility today.

When World War I ended, so did the need for such an immense, special-purpose facility. In just a matter of years, the Boston Avenue factory became obsolete.

But not for long. In the 1920s GE decided to relocate some of its business operations to the unique Bridgeport facility, and a small group of managers arrived to establish the "Bridgeport Works." Over the next ten years a few businesses expanded and filled several of the buildings in the complex.

Operations began with the manufacture of phonograph motors. Soon after, the manufacture of GE switches, sockets, receptacles, plugs, fuses, and other wiring devices also swung into production. And, in the years that followed, many other GE operations settled in the Bridgeport plant, including insulated wire and cable products, household appliances, construction materials, electric fans, washing machines, and radio receivers. Even GE's wholesale distributing business consolidated in Bridgeport under the name General Electric Supply Company (GESCO).

In the 1940s the facility's role changed once more. During World

Large bays have been renovated, many as attractive, modern office facilities. Operations in Bridgeport support company-wide marketing and market development efforts directed toward promoting GE products, services, and technologies in a variety of media.

Corporate Pooled Services (CPS) provides finance, accounting, and customer service for a variety of GE businesses. The CPS integrated computer system, housed in Bridgeport, supports more than 200 computer terminals being used by CPS employees in the Boston Avenue facility.

Switches for small appliances and major appliances, fluorescent lamp holders, appliance wires, and cords are manufactured in Bridgeport. Here an employee tends a fully automatic lamp holder assembly machine. Fifty million lamp holders for fluorescent lighting fixtures are manufactured on this equipment each year.

War II all consumer production ceased and GE began manufacturing military radios, anti-aircraft gun mounts, new-design bazookas, electrically heated aviation suits, and other U.S. military products.

The war ended, but not the plant's evolution. Indeed, building alterations have never ceased since GE first occupied the facility in the early 1920s. While appliance components are still manufactured at the Bridgeport plant, the emphasis has turned increasingly to high-tech, service-oriented work environments. Today approximately 1,500 people are employed by more than a dozen different GE businesses, including company-wide operations providing accounting, customer service, sales, marketing, and information systems, plus engineering and manufacturing consulting. Corporate Sourcing and General Electric Technical Services Company, Inc., are headquartered in Bridgeport, in addition to the General Electric Supply Company. An area

employee relations and facilities support operation provides central employee relations, community relations, and "landlord" services for the General Electric operations located in Bridgeport.

For more than sixty-five years of dynamic change, GE has remained a major employer in the Bridgeport area. The company continues to make substantial investments in the Bridgeport facility to respond to changing business needs and to attract new business operations to this location.

When the giant factory on Boston Avenue was first completed, no one could have imagined what lay ahead for this facility. Although today's businesses still can't be certain about what the future holds, some things won't change. GE's standards will always be guided by excellence—excellence in its personnel, in its products, and in its services. General Electric looks forward to an exciting future for its employees, its businesses, and Bridgeport.

BUNKER RAMO CORPORATION

Bunker Ramo headquarters in Trumbull, Connecticut

From its idyllic surroundings in Trumbull, Connecticut, Bunker Ramo has become a leading force in the high-powered worlds of Wall Street and banking—where it has pioneered many of the groundbreaking technologies on which the financial services industry depends.

Bunker Ramo was established in 1928 as the Teleregister Corporation with one significant product: the first electronic stock quotation board for brokerage firms. Today Bunker Ramo is a leading supplier of market information services and branch automation systems for the brokerage, banking, and thrift industries. As an international high-technology company, Bunker Ramo has built its reputation on the reliability and innovative thinking behind its products.

It was in the spring of 1928 when Robert Daine, a pilot for the French Air Corps, immigrated to the United States with patents for an electronic stock quotation board he had purchased in Europe. Bunker Ramo was founded as the Teleregister Corporation, with Daine and several coworkers operating out of an office on Chamber Street in New York City.

While the company was based in New York City, it developed and marketed the first electronic stock quotation board for major stock exchanges. This system was a significant breakthrough for the securities industry, combining advanced communications techniques and new display technologies. The first major advance in market information since the Edison ticker, the boards became operational in 1929 and the system eventually reached over 700 brokerage offices from coast to coast, serving the securities industry well into the 1970s.

By 1930 the Teleregister Corporation was flourishing, despite the dire circumstances of the stock market crash in 1929. That initial venture laid the foundation for the organization's continuing reputation as a pioneer in on-line computer system development and in data communications. A year before Daine's death in 1955, the company moved to Stamford, Connecticut.

In 1964 George Bunker, who was working at the electronics division of Martin Marietta, and Simon Ramo, an official at Thompson Ramo Woolridge, acquired the Teleregister Corporation and formed Bunker Ramo Corporation. In 1971 the firm moved to its current location in Trumbull.

Bunker Ramo has since established a history of developing new technologies and setting industry standards. George Bunker and Simon Ramo upheld the tradition of developing industry "firsts" and since its milestone year of 1928, and from 1981 until recently, while still a division of Allied-Signal Corporation of Morristown, New Jersey, Bunker Ramo established itself as a leader in developing new computer system technologies. Thus, the company has become a major force in providing information services and systems to financial institutions.

On the brokerage side, the company introduced the first voice-response system for the American Stock Exchange; the first desktop distributed processing system for on-line quotes; the first electronic stock market quotation board for NASDAQ, the first branch-level quotation system for brokerages; and (in 1985) the first financial information computer networking system to embrace industry standard communications—SuperNet™.

On the banking and commercial side, Bunker Ramo introduced the first on-line airline reservation system in 1952, which helped to set the standard for on-line financial systems used worldwide. Because of the uniqueness of this product, the achievement was nominated by various scientific organizations for entry into the Smithsonian Institution, where the terminal system now resides on display. In the early 1970s Bunker Ramo introduced the BTS 2000, the first CRT-based terminal for the thrift industry. Not content to rest on its laurels, Bunker Ramo announced Bank Control System 90® (BCS 90) in 1974, the first truly modular banking terminal system. In subsequent announcements Bunker Ramo introduced major feature enhancements to BCS 90, which included the first Electronic Journal Package and the first full-function platform automation package, ADTRAN™. The successor to the very successful BCS 90, the Aladdin microcomputer system, has set a new pace for branch bank technology. Aladdin is based on the Unix operating system and a high-performance 32-bit microprocessor architecture. The unique strength of the Aladdin system, however, is in its software. ADTRAN is one of the most powerful and flexible software packages available today, BANKTRAN PLUS, Bunker Ramo's transaction-oriented application software package, automates ALL teller activities from the simplest to the most advanced application. Both ADTRAN and BANKTRAN PLUS use a powerful software tool, the Transaction Generator, to create and modify applications to meet the changing needs of the branch. Thus, Aladdin satisfies the needs of the banking and thrift industries today, while providing substantial capacity for future expansion.

These systems and services are marketed and maintained by highly trained and experienced professionals nationwide.

THE BANK MART

"How do they do it?" is the question that people ask about The Bank Mart not only today but also throughout the bank's entire history, which spans over 125 years. The Bank Mart has weathered countless storms during those many years, thriving through them all.

Chartered in 1859 as City Savings Bank of Bridgeport, The Bank Mart was founded by Bridgeport's major philanthropists and public figures of the mid-nineteenth century. Through recessions and depressions, The Bank Mart has always been there, always with its doors open, always ready to meet the needs of its depositors.

Formerly known as City Savings Bank of Bridgeport, The Bank Mart is shown second building from the right. Photo circa 1903

In 1911 The Bank Mart purchased the old Bridgeport National Bank property and constructed the magnificent building that is still its headquarters at 948 Main Street in Bridgeport.

The Bank Mart continues this tradition today. It emphasizes financial strength—its capital-to-assets ratio of over 8 percent makes The Bank Mart among the financially strongest banks in the nation. It pays top rates for deposits, a feat made possible by The Bank Mart's sharp control of nondeposit expenses. The Bank Mart has neither merged with nor acquired any other bank, and it is committed to remaining independent as it has for its entire history.

The Bank Mart—throughout its many years—has been the bank of quality.

UNIVERSITY OF BRIDGEPORT

In 1925 New York University Professor E. Everett Cortright defined a serious need for the city of Bridgeport. "Bridgeport is the only city in the United States with a population of more than 100,000 that does not have some kind of higher educational institution," he stated in a speech to fellow Bridgeport Rotarians. "We need a college."

Cortright persuaded Dr. Alfred C. Fones, past president of the school board, to join him in his effort to form a junior college. The two men then encouraged other community leaders to form a board of trustees, and the Junior College of Connecticut was formed. In February 1928 twenty-seven students enrolled at the new school, which was housed in a small building on Fairfield Avenue. Cortright's dream had become a reality.

Except for the Depression years the college continued to grow and expand. In 1940 there were about 400 full-time students being well prepared in the liberal arts. A year later

The sixteen-acre Marina estate at Seaside Park was purchased in 1941 for the Junior College of Connecticut. The institution has evolved into the University of Bridgeport, with a faculty of 540 and a student body of 6,300.

the institution purchased the sixteen-acre Marina estate at Seaside Park, once owned by P.T. Barnum.

During that same period the school was evolving from a junior college to a four-year institution. In 1947 it officially became the University of Bridgeport. At first UB offered the traditional liberal arts degrees; as the years progressed business administration, arts and sciences, education, engineering, nursing, and dental hygiene degrees were added.

By 1950 enrollment at the University of Bridgeport had leaped to 3,500 students, taught by 183 faculty members. This growth continued in the 1960s under president Henry W. Littlefield and chancellor James H. Halsey. A highlight from that period was the addition of the nine-story

Arnold Bernhard Arts and Humanities Center with its 900-seat Mertens Theater and the Carlson Art Gallery. Presently directed by a professional in the performing arts, the Bernhard Center is a showcase for area performers and artists. In recent seasons the Philadelphia Pops Orchestra, the New York Gilbert & Sullivan Players, artists James McGarell and Frederick Sommer, and composer Stephen Sondheim have all been featured at the facility.

When Leland Miles became the university's president in 1974 he emphasized the importance of long-range planning and reorganization to ensure the school's continued success. One of his major accomplishments was the creation of the Connecticut Technology Institute (CTI) in 1983. The institute is a prime example of the university's response to a stated community need. CTI was established to enhance and expand science and engineering, and the Technology Business Development Unit was formed to assist new entrepreneurial

The university offers degrees in business administration, arts and humanities, law, science and engineering, nursing, and dental hygiene, as well as the traditional liberal arts.

Connecticut residents in UB's electrical engineering program for the 1985-1986 school year.

The present University of Bridgeport, with its 540 faculty members, serves the needs of more than 6,300 students as well as the community at large. Its academic programs range from science and business to fine arts and humanities. In addition, its faculty, students, and administrators continually volunteer their time to help build a better Bridgeport.

UB is currently playing a major role in both the revitalization of the south end and in the Gateway to the Sound program, which is specifically interested in the renovation between Wheeler Fountain and Perry Arch on Park Avenue. The institution has also proposed plans for a pedestrian mall that would eliminate traffic from University Avenue and the campus section of Myrtle Avenue.

Several university buildings are currently being used as headquarters for local community organizations. The School of Law, College of Health Sciences, and Fones School of Dental Hygiene provide ongoing free services to low- and moderate-income residents. As part of the Bridgeport Area Chamber of Commerce Adopt-A-School Program, UB faculty and students are working with the teachers and pupils of Roosevelt Elementary School on curriculum development.

In the future the University of Bridgeport's main objectives will be the same as they have been for the past six decades: to provide programs that meet the needs of the students and the community, to develop future leaders for area commerce, and to be a resource and partner in the ongoing development of the city of Bridgeport.

technology corporations.

The Cooperative Education Program (Co-op) is also an important aspect of the university. It integrates academic studies with supervised work experience in an engineering, science, business, or art environment provided by business and government organizations such as Pitney Bowes, Sikorsky Aircraft, and the Internal Revenue Service.

In 1983 Miles initiated another first. That year the university won the first contract for a state subsidy under a law that permits Connecticut to provide financial assistance to students enrolled in key programs at private colleges. In 1984 some $47,000 in state subsidies was provided for the education of fifteen

SPRAGUE METER COMPANY

Henry Hezikiah Sprague, a graduate in architecture from Yale University, returned to his native Ohio in 1881 and began working for the Equitable Gas Company. Quickly foreseeing the future needs of the rapidly developing gas industry, he became interested in the design of gas meters. His hope was to design a meter that would not only satisfy the gas company's present needs, but would also bring a completely new idea to an old industry.

In 1903 he patented his first three-chambered meter, which measured accurately at low rates of flow, was relatively inexpensive to manufacture, and was less expensive to maintain than other types of gas meters. It was around this sound, basic design that the Sprague Meter Company was built.

The firm expanded, and soon Sprague moved all operations to Bridgeport. At first its then five employees worked in a two-room, second-floor shop on the corner of Water Street and Fairfield Avenue. In 1907 larger quarters were needed, and the business moved to its present location on South Avenue and Water Street.

During World War II Sprague Meter Company, like most other manufacturing plants in Bridgeport, directed its energies toward the war effort and produced precision instruments and mechanisms for use in artillery shell fuses, Navy convoy lights, and Air Corps radar units.

Throughout its history Sprague Meter Company has been responsible for many innovations in the meter industry. During the 1960s, for example, it pioneered several major product developments for the gas industry, its principal customer. It perfected special lubrication-free parts that increase the durability of meters and improve their accuracy. It also developed a compact combination regulator and meter unit that eliminated nearly all unsightly piping.

In 1961 Sprague Meter Company was acquired by Textron, Inc., a Providence-based conglomerate. This ownership continued until July 1985, when the firm was purchased from Textron by Schlumberger. Headquartered in both New York City and Paris, France, Schlumberger is a worldwide corporation principally

Sprague Meter Company has been located at South Avenue and Water Street since 1907.

involved in the area of oil field services, measurement control, and components, and has sales of over six billion dollars.

Today Sprague Meter Company is the third-largest U.S. manufacturer in its field. Its major plant is on South Avenue. In addition to gas meters, gas regulators, and calibration equipment, it also produces pipeline items such as repair clamps and service fittings, patented Electronic Meter Provers and is a distributor for Firomatic security items such as tamper-resistant clamps, lock seals, and lock plugs and caps that eliminate the problem of theft and tampering of gas service.

In addition to its South Avenue plant, the firm has a facility in Kentucky that manufactures gas meters and regulators, meter parts, and pipeline products.

Currently the Sprague Meter Company turns out up to 2,000 die-cast aluminum meters per day, supplying markets in the United States, Canada, and overseas. Surely this is an impressive accomplishment when considering the firm's early days, when about 100 then-unique, cast-iron meters were produced each week.

LOUIS A. ABRIOLA & SON FUNERAL HOME

The name Louis A. Abriola & Son Funeral Home, located on East Washington, has long been synonymous with care and compassion. And rightly so. This establishment has provided these qualities to Fairfield County residents during times of need for more than eighty years.

Founder Louis Abriola immigrated to New Haven from Italy with his family in 1881. Several years later, when he was old enough to set off on his own, he barbered first in New York City, and later with his brother in Bridgeport.

One of Abriola's regular customers was Fred Coughlin, who was involved with a funeral business in Bridgeport. Conversations with Coughlin in the barber chair encouraged Abriola to change careers. He enrolled in the Lewis Barnes Embalming School and, upon graduation in 1906, started his own parlor on Hamilton and Gilmore.

Those early years marked the beginning of funeral homes as we know them today. Up to that time most wakes were held in private homes, and a funeral parlor was just a storefront to handle preparations. Louis Abriola's funeral home, therefore, was one of the earliest such establishments in Bridgeport, and the first to serve the Italian population.

The sense of compassion and service Abriola showed to his patrons also led to his involvement in political life. He was the first Italian American in Bridgeport to be elected to public office, serving as alderman for the tenth district.

When Louis Abriola died his wife, Maria Antoinette, assumed ownership of the business. Later her grandson, Kenneth, decided to carry on his family's tradition of service. He attended Renouard Training School for Embalmers in New York in 1949, and became owner of the company in 1983.

Director Kenneth L. Abriola

The newly remodeled Louis A. Abriola & Son Funeral Home at 426 East Washington Avenue.

carries on another family tradition—service to the community and its Italian population. For many years he was manager of the Highlanders baseball team of the Bridgeport Senior City Baseball League, and received the Bridgeport Oldtimers' Award for Sportsman of the Year.

The list of Abriola's civic involvements includes his membership in such diverse organizations as Mother Cabrini Council #4096 of the Knights of Columbus—Third Degree, the Anchor Club for Professional and Business Men, the Fairfield County Heart Club, the Washington Park Association, the Trumbull Historical Society, the Mens' Club of Holy Rosary Church, the Holy Rosary Church Parish Advisory Board, and the Boys' Club Alumni Association.

His affiliations with Italian associations are numerous. He is a past officer of the Trumbull Italian Club and the Trinacria Society, a fraternal group that aids Italian immigrants. Abriola is also a member of Roma Club, the Sons of Italy, and the University of Bridgeport's foreign ex-

Kenneth L. Abriola, director.

change program with Italy. He also serves as president of the Bridgeport Funeral Directors' Association and is involved with the Connecticut and national chapters of that organization.

Since Louis A. Abriola & Son Funeral Home was first established, many of the families in the neighborhood have moved to other parts of Bridgeport, nearby cities, or the suburbs. However, at their time of need, they come back to Abriola & Son because of its long-standing reputation for compassionate service.

COMO & NICHOLSON, INC.

What better time to start a business than when there's a definite need for the service? Such was the case in 1961, when Vincent Como and Roderick Nicholson began a firm specializing in insurance and bonding contractors.

Both partners of Como & Nicholson, Inc., had extensive experience in the insurance industry before setting out on their own. After taking numerous insurance courses at the University of Rhode Island, Como was hired by Aetna Casualty Insurance

Vincent J. Como, president and owner of Como & Nicholson, Inc.

Company. He was located first in Hartford and later, Bridgeport.

Nicholson had a similar entrance into the field, graduating from Bates College, becoming a state agent for Aetna, and then being assigned to a Bridgeport office.

The men specialized in different areas—Vince in casualty and Rod in fire insurance—but worked together on many cases. After some job shifts, the pair "decided it would be better to team up and start on our own,"

recalls Como, who is now president and sole owner of the firm following his partner's death in 1983.

But why did they choose bonding since neither was well versed in this area? Both Como and Nicholson had worked with a bonding manager who started his own office in Boston. He suggested that the pair also specialize in insurance bonding for contractors since no agency offered the service in Bridgeport. It took the new partners a while to learn the trade, but as soon as they did the business grew rapidly.

Como & Nicholson, Inc., now with over twenty employees, is in the forefront of contractor bonding and insurance in Connecticut. This distinction exists for several reasons, but primarily because the firm continues to expand its expertise in the construction field and also because of its ability to respond to contractors' round-the-clock needs.

In addition to being past president of the National Association of Surety Bond Producers, Como has served on the boards of several construction industry organizations, and rose to the prestigious position of chairman of

Now with over twenty employees, Como & Nicholson, Inc., is in the forefront of contractor bonding and insurance in Connecticut. Pictured in front of the firm's office are Vincent J. Como (left) and Roderick M. Nicholson.

the National Construction Industry Council. He continues to be active in the National Association of Surety Bond Producers and is currently chairman of a committee that developed a computer software system for surety bond producers that is being expanded to include surety companies and other segments of the surety industry.

Como's record of community service is just as extensive. With over twenty years of public service in Fairfield, he was nominated as the town's Democratic candidate for first selectman in 1985.

Como is proud of his company's reputation of high quality, extensive knowledge, and unquestionable integrity. "Como & Nicholson, Inc., is a nationally recognized firm," he states. "I can call any bonding agency in the country, and they will know who I am and be pleased to speak with me on any bonding issue."

WRIGHT INVESTORS' SERVICE

In 1960 John Winthrop Wright took the saying, "If you want something done right, do it yourself" to heart. Not long after selling a couple of manufacturing businesses he had owned, he realized that there was no place to invest his funds with satisfactory assurance of safety and profitability. "I was just not getting what I considered satisfactory information from the usual sources—New York brokerage firms and investment companies—in order to make sound investment decisions," Wright recalls. To resolve his dilemma, he began to do his own investment research.

Within a year Wright realized that he wasn't the only one who was dissatisfied with the prevailing investment services. As a result, he formed Wright Investors' Service, which today has about 110 investment professionals and staff managing a total portfolio of about three billion dollars out of modern offices in Park City Plaza.

Wright Investors' Service professionals and staff are situated in modern offices in Park City Plaza. Here the senior officers meet in the firm's boardroom.

Over the past twenty-five years the company has emerged as the "blue chip" of the nation's leading professional investment organizations, offering a full range of financial services and concentrating on the high-quality blue chip investment securities. Today, for example, WIS manages assets of pension funds for major corporations, nontaxable institutions, and municipalities throughout the United States.

WIS uses sophisticated computer analysis to manage these funds. The firm continually feeds statistics on 1,500 New York Stock Exchange firms plus 500 companies in the American Stock Exchange, over-the-counter, and National NASDAQ into a computer. Only the 350 companies that pass Wright Investors' stringent tests are then put on an Approved Wright Investors' List (AWIL); the funds the company manages are placed only in these equities. This list is continually updated and changed to guarantee the firm's philosophy that "Wright blue chip investment quality produces superior investment performance."

WIS also provides bank trust departments throughout the country with a variety of analytical and advi-

sory services. A series of investment publications called Wright Bankers' Service provides information on investment recommendations, analysis of each stock approved by WIS, and an evaluation of recent and forecasted developments in the investment world. In addition, with Wright Subordinated Investment Management, bank trust departments are provided the same high-quality investment management that WIS offers directly to its own multimillion-dollar corporate clients. In 1982 the firm introduced to client trust departments a family of mutual funds for fiduciary use that meet a wide range of account objectives and provide a diversity of investment management styles.

WIS also offers custom-tailored services to meet the specific needs of major institutional clients, international business development services that assist foreign corporations in search of qualified U.S. partners, corporate financial services that provide consultation with businesses and help them raise the quality and value of their investment attraction to sophisticated, long-term investors, and "Stat-Scan," an investment data and evaluation service delivered through computer-operated wire distribution networks.

In short, over the past quarter-century Wright has indeed "done it right" first by himself and now through a highly organized, solidly established company of over 100 investment professionals and staff. His firm's investment data base and extensive operating facilities are believed to comprise the most advanced investment data-processing capability in the industry. And Wright Investors' Service investment data resources, research capabilities, and personnel organization are now believed to constitute one of the world's largest independent investment management and advisory facilities.

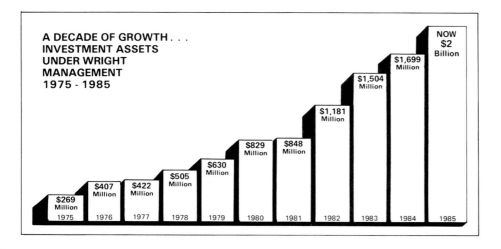

A DECADE OF GROWTH...
INVESTMENT ASSETS
UNDER WRIGHT
MANAGEMENT
1975 - 1985

$269 Million 1975	
$407 Million 1976	
$422 Million 1977	
$505 Million 1978	
$630 Million 1979	
$829 Million 1980	
$848 Million 1981	
$1,181 Million 1982	
$1,504 Million 1983	
$1,699 Million 1984	
NOW $2 Billion 1985	

THE SCHWERDTLE STAMP COMPANY

The business journal read:
Louis F. Schwerdtle
Bridgeport, Connecticut
June 12, 1893

Commenced business this day at
35 Fairfield Avenue, Room 4.
Hawes Opera House block.
Used as capital: Mrs. C. M.
Schwerdtle $256.88.

That marked the beginning of a business passed down through four generations that is known today as The Schwerdtle Stamp Company, specializing in rubber stamps, hot stamping dies for marking plastics, and steel stamps for indent marking metal products.

As a young man, Bridgeporter Louis Ferdinand Schwerdtle learned the art of die engraving while working for the Andrew Krause Company, a manufacturer of white metal-plated novelty goods. In time Schwerdtle became disenchanted with the lack of opportunity for advancement and decided to start his own engraving business.

In the early years, Schwerdtle worked with metal engraving, producing dies and tools for products like carriage lamps and silverware manufactured by such companies as Bridgeport Brass, Scovill Manufacturing, Turner and Seymour Company, and American Brass. The rubber stamp side of the business was added in 1904, when Louis and his younger brother, Edward, bought out the Bridgeport Stamp Company which dated to 1879.

Throughout the following decades The Schwerdtle Stamp Company continued to expand its capabilities to meet both industry and consumer needs. During World War I the firm made steel stamps for marking ammunition shells. Later the customer list expanded to almost every segment of American industry including automotive parts, housewares, and

Here in the early days of The Schwerdtle Stamp Company (circa 1930), all engraving was done by hand by skilled craftsmen mostly from Germany. Today this work is done just as meticulously by pantograph engraving machines, computer-controlled engraving and electrical discharge machines.

machine tools.

In 1929 Louis Schwerdtle died and soon after Hubert, Edward's son, who had recently graduated from Wesleyan University, joined his father in the business. During the Great Depression in the early 1930s, they managed to keep all their workers employed by dividing up whatever work was available.

Gradually the situation improved, reaching a high point toward the end of World War II when the company, in order to expand, moved to its present location on Elm Street in Bridgeport. The 1950s, increasingly under Hubert's leadership, brought modernization from handwork to mechanization in both engraving and typesetting.

That trend continues today where the most up-to-date equipment now does the work just as meticulously as it once was done by hand. For example, rubber stamps now are typed out on a phototypesetter using a light-

sensitive material called photopolymer, which greatly speeds up completion time.

Today, under the direction of Louis' grandsons, John and Edward, The Schwerdtle Stamp Company has thirty-five employees and is a multi-million dollar business. It continues to provide custom service, offering a wide range of expertise in the marking field. The firm produces silicone rubber and metal hot stamping dies and steel stamps for just about every industry. Its dies decorate or mark a variety of products including cosmetic containers, industrial tools, medical and research equipment, electronic parts, appliances, and automotive parts, as well as type pieces for dating and coding consumer products.

In the future The Schwerdtle Stamp Company will remain a family business in touch personally with both customers and employees. With Sarah Schwerdtle McCann and John Schwerdtle II representing the fourth generation of the family to be involved in the business, The Schwerdtle Stamp Company will continue to provide state-of-the-art services to meet the varying needs of both industry and consumers.

PHYSICIANS HEALTH SERVICES

In 1975 a group of area doctors, led by Robert W. Doering, M.D., defined a need for a new form of health management system that could deal with the problems of escalating health care costs, lack of access to available health care resources, and the need to assure effective, high-quality care in the greater Bridgeport area.

Two years later they launched a prepaid health plan called Physicians Health Services (PHS). It was unlike any other Health Maintenance Organization (HMO) in Connecticut. Up to that time almost all HMOs were the "staff model" type, where physicians are salaried employees of the HMO, provide care from a central facility or clinic, and have a primary relationship with just one hospital. PHS, however, was formed as an Individual Practice Association (IPA), where the physicians continue their private practices and see patients in their own offices. In addition, IPAs have relationships with a number of hospitals depending on the physicians' affiliations.

The next several years were not easy for the new organization. In spite of the generous contributions of participating physicians, PHS's early growth was stymied due to insufficient funds for broad marketing plans and the skepticism of employers who were still hesitant to offer a new health service to their employees.

All that changed in 1980, when PHS became the first federally qualified IPA/HMO in all of New England and began to be offered to major local employers such as Sikorsky Aircraft and Harvey Hubbell. Under the direction of company president Michael E. "Mickey" Herbert and with the support of the state's medical leadership, PHS grew rapidly, becoming the largest HMO in the state. Its service area expanded to all of Fairfield, New Haven, and New

Reviewing notification of federal qualification in December 1980 are (seated) Michael E. Herbert, current president of PHS, and (from left) Robert W. Doering, M.D., then medical director; John R. Gulash, M.D., then president; Raymond Builter, treasurer at that time and then business manager of the University of Bridgeport; and Norman Weinstein, M.D., then chairman of the Greater Bridgeport Individual Practice Association.

London counties, the greater Danbury area and, most recently, to Windham, parts of Tolland County, and into Westchester County in New York.

The number of employees expanded from six to over 100, PHS members from 10,000 to 70,000, and participating physicians from 350 to more than 1,500 located across Connecticut. In addition to its Trumbull headquarters there are regional offices in Stamford, Danbury, Waterford, and White Plains.

One reason for PHS's rapid growth has been the initial and ongoing support of physicians across the state. Acting on a conviction that PHS represented an opportunity for the physician community itself to control health care costs, they also saw it as a guarantor of quality health care provided in the traditional office setting.

Another factor in PHS's success has been the high quality of its staff. Michael Herbert has been a leader in the HMO industry for the past sixteen years despite his relatively young age. Charter president of the state HMO association, Herbert is a board member of the American

PHS's corporate facility, at 2440 Reservoir Avenue in Trumbull, serves as administrative headquarters for operations extending from Westchester County east to the Rhode Island/ Connecticut border.

Medical Care and Review Association.

He is also a former All-American player for the Franklin Cardinals (formerly the Raybestos Cardinals) fast-pitch softball team. In 1984 he was America's leading hitter in the World Championship, when the United States took a bronze medal.

PHS itself will be a big hitter in the years to come. Herbert sees an even brighter future for HMOs and particularly for PHS. "In 1981 people in Connecticut were questioning if HMOs were an idea whose time might never come," he says. "Now, only five years later, total Connecticut HMO membership exceeds 250,000—more than 8 percent of the total population, and we can confidently predict that 20 percent of Connecticut's population will be in these types of prepaid health plans by 1990."

271

THE SWAN ENGRAVING COMPANY

J. Reece inspects the etching of a relief printing plate.

Changing with the changing times: That phrase describes the history of The Swan Engraving Company. As the industry and its capabilities have expanded over the years, so too have the services of this Bridgeport photoengraving business. In fact, it has expanded into much more than just engraving, pioneering whole new areas of the craft. Thus, it now calls itself a "graphic preparatory house."

Walter Swan, founder of the company, got his first taste of the printing business when he was working on a paper in Battle Creek, Michigan. He later moved to Bridgeport on Cannon Street to start a business in the field he knew best—photo engraving. At that time all newspapers were printed using the letterpress method. Swan did the advertising letterpress plates for department stores such as D.M. Reads and Howlands and Meigs, which were then placed in daily newspapers. He also did copper plates for printers for use on folding cartons—an area for which Swan Engraving is still well known today.

In the early days the etching process was long and involved. Copper plates were etched with acid, banked with a fine resinous powder called "dragon's blood," and then heated. All this took many hours.

Now, with the latest equipment, Swan Engraving can repeat this process in a matter of minutes. In addition to letterpress, there is the faster,

S. Bedient producing four-color separations from a transparency on a Hell CP 340 Scanner.

more efficient offset process. Working from a 35-millimeter slide, Swan Engraving makes films that can be used for pictures in a magazine or catalog, or on the front of a carton in the grocery store, or on a poster. This is done by putting the slide on a laser scanner. The scanner beams light through every inch of the slide. The computer in the scanner then determines what percentage of yellow, red, blue, and black is in every portion of the slide. It then generates

With the use of a computerized art and film system, R. Leigh creates rules, windows, and grids that formerly were created by hand.

dots onto a piece of film (22,500 dots per square inch). The dots vary in size depending on how much color the scanner sees in each area on the slide. The finished product is four pieces of film (yellow, red, blue, and black), each one with thousands of varying-size dots on it. From these films are made printing plates, which are then used on printing presses. If you look with a magnifying glass at pictures in magazines, you will notice all the little yellow, red, blue, and black dots that create the picture.

Walter's son, Robert, president of Swan Engraving, uses many new processes in the company's four plants. Swan Color Graphics, on Wordin Avenue, has two electronic laser scanners and a CAD/CAM system for making color separations onto film. Swan Engraving, on Hanover Street, specializes in platemaking for both letterpress and offset printing. Swan Laser Die, on Norman Street, does large metal sculpting. Micro Etch Products, in Stratford, makes very fine metal parts used for jewelry and the electronic industry.

"Most engraving companies have one focus and thus, only one product line," says Robert Swan. "The name 'Swan Engraving' is misleading. We do engraving, but also a lot more. People come to us for a number of products."

Swan is involved in the fine art field, printing limited editions of art reproductions. The firm does commercial color separations for local advertising agencies and makes etched dies for plastic tablecloths. Swan even helps a local sculptor complete his museum pieces made out of magnesium, aluminum, and steel.

Although The Swan Engraving Company's primary market is New England, it is known nationally and internationally. Says Robert Swan, "We have such diversity of equipment and expertise that people come to us from throughout the world."

COMPUTER PROCESSING INSTITUTE

The business application of computers started in the mid-1950s and expanded so rapidly that in ten years there were severe shortages of computer programmers and operators. David S. Shefrin, an MIT-educated electrical engineer managing a computer payroll and accounting service for Hartford-area businesses, was one of the first to experience the shortages. He decided to start training computer operators to meet the needs of the local insurance industry, which was employing data processors as fast as they could be produced.

In 1965 Shefrin founded the Computer Processing Institute in West Hartford, offering one six-month program in computer operations for thirty students. The demand exceeded his expectations. In 1966 he moved to larger quarters, added computer programming and data-entry courses, and enrolled several hundred students. Continued demands resulted in a second relocation in 1969 to the 30,000-square-foot building that is now the main school of a chain of four located in three states.

The school's success was due to its concentrated courses, frequently revised in response to technology changes and job market demands, and the fact that it produced work-ready graduates in either three or six months. It also gave young adults career opportunities unavailable in public schools and colleges. Unemployed college graduates and persons with two or more years' work experience made up the bulk of CPI's student body then, as today.

In 1977 Shefrin opened a branch school in Stratford, which was moved two years later to a 20,000-square-foot building at 830 Broad Street in Bridgeport. The location was selected, in part, to enable inner-city citizens to receive training without traveling long distances. In the first year about 550 students graduated and became employed, many for the first time.

The modern CPI office building in the heart of downtown Bridgeport.

By 1984 CPI offered a broad range of data-processing programs including computer operations, programming, data entry, word processing, electronic technology, computer repair, and electronic assembly technology. Students were coming to the institution from an area including Norwalk, Danbury, Meriden, and New London.

CPI has become one of the largest independent data-processing schools

David S. Shefrin, founder of Computer Processing Institute.

in the country, each year graduating over 1,300 students. Many graduates have gone on to be employed by companies nationwide including Exxon, Xerox, Duracell, Pitney Bowes, WaldenBooks, IBM, Automatic Data Processing, Aetna, and The Travelers.

CPI is accredited by the Association of Independent Colleges and Schools and is approved by the Connecticut Department of Education. In 1985 it entered into a unique credit articulation agreement with Housatonic Community College, providing for the acceptance of CPI credits toward requirements for an associate's degree from Housatonic.

Today Shefrin also owns schools in

New Jersey and Massachusetts. Bridgeport CPI will soon become the center for one or more small extensions in neighboring communities along the Connecticut shoreline.

Shefrin believes that Computer Processing Institute provides a major service for large and small businesses and for men and women seeking to change careers or start new ones. He has believed from the start that the true measure of quality in vocational education is the extent to which the graduate becomes self-sufficient and economically independent.

DIOCESE OF BRIDGEPORT

In 1830 the Reverend James Fitton celebrated Mass with his congregation of seventeen in a private home on Middle Street. That was the beginning of St. James (later St. Augustine), the first of over twenty Roman Catholic parishes now located in Bridgeport. Today all are part of the Diocese of Bridgeport, representing parishes throughout Fairfield County.

Located on the corner of Arch Street and Washington Avenue, the original St. James Church was dedicated in 1842 by Bishop Benedict Fenwick of Boston. Ten years later, with a growing congregation of more than 300, the structure was enlarged to double its size. Then, in 1869, a

Lawrence Cardinal Shehan, D.D., served as the first bishop of Bridgeport from 1953 to 1961.

language and culture. The Catholic parishes representing various nationalities were a natural extension of this tendency.

In 1874, for example, there were about twenty-five German Catholic families in Bridgeport. Originally, Father Joseph A. Schaele said Mass in the T.A.B. Hall over Harral's Tea Store on Main Street where the arcade is now located; the congregation later moved to St. Joseph's Church on Madison Avenue. Other ethnic groups likewise formed their own parishes. These included the Hungar-

Bridgeport's St. Augustine Cathedral was dedicated in 1869.

new church was dedicated on Golden Hill, today's St. Augustine Cathedral. Throughout the following decades, as the Catholic population in Bridgeport grew steadily, many parishes developed from the original St. James, including St. Mary's, Sacred Heart, St. Patrick's, Blessed Sacrament, and St. Charles.

The majority of parishes that were founded in Bridgeport during the nineteenth century had congregations with similar ethnic backgrounds. When immigrants came to the United States, they tended to live in neighborhoods with people of similar

The Most Reverend Walter W. Curtis, S.T.D., has been bishop of Bridgeport since 1961.

ian St. Stephen's, the Slovak St. John Nepomucene, the Italian Holy Rosary, the French St. Anthony's, the Polish St. Michael's, the Irish St. Patrick's, the Lithuanian St. George's, and the Slovenian Holy Cross.

Parishes are normally founded to serve the needs of Catholics within a certain territory or area of a city. During the nineteenth and early twentieth centuries, the Catholic population grew at an unexpected rapid rate as a result of European immi-

The interior of St. Augustine Cathedral.

always welcomed immigrants, opening its doors to the Irish, Slovaks, Poles, Hungarians, and now the Spanish. A new St. Mary's Church is being rebuilt with funds raised by a strongly unified Spanish community. St. Charles on East Main Street now has a very active Spanish and Laotian congregation, and St. Augustine's has many Portuguese and Spanish parishioners.

In years to come the Bridgeport parishes in the Diocese of Bridgeport will continue to reach out, offering a home to immigrants, strengthening the faith of American-born Catholics, and providing necessary community social services.

gration. Since these Catholics arrived speaking no English and carrying their own customs with them, certain parishes were established to care for individual national groups, regardless of the area or territory in which they lived.

The churches also opened schools, and many of them still instruct parishioners today. In addition, through Catholic charities, the Diocese of Bridgeport offers a variety of social services to all members of the community.

Some things change, yet some things remain the same. Today the city of Bridgeport's parishes are made up of second-, third-, and fourth-generation Americans. However, just as in the past, the Roman Catholic Church opens its doors to new ethnic groups coming into the city. Hispanics, Laotians, and Haitians are now counted in congregations of parishes that were once the houses of prayer for various European settlers.

St. Mary's on Pembroke Street has

St. Augustine Cathedral's Eucharistic Shrine.

THE SOUTHERN CONNECTICUT GAS COMPANY

The former West Works of The Southern Connecticut Gas Company. This is the present location of the firm's service center on Pine Street.

When gas was first used in Bridgeport, it took a little getting used to. Many greeted the coming of gas with initial contempt and ridicule. Some even said it was ungodly. "The Creator meant night to be dark," they said.

Some believed that gas lighting of streets would make people ill, encouraging them to walk about at night and catch cold. And would not drunkenness and evil of all kinds increase? Also, horses would be frightened. Despite all these objections, gas soon became popular, and thus, The Southern Connecticut Gas Company and its forebears went on to introduce generations of residents and industries to the benefits of gas.

The history of The Southern Connecticut Gas Company goes back to the founding of both the New Haven Gas Light Company and Bridgeport Gas Light Company in the mid-1800s. These two businesses merged in 1967 to become The Southern Connecticut Gas Company, now headquartered on Broad Street in Bridgeport.

The Bridgeport Gas Light Company was formed in 1849 by a charter of the Connecticut General Assembly. The East Works, one of the firm's original operation centers, was locat-

ed on Housatonic Avenue. Despite residents' early reservations, by 1851 the company had seventy-six private customers and operated twenty-six public street lamps. And by 1859 gas was used for much more than just lighting. Toasters, gas furnaces, laundry stoves, hatters' irons, bathroom stoves, and gas ovens all were advertised.

A new product called "cooking gas" became popular in the late nineteenth century, and it led to the production of the first gas ranges in 1899. Gas refrigeration followed in 1915.

In 1934 the firm took advantage of the popularity of gas appliances and began its own merchandising operations by buying out the Gas Appliance Exchange. Three years later Bridgeport Gas achieved record sendouts of manufactured gas, with an average of four million cubic feet of carbureted gas being used.

After World War II the present

The gas company's service fleet of an earlier era.

The present-day headquarters of The Southern Connecticut Gas Company at 880 Broad Street.

262-foot-high gas holder was built, more than doubling storage facilities. The conversion to natural gas in 1952 ushered in a new era. Mayor Jasper McLevy opened the valve that allowed the natural gas from Texas and Louisiana to enter the mains.

Conversion to nontoxic natural gas provided the company with a tremendous opportunity for growth. About 200,000 appliances had to be converted. New appliances were being sold by the carload, and miles of new main were laid in the greater Bridgeport area including Fairfield, Trumbull, Stratford, Easton, and Westport.

The New Haven Gas Company had a history similar to that of its Bridgeport counterpart. Founded in 1847, the first offices were located in a single upstairs room at the corner of Chapel and State streets. Currently its offices are located on Church Street.

In 1979 the Connecticut Energy Corporation, a holding company, was formed with The Southern Connecticut Gas Company as the principal subsidiary. Today Southern serves 140,000 residential, commercial, and industrial customers in southern Connecticut. Other Connecticut Energy Corporation subsidiaries engage in natural gas and oil exploration and the transportation of natural gas.

The Southern Connecticut Gas Company is continually searching for new forms of energy and energy conservation. One answer is cogeneration, where both electricity and hot water or steam are produced by burning gas. This results in a money-saving overall reduction in fuel.

Southern also devotes much of its time to community needs. Presently the company is involved with revitalization efforts in Bridgeport. In 1984

it purchased the Augustus Dupée mansion in the historic Washington Park area. The classic French Second Empire exterior is being preserved, and the interior will be subdivided into four condominium units. These units will be sold to people with low or moderate incomes.

The firm also contributes to the growth of the community in other ways. A grant given to Family Services-Woodfield for the agency's Handyman program helps to provide weatherization, home repair, and maintenance services to low-income

elderly and handicapped persons in the greater Bridgeport area. In June 1983 Southern began a program of commercial and industrial energy audits. These have led not only to a reduction of gas consumption but also of all energy usage—in some cases by as much as 40 percent.

The Southern Connecticut Gas Company confidently expects to continue to meet the expanding needs of its customers by acquiring additional gas supplies when necessary. At the same time it will always place energy conservation as a top priority.

TREFZ CORPORATION

The Trefz brothers, Ernie (left) and Christian (right), welcome their father to Trefz Corporation headquarters.

There are three types of individuals: those who do not know an opportunity when they see it, those who recognize an opportunity only after it passes and say, "I should have," and those who, like the Trefzes of the world, spot an opportunity, act on it, and reap the benefits. Because of answering "when opportunity knocked," the Trefz brothers are now the principals of Trefz Corporation, a Bridgeport-based firm that includes in its holdings forty-two McDonald's restaurants and is one of the five largest franchise groups in the 9,000-unit worldwide McDonald's system.

Ernest Trefz, president and chief executive officer of Trefz Corporation, began his "Horatio Alger" career during his high school years. While his contemporaries studied or played sports after school, Ernie was driving truckloads of cider and corn from his hometown of North Haven to Boston. He was quickly immersed in the world of business, and, as a result, got an education unequaled by the Harvard Business School. Christian Trefz, who is now executive vice-president of Trefz Corporation, followed in his older brother's footsteps.

At a very young age he launched a number of businesses, including a lawn-mowing service and a bicycle sales and repair business.

Following stints in the Army, both brothers joined their father, Christian, at the Roessler Packing Company, a major Fairfield County provisions supplier, located where the Bridgeport train station is today. The elder Christian was with Roessler for over fifty years, until his retirement as president in 1975.

Roessler Packing Company was where opportunity came knocking. Ernie established a new relationship through which the firm supplied ground-beef patties to the first McDonald's outlet in New England, located in Hamden. Not only did this initiative open an entire new business arena for Roessler—the ground-beef patties and portion-control business—it also provided Ernie with some new aspirations of his own. "It

Ernie Trefz opened his first McDonald's restaurant in Waterbury, Connecticut, in 1964. Today the Trefz Corporation owns forty-two restaurants.

didn't take me long to realize that I was on the wrong side of the hamburger," Ernie says. "When the first McDonald's opened in the late 1950s, I could see such great opportunity for this crazy red and white building with the hoola hoops that sold hamburgers for fifteen cents. It was perfect for me. I knew the food business, and I was ready to get in on the ground floor of a brand-new enterprise."

It was just a matter of time before Ernie could act on his hunches. During the next few years the McDonald's organization began expanding, and in 1964, while still employed at Roessler Packing Company, Ernie opened his first McDonald's restaurant in Waterbury. Christian joined Ernie in this new venture and by 1969 the brothers owned and man-

aged three additional McDonald's restaurants. By this time the business had grown to such an extent that it required Ernie's full attention. He resigned from Roessler Packing Company to devote his full time to McDonald's.

Today the Trefz Corporation employs 2,800 people in its network of forty-two McDonald's restaurants, located throughout Fairfield and New Haven counties in Connecticut and in Westchester, Putnam, Bronx, and Dutchess counties in New York State. In addition, the corporation-owned T/C Distribution Company in Stratford provides, on a completely computerized basis, the total distribution of food, paper, and related products to each McDonald's location. This distribution concept was a "first" for McDonald's licensees.

The Trefz brothers are used to firsts. Through the years the corporation has received a succession of awards for excellence in the areas of restaurant management, employee

Ernest and Christian Trefz in front of Bridgeport's Park City Plaza, headquarters for the Trefz Corporation.

development, decor and landscaping, and marketing. McDonald's Corporation has strict guidelines for awarding franchises. "There is no geographical exclusivity, so you must demonstrate superior management ability to earn every franchise you get," stresses Ernie Trefz. Because of its exemplary performance, Trefz Corporation was the first company to be awarded as many as five McDonald's franchises at one time. These restaurants opened on May 22, 1985, along Interstate 95 in Darien, Milford, and Branford.

Both brothers have been officers of the two McDonald's cooperatives responsible for advertising and public relations. Ernie has also served as chairman of McDonald's National Advertising Board, which approves and controls all national creative advertising material.

The Trefz family is optimistic about the future of Bridgeport and deeply committed to the city's revitalization. This commitment is evidenced by the family's substantial investments in Bridgeport, which include the Woolworth Building, numerous apartment buildings, and other real estate holdings. In addition, Trefz Corporation is headquartered on the seventeenth floor of the Park City Plaza, a building that was purchased by the brothers in 1984.

Both men are also involved with numerous community and business activities. Ernie serves on the board of directors of Citytrust Bank, and is a member of its executive committee. He is also a board member and member of the executive committee of the University of Bridgeport, a board member of the Downtown Council of the City of Bridgeport, a board member of Bridgeport's 150th-anniversary committee, a board

member of Goodwill Industries, a trustee of the St. Vincent's Medical Center Foundation, and a member of the international board of the Up With People organization. Christian serves as vice-president of the board of associates of the University of Bridgeport.

In keeping with the family tradition, Ernie and Christian both have sons who work in the organization and related businesses, with the expectation of making future contributions to the company. And Trefz Corporation's future looks bright indeed. It will surely include more hard work, more recognition from McDonald's Corporation, and most likely, more franchise awards. McDonald's Corporation, like the Trefz brothers, knows a good opportunity when it sees one.

THE BRIDGEPORT AND PORT JEFFERSON STEAMBOAT COMPANY

The M/V Grand Republic, *which was christened on the firm's 100th anniversary, has a capacity of transporting 1,000 passengers and 85 vehicles, and has a cruising speed of sixteen knots.*

Since the early days of America, a link between agricultural Long Island and industrial New England was considered essential. Sailing packets covered the route between Bridgeport and Port Jefferson, about seventeen statute miles, since the 1830s. By the 1870s two sloops were carrying passengers and freight between these Connecticut and Long Island ports a couple of times a week. However, there was a persistent demand for a more reliable and comfortable vessel.

"A steamboat is the answer," said Captain Charles E. Tooker, a deep-water sailor from Port Jefferson. Thus The Bridgeport and Port Jefferson Steamboat Company was born, with twenty-seven stockholders, P.T. Barnum as president, and Captain Tooker and his brother-in-law, Edward Davis, having majority interest. *Nonowantuc,* a utilitarian steamboat, was the company's first vessel. Captain Tooker's suggestion surely proved right. More than a century later the route is still going strong.

At first the steamboat's passengers were Long Island farmers bound for Bridgeport, and Park City merchants and salesmen traveling to Port Jefferson to take orders. In the 1890s the firm promoted tourist trade: Port Jefferson was established as a recreational mecca, and Bridgeport as a great entertainment spot with trolley rides, resorts, and a scenic zoo.

While the automobile was the death knell for many steamboat lines in the 1920s and 1930s, it stabilized the Bridgeport-Port Jefferson operation. In 1921 the company's second boat, *Park City,* was remodeled to transport automobiles. However, the firm was not so fortunate during the Depression, and it was not until World War II that it again began a brisk business, boosted by gasoline rationing.

The descendants of Captain Tooker remained in control of the business until 1961, when Vail Tooker sold his family's interest to Edward Acker, a Long Island businessman, and the McAllister Tugboat Company. The McAllister family had roots in

---

The diesel-powered Martha's Vineyard *(below), docked beside the M/V* Grand Republic, *replaced the steamboat in 1968.*

American water transportation, and today McAllister Brothers, Inc., is one of the largest towing and transportation companies in the United States.

Although the word "steamboat" still remains a part of the company's official name, the diesel-powered *Martha's Vineyard* replaced the steamboat in 1968 to make the trip shorter. For similar reasons, the *Grand Republic* was christened on the firm's 100th anniversary. With a cruising speed of sixteen knots, this vessel could make the crossing twenty minutes faster than *Martha's Vineyard.* She also could carry 1,000 passengers and 85 cars, recreational vehicles, and boat trailers.

Today high automobile costs and increasing traffic congestion make ferry travel more attractive than ever. Captain Brian McAllister, president of The Bridgeport and Port Jefferson Steamboat Company, expects to meet this increased demand with the addition of new vessels. In the future he hopes to preserve what has best served the area, while continuing to provide every appropriate convenience.

CABLEVISION SYSTEMS OF SOUTHERN CONNECTICUT

On October 27, 1976, Southern Connecticut Cable received certification from the Connecticut Department of Public Utility Control stating that its franchise license had been approved. That was a landmark day for Bridgeport. The city was entering the new age of cable communications. Approximately a year later cable television service was initiated to the first subscriber, and SCC was on its way.

In the early years many people were under the false impression that cable television was developed only to enable suburban residents to have better reception. "This just isn't the case," said a few cable pioneers. "Cable television is much more than the retransmission of broadcast channels. It is a means of opening up a whole new world of programming and family entertainment right in the subscribers' homes."

One of the cable industry's innovators was Charles Dolan, originator of Home Box Office and general partner of Cablevision Systems, the nation's largest privately owned cable television organization. In 1983 Southern Connecticut Cable was acquired by Dolan's progressive, farsighted company and was reborn as Cablevision Systems of Southern Connecticut with a whole new range of programming including sports, music, and educational and cultural offerings. The management believes its service contributes significantly to the lives of the people and the vitality of the communities it serves.

Currently, due to Cablevision's primary goal of customer satisfaction, 60,000 subscribers in the six towns of Bridgeport, Stratford, Milford, Orange, Woodbridge, and Fairfield enjoy a package of programming services at an affordable price. New national entertainment programming services, some produced by Cablevision System's Rainbow companies, are adding more exciting choices to

Cablevision News 12, "Fairfield County's own nightly news," is highly regarded by news organizations and broadcasters nationwide and throughout the world. Pictured are members of the award-winning evening news staff.

both basic and premium program packages. In addition to an extensive offering of entertainment programming, Cablevision subscribers receive a variety of local programming.

Cablevision News 12, a United Press International Award recipient and two-time winner of the ACE Award, cable television's Emmy, provides comprehensive coverage of the events, issues, and items of interest that most affect the lives of southwestern Connecticut residents. The "Fairfield Exchange" is a local talk show offering viewers an in-depth look at the interesting people and events of the area as well as national personalities traveling through Connecticut. There is also local-origination programming of such events as area elections, the Barnum Parade, school sports, and Fairfield University activities. In addition, an active public-access program, in association with the University of Bridgeport, allows any individual to produce his/her own programming in the university's production studio.

Because customer service is another priority of Cablevision, a new Cable Center was recently opened at 3782 Main Street in Bridgeport. This center has been designed to better accommodate subscribers and to give customers easier access to the cable

company.

Through the firm's addressable converters, Cablevision subscribers have even more programming choices. A "Pay-Per-View" programming system will allow future viewers to enjoy sneak previews of popular films and live national sporting events. Also, interactive services and cost-effective high-speed data transmission are among the promising programs the system has been designed to bring to the homes and businesses in the region.

The cable television industry is in its infancy, and Cablevision Systems of Southern Connecticut is expecting to participate in its additional growth and numerous changes in the future as described in its corporate goal: "The primary purpose of Cablevision is to develop into a quality cable television company with unsurpassed competence to manage the cable systems, program syndication, and advertising sales businesses. Our goal is clear—industry leadership in service to subscribers, creative marketing, and profitable growth."

MODERN PLASTICS

In the 1960s movie *The Graduate* a man said to Dustin Hoffman, "I have one word for you . . . 'plastics.'" It was to be the material of the future. However, nearly two decades earlier there was a company that was already thinking plastics and saw its potential.

Joseph C. Carbone, founder of Modern Plastics, moved to the east end of Bridgeport with his family in 1925. He later served in the Navy, first as an aviator machinist, where he came in contact with a new material called plastic. In 1946 he joined his brother-in-law, Victor Chesto, who was running what was then called Modern Glass Company on Howard Avenue. Carbone assumed ownership of the business a year later.

Although Carbone kept the glass

Joseph C. Carbone assumed ownership of Modern Glass Company, at 678 Howard Avenue, in 1947. This facility is the retail store for Modern Plastics today.

business going, specializing in auto glass replacement, mirrors, and storefront glazing, he was more interested in plastics. Some of the first machinable plastics in Connecticut had their beginning in his three-car garage on Howard Avenue.

In the years that followed the business turned increasingly toward plastics and away from glass. Plastic was quickly becoming accepted as a replacement for glass because of problems with safety and vandalism. More and more applications for plastics were being found in various in-

the Northeast. In addition to distribution, it fabricates large quantities of plastic material, cutting it to order for customers. It now deals with more than eighty types of plastic. The company also operates a retail business, selling specialized plastic items, as well as providing the product to industries for the replacement

Robert J. Carbone, vice-president; Bing J. Carbone, vice-president; James A. Carbone, president; and Joseph C. Carbone, chairman of the board, in front of the firm's corporate headquarters at 706 Howard Avenue.

dustries. For example, an automobile in the 1970s carried about twenty pounds of plastic in its body; today the average is over 150 pounds.

Because of the increasing use of plastic, Carbone's business has remained in a constant state of expansion. Today, under the direction of Jim Carbone, who assumed corporate leadership upon his father's retirement in 1977, the firm has 35,000 square feet of floor space, including sales offices and warehouses in Rhode Island and Massachusetts, and currently employs sixty people.

Modern Plastics, as it is known today because of its primary product, is the largest supplier of plastic in

of metal parts.

In 1982 Modern Plastics purchased the Defender Corporation, a firm that manufactures a plastic storm window for industrial and consumer use. The company now manufactures and distributes this energy-efficient and durable product.

Modern Plastics currently employs its third generation of Carbones in the persons of Robert and Bing. And there's no reason why it won't remain a family business for years to come. The plastics industry continues to grow as new uses, and new plastics, are being discovered daily. And as the industry grows, Modern Plastics will grow with it.

CHAPIN & BANGS COMPANY

In 1888 William Chapman established in Bridgeport a branch of the Congdon & Carpenter Co., iron merchants from Providence, Rhode Island, whose business was founded in 1790. This store on Cannon Street dealt in supplies for blacksmiths and wagon makers and other articles known in the trade as "heavy hardware." In 1895 Walter Bangs was sent to help in the management of the business, and in 1902 the two men bought control from Congdon and Carpenter and incorporated as the Chapman & Bangs Company.

In the years that followed, steel bars, sheet metal, and tinning and heating supplies were added to the merchandise stocked. With the advent of World War I the volume of business grew so much that larger quarters were needed. As a result, the company moved to Water Street near the railroad freight station. This was a convenient location as out-of-town shipments were made by rail and trolley. Local delivery was by horse and wagon. About 1918 the firm bought its first motor truck, a chain-driven Mack with solid tires and side curtains for bad weather.

In 1918 Murray Chapin bought

Chapman's interest in the business, and two years later its name was changed to the Chapin & Bangs Company. William Boyd, Chapin's son-in-law, joined the firm in 1934. At that time its stock consisted of H.R. steel bars; tool steel; black and galvanized steel sheets; and plumbing, heating and tinning, and blacksmith supplies.

Boyd saw the market and profitability of the blacksmith articles fading and worked to phase them out while building up the steel part of the business. He added C.F. bars, structural shapes, and plate to the stock and introduced the flame cutting of plate, thus beginning the firm's transition to a steel-service center.

In 1954 A. George Lindquist bought controlling interest in the company from Chapin. Lindquist, the entrepreneur and financial man, and Boyd, in charge of operations and planning, proceeded to complete the firm's metamorphosis into a full-fledged steel-service center. They constructed a modern warehouse and office building on River Street and moved the business there in August 1955. Since then the plant has been enlarged five times, the material-handling equipment and the production machinery have been continually upgraded and added to, and the inventory has been greatly enlarged in both tonnage and range of sizes and grades.

A. George Lindquist, owner and chairman of the board.

Boyd retired in 1972, and Lindquist is still active in the business on a part-time basis. Chapin & Bangs is now run by Richard Hoyt, who serves as president and Morely Boyd, son of William Boyd, vice-president. Hoyt and Boyd have continued the process of growth and improvement. Today Chapin & Bangs is the largest independent steel firm in New England.

In the near future Chapin & Bangs Company will again be expanding its facilities on River Street—another example of the firm's tradition of growth and improvement and its continuing commitment to the city of Bridgeport.

Employees handle warehousing and material handling with ease as Chapin & Bangs has continually upgraded its equipment. This extra-long-bed truck is in marked contrast to the company's first motor truck, a chain-driven Mack with solid tires and side curtains purchased in 1918.

JOHN L. SIMPSON COMPANY, INC.

Ever since the John L. Simpson Company was founded in 1927, it has been expertly led by self-made men with an extensive knowledge of the general contracting business— from the ground up. As a result the firm has been able to continually live up to its motto: Simpson Superior Service Satisfies and Saves.

Founder John L. Simpson was born in Bridgeport in 1893. After losing his mother at an early age, he moved to Scotland to live with his grandmother. There he began his trade in the plastering business. As a teenager, he returned to the Park City, working as a tradesman for a local building contractor.

The original residence and office of John L. Simpson, founder of the firm, on Putnam Street in Bridgeport.

President Donald C. Keegan in front of the present office and mill of the John L. Simpson Company, Inc.

After World War I Simpson opened a small plastering business that was expanded to general contracting in 1930. He quickly established himself as a quality contractor by completing alteration jobs on storefronts for such businesses as Lerner, Reid and Todd, and Howlands; remodeling the interiors of factories such as Underwood, General Electric, and Bridgeport Fabrics; and doing extensive interior work in the Stratfield and Barnum hotels.

The John L. Simpson Company has been involved in bank construction and remodeling since its early years. At first, Simpson renovated the main offices of leading area financial institutions. Then it expanded its expertise with the advent of the branch system in the 1940s, constructing new offices, reconverting other buildings such as gas stations into branches, and remodeling existing banking facilities. Later, automatic teller machines and drive-up windows were added to the firm's service credentials.

When Simpson passed away in 1970, his nephew Clifford capably led the firm until his retirement in 1980. At that time the John L. Simpson Company was purchased and incorporated by today's president, Donald Keegan.

Like Simpson, Keegan learned the business from the job site to the office. He joined the firm in 1959 as an apprentice following service in the Navy in the construction battalion. He worked his way up to supervisor and later to estimator, overseeing the building of two new bank branches and several bank remodeling jobs.

Today the John L. Simpson Company, located on Huntington Road, continues its tradition of superior contracting. Although still specializing in bank remodeling, contracts, ranging from Greenwich to Hartford, also cover work for office buildings, factories, and educational institutions.

The firm's thirty employees, with an average of fifteen years' service with the John L. Simpson Company, are all skilled craftsmen and mechanics, capable of handling a variety of commercial work. Much of the mill work for major projects takes place right in the Simpson workshop. For the past fifteen years the business has done all its formica fabricating on the premises, building custom-made cabinets and counters.

Donald Keegan and his employees can boast that their fine reputation precedes them. Word-of-mouth recommendations and repeat client business keep the firm very busy. People know they can turn to the John L. Simpson Company, Inc., for superior work.

SACRED HEART UNIVERSITY

Sacred Heart University in Fairfield was founded in 1963 by the Most Reverend Walter W. Curtis, Bishop of the Diocese of Bridgeport, with a goal of providing a liberal arts education to the commuting student of southwestern Connecticut. Since its founding over 7,000 men and women have graduated from the institution.

From the original 173 students and a faculty numbering 12, the university has grown to more than 5,000 full- and part-time students and over 300 full- and part-time faculty. Students can earn undergraduate degrees in twenty-two majors encompassing business, the humanities, and the sciences. In addition, master's degrees are offered in business administration, teaching, applied operations research, and religion.

Nearly 90 percent of Sacred

Heart's students are employed either full or part time, yet they find time for a variety of extracurricular activities, including sororities/fraternities, clubs, honor societies, publications, student government, and athletics. Campus facilities include an academic center, a modern library housing 120,000 volumes, a well-equipped computer center, studios for art and media studies, language labs, science labs, and WSHU-FM, a 1,000-watt radio station.

Sacred Heart University sponsors a wide variety of cultural activities open to the community. In its 23-year history many distinguished persons have appeared on campus, including Isaac Bashevis Singer, Vice-President George Bush, former United Nations Secretary-General Kurt Waldheim, Edwin Newman,

Conveniently located just south of the Merritt Parkway at Exit 47, the 53-acre campus at 5229 Park Avenue on the Bridgeport-Fairfield line is easily accessible to the community it serves. The library is shown here.

Dr. Mary Leakey, Rollo May, James Buckley, Jackie Robinson, and Cardinal John J. O'Connor.

Three men have served as president: Dr. William H. Conley, Robert Kidera, and Dr. Thomas P. Melady.

FAIRFIELD UNIVERSITY

When a guide to colleges reported that students rave about Fairfield University and "the solid liberal arts education and relaxed setting that it provides," it was no surprise to either undergraduates or alumni.

In 1942 Fairfield University was chartered as the twenty-sixth Jesuit institution of higher learning in the United States, and the first class was graduated in 1951. Today a coeducational institution with 2,800 undergraduates from thirty-three states and five countries, Fairfield University is respected for programs in the natural and behavioral sciences, especially the pre-medical and pre-dental curriculum, as well as the pre-law program. There are also new majors in computer science and communication arts. Also acclaimed are the School of Business, which offers majors in accounting, finance, management, marketing, and computer information systems, and the School of Nursing, which offers three years

of clinical experience.

Among the keys to Fairfield's reputation is the commitment to keep enrollment at manageable size. The fifteen-to-one student-faculty ratio assures close student-faculty contact.

Graduate courses have been offered since 1950; currently degrees are offered by the School of Graduate and Continuing Education, the Graduate School of Communication, and the School of Business. Diverse programs are also available in the evenings and on weekends for adults to attend on either a credit or non-credit basis as part-time students. part-time students.

The 200-acre wooded campus has twenty-six buildings including the modern Recreational Complex, the Alumni Hall, the Nyselius Library, and the Center for Financial Studies, built cooperatively by Fairfield University and the National Council of Savings Institutions.

The 200-acre campus of Fairfield University has twenty-six buildings, including Bellarmine Hall (shown here), eight modern residential halls, a science center, a library with more than 200,000 volumes, a recreation complex with an Olympic-size swimming pool, and a campus center.

BLUE CROSS & BLUE SHIELD OF CONNECTICUT

Joseph F. Duplinsky, a Bridgeport native and leader of the health insurance company for more than forty years.

In 1936 a group of New Haven-area businessmen founded the Hospital Service Fund, Inc. Beginning in a rented corner of the New Haven Chamber of Commerce headquarters and equipped only with a chair, a desk, and a typewriter, the fledgling company represented a pragmatic assessment of the marketplace, a willingness to test new ideas, and a

The present corporate headquarters of Blue Cross & Blue Shield of Connecticut in New Haven.

determination to provide a service for a changing society.

Today that company is Blue Cross & Blue Shield of Connecticut, processing over ten million health benefit claims totaling over $700 million annually. With approximately 1.5 million members, it is the state's largest health insurer.

Through almost five decades the country, the state, and the city of Bridgeport changed markedly. The neophyte insurance company changed with it.

In 1937 the firm, renamed Plan for Hospital Care, Inc., offered a health insurance contract that provided twenty-one days of semiprivate hospital care each calendar year and cost $1.50 per month for family coverage.

Through the late 1930s and early 1940s the Plan's enrollment grew by 45 percent. By 1938 the first Blue Cross baby was born. By 1943 the company had enrolled 300,000 members.

After World War II the firm, now known as Blue Cross, evolved and grew as rapidly as did the postwar society. Connecticut Medical Service (CMS), a sister corporation, was founded to insure physician and medical costs outside the hospital. By 1950 there were 250 Blue Cross em-

ployees and a new headquarters on Whitney Avenue in New Haven. Membership also passed the one-million mark as employers such as those in Bridgeport began to subscribe to the insurance plan on behalf of their employees.

Responsive to the needs of its members, Blue Cross added new benefits for catastrophic illness, new-born babies, dental plans, prescription drugs, home care, supplements to Medicare, hospice coverage, and more.

At that same time the company moved swiftly with the advancing computer age. By 1960 electronic data-processing equipment was in use and a computer system was established to link hospitals directly with Blue Cross. By 1977 Blue Cross had merged with CMS to become Blue Cross & Blue Shield of Connecticut.

As the firm continued to grow and to meet the needs of its members, medicine and technology leaped forward. Blue Cross & Blue Shield responded.

Today, built on five decades of strength, the health insurer remains the largest in the state and continues to evolve. In 1984 Blue Cross & Blue Shield of Connecticut converted from a hospital and medical service corporation to a domestic mutual insurance

The original location of the fledgling company that eventually became Blue Cross & Blue Shield of Connecticut.

company. Bound by fewer regulatory restraints, it is now developing a more flexible structure, one that can bridge the past and the present with the future.

Because Connecticut citizens require more and different types of health care today, Blue Cross & Blue Shield of Connecticut is affiliated with Constitution Health Network, an independent practice association model health maintenance organization.

At the same time, the health insurer is affiliated with Community Health Care Plan (CHCP), a staff model health maintenance organization in Connecticut. As health care and the delivery of health care

changes, Blue Cross & Blue Shield of Connecticut changes as well.

The organization also operates a wholly owned subsidiary—ProMed Systems, Inc. ProMed Systems brings affordable state-of-the-art computer technology into the physician's office. The new venture represents a matching of two corporate objectives—a commitment to minimize its benefits administration costs and a willingness to test a new product in a new market. Another departure from the insurer came with the establishment of Connecticut American Life Insurance Company, a domestic mutual life insurance company that allows Blue Cross & Blue Shield of Connecticut to expand its market share by offering a more complete package of benefits to employers and employees.

Just as Bridgeport has been a cor-

nerstone of the state's past, just as the city has grown, changed, and prospered, so too has Blue Cross & Blue Shield of Connecticut—in the belief that innovation, evolution, and development are needed to sustain progress.

The link between Bridgeport and Blue Cross & Blue Shield of Connecticut goes beyond its benefit plans. Joseph F. Duplinsky, a Bridgeport native, guided the emerging corporation for more than forty years. His service included roles as general manager, president, and chairman of the board. His achievements included membership and financial growth, consolidation with CMS, pioneering programs such as home care, prospective reimbursement, and hospice care, and conversion of the firm into a domestic mutual insurance company.

PEOPLE'S BANK

New England's largest mutual savings bank, with sixty-five offices in five Connecticut counties, began in 1842 as Bridgeport Savings Bank in the store of iron merchants George and Sherwood Sterling on Water Street. The first account was opened on December 24, 1842, by the Fairweather lighthouse keeper for his daughter, Helen Moore. Four months passed before a single depositor withdrew any money—one dollar.

The bank's charter set a $400 limit on the amount any one person could deposit at a time, and no deposits could be made to an account after it had reached $1,000. This policy, in effect for fifty years, discouraged deposits from wealthy people. Needless to say, People's is no longer so conservative in receiving deposits.

In 1843, for an annual rent of twelve dollars, the little savings bank moved to a second-floor room near the corner of Water and Wall streets. In 1845, two weeks before Christmas, a fire spread from an oyster saloon and burned half the downtown section to the ground. Virtually overnight the business center moved from Water Street to Main Street, where it remains today.

The bank purchased its present facility at Main and State streets in 1850 for $2,100. Today on that same site stands the classic three-story columned bank building that was erected in 1918, and next to it stands the modern eleven-story glass-and-steel structure completed in 1965.

After the Civil War famous showman P.T. Barnum bought six big farms in East Bridgeport and became the first large-scale developer the institution helped to finance. Barnum would supply a Bridgeporter with at least 80 percent of the cost of home construction—so long as that individual gave up smoking and drinking.

In 1927 Bridgeport Savings and another local bank, People's Savings, merged to become Bridgeport-People's Savings. During the Depression the institution advanced more than one million dollars to pay the delinquent taxes of borrowers so they wouldn't lose their homes. It also made the first FHA loan in the state.

After merging with Southport Savings in 1955, the bank continued to expand aggressively, greatly increasing its number of offices. In 1981 it acquired First Stamford Bank and Trust Company; the following year it acquired Guardian Federal Savings and Loan Association; and in 1983 it

In 1843 the bank paid twelve dollars a year rent for this second-floor room (stars in windows) near Water and Wall streets in Bridgeport.

merged with National Savings Bank of New Haven, State Bank for Savings in Hartford, and People's Bank of Vernon.

In 1974 People's became one of the first two banks in the nation to provide pay-by-phone service to its customers, and in 1981 it established its first commercial banking department. Today People's has five regional commercial banking offices located throughout Connecticut.

In 1983 the institution's name was shortened to People's Bank. Its discount brokerage subsidiary, People's Securities, Inc., was admitted to the New York Stock Exchange in 1984. In 1985 People's Trust and Financial Management Department was formed.

Today, with assets of over four billion dollars, nine offices in Bridgeport alone, and 2,000 employees, People's Bank is in the top ten of savings banks nationwide and is also New England's largest residential mortgage lender. Its original philosophy of personalized individual service has been strengthened and expanded to include new dimensions of consumer and commercial banking services.

People's Bank's current corporate headquarters at the corner of Main and State streets. Construction will soon begin on a new headquarters building on Main Street. Architect Richard Meier has designed a 440,000-square-foot building encompassing nearly three acres surrounding the historic Barnum Museum.

ELMER R. CRAW REALTORS

In 1959 Elmer R. Craw opened a one-man real estate office with a card table, two folding chairs, and a telephone at 4007 Main Street in Bridgeport. After spending the five previous years working in his brother's real estate office, he knew this would be his lifelong career and was ready to get started on his own.

Over twenty-five years later that office on Main Street is still standing. However, it is now three times larger and only one of three Elmer R. Craw offices in Bridgeport; the firm has a total of ten offices located in eight towns throughout New Haven and Fairfield counties. The one-man staff is now enlarged to 120 sales people and 12 administrative assistants, serving clients from Westport to New Haven. In addition, Craw is now assisted by his sons, David and Jeffrey, and John Cannone, general manager.

Elmer R. Craw Realtors goes beyond the typical run-of-the-mill real estate business. In 1978, for example, Craw opened the first real estate sales training school. Experts in the field supply incoming agents the most up-to-date information on real estate practices, time utilization, goal development and achievement, financing, advertising and marketing, and real estate law. The firm also has seminars throughout the year for its staff on the latest financial and real estate news and services.

Elmer R. Craw Realtors is the only local real estate business to provide daily, on-site mortgage approvals. Each day an area savings bank officer is present to underwrite loans for prospective home buyers. In addition, Craw's full-time relocation department in Monroe provides all the assistance any newcomer would need, including information on education, medical care, retail shopping, and community services. Similarly, when someone is leaving the area, Craw's countrywide network of contacts helps make the move a comfortable one.

The firm's deep commitment to Bridgeport makes it stand out from other agencies. In addition to the office on Main Street, there are recently

Standing in front of his original Bridgeport office at 4007 Main Street, Elmer R. Craw (left) congratulates the winner of the first of three cars in the 1985 Sales Associates Listing Contest.

opened locations on East Main Street in the Beardsley Park area and in Black Rock in the Beverly Theater building.

Elmer R. Craw Realtors' services extend well into the community. Every year its agents collect for Muscular Dystrophy research. Each dollar that is raised is then matched by the firm itself, making Elmer R. Craw the largest local contributor to the fight against MD.

The community's response to Elmer R. Craw's commitment and professional services speaks for itself. Since it first opened, the firm has only experienced one year when the number of housing units sold did not increase. And, in fact, during the 1980-1981 recession when the real estate market fell so dramatically, the phones never stopped ringing at Elmer R. Craw Realtors, and business increased. It's in situations such as these that the agents really prove their worth. As Elmer R. Craw states: "When the market is good, any one can sell real estate. It's when the going gets tough that Elmer R. Craw's professional sales people really motivate themselves and show how exceptional they are."

MECHANICS AND FARMERS SAVINGS BANK FSB

David J. Sullivan, Jr., president and chief executive officer of Mechanics and Farmers Savings Bank FSB.

In the 115 years since the Connecticut Legislature chartered Mechanics and Farmers Savings Bank of East Bridgeport, as it was first known, the bank has dedicated itself to serving its immediate community and staying tuned to its next logical direction of growth and service.

Right from the beginning, the name the founders selected for the bank reflected this philosophy. Opening its first office at 189 East Washington Avenue, just off East Main Street, the bank chose the busy center of East Bridgeport's growing industrial mosaic. "Mechanics" was the name given to workers in the city's factories, which were moving from serving the horse-and-buggy days, producing whips and carriage trim, to turning out sewing machines, metallic cartridges, and factory machinery, the new wonders of Yankee ingenuity.

As the bank's founders focused on serving the growing industrial development of East Bridgeport, they must have been keeping an eye on the surrounding agrarian region. By including "Farmers" as the other element in the bank's name, and featuring beehive and wheat shaft designs on its bankbooks and reports to depositors, those earliest Mechanics and Farmers leaders demonstrated a vision that looked beyond the smokestacks to the next logical group of families to be served: those who earned their living off the land.

Staying alert to new markets and new ways to serve has been the continuous thread running through Mechanics and Farmers' 115-year history.

The bank opened for business on the first day of October 1873, in its new temporary quarters rented for twelve dollars a month. With a ten-cent minimum required to open an account, the first of the three accounts opened that first day was Judge David B. Lockwood's. It amounted to ten dollars, a large sum in those times.

The Mechanics and Farmers bank remained five years at its east side location. It moved across the river in 1878, to downtown Bridgeport's bustling business and banking center located in the Main and Wall streets region. The bank changed locations a few times more to gain additional space to match its growth.

Then, in 1915, it finally settled at 930 Main Street, its present address. It continued to acquire adjacent space as its business expanded, until today it occupies the entire block at the northeast corner of Main and State streets.

It remained largely a Bridgeport-area bank until 1970, when it began developing its present wide network of branches extending throughout Fairfield and New Haven counties. Mechanics and Farmers opened its first office outside the Bridgeport region in Westport to serve that town's substantial home mortgage business.

The subsequent extension of services along the shoreline to Greenwich, and north to Bridgeport's neighboring towns, continued through the 1970s. Then, a major event took place that was the key to the expansion of Mechanics and Farmers into the upper western part of Fairfield County: two great old banks merged. Mechanics and Farmers and the New Canaan Savings Bank joined in December 1982. In addition to New Canaan, this landmark event extended the bank to Wilton, where the New Canaan Savings Bank maintained a branch office.

This broader market area, which resulted from the merger, enabled the bank to gain mortgage customers in northern Fairfield County. In order to serve these new customers, the bank switched its charter from state to federal in 1984 so it could open offices in Ridgefield, Danbury, and, later, in Milford. The Milford office, which was opened in June 1985, was Mechanics and Farmers' first office in New Haven County. In January 1986 the bank purchased an attractive brick building in the historic village section of Southport. A full-service branch office is planned for that site to serve the surrounding area.

Underlying the bank's progress over more than a century has been its dedication to the home mortgage business. Mechanics and Farmers' first mortgage loan of $200 on Bridgeport's east side is the tiny base upon which today's $275-million annual mortgage business is built. Ever-new mortgage concepts to meet current needs have brought innovations like the bank's new SMART Mortgage(sm), which features biweekly payments to save families huge amounts of interest.

Mechanics and Farmers is unusual in that it has had only eight presidents over the past 115 years. Beginning in 1873 with George W. Hayes, the bank's chronology of presidents includes Lyman Catlin, John Otis, Philip S. Davison, Carl R. Switzgable, Victor C. Cogswell, Edward R. Kasparek, and David J. Sullivan, Jr., the current president and chief executive officer.

These leaders of the bank have guided it through good times and bad, and two world wars. They have brought creative solutions to the ever-changing needs of families buying homes, managing finances, and educating children, from Bridgeport's colorful post-Civil War days to these closing years of the twentieth century.

REMINGTON ARMS COMPANY, INC.

Eliphalet Remington was not at all pleased with any gun that could be purchased in 1816. So he decided to manufacture his own gun, one that would be better than any he could buy. Following the completion of his first rifle, Remington was not the only one happy with the results. It was such a good product that at first his neighbors and later customers worldwide ordered others like it. Soon Remington and his son were creating a new American industry.

The business quickly outgrew its first little shop and moved to a large farm near the Erie Canal—the site of the current Remington plant at Ilion, New York. The company continued to expand, and played an important role in the westward movement of the frontier during the nineteenth century.

In 1888 Bridgeport businessman Marcellus Hartley purchased controlling interest in the firm. He had previously acquired two small businesses in Bridgeport and had combined them to form the Union Metallic Cartridge Co., Inc. (UMC). This venture was the beginning of the first successful manufacture of metallic cartridges in the United States.

At first the emphasis was on rim fire ammunition, but before long UMC revolutionized the industry with the introduction of the center fire cartridge. In the 1880s the firm also developed paper shot shells; later, when smokeless powder came into being, UMC pioneered that product's use in metallic cartridges.

In 1916 Remington, as a manufacturer of firearms, and UMC, as a producer of ammunition, combined with the M. Hartley Co. to form Remington Arms Company, Inc. Later, in 1933, E.I. du Pont de Nemours and Co. purchased a controlling interest in Remington Arms. Du Pont purchased the remaining 30 percent of outstanding stock in 1980.

During World War II, for the fifth time in Remington's history, the U.S. government asked the company to help arm the nation in time of war. The program undertaken far surpassed any similar activity in the past. It required a twentyfold expansion in personnel to 82,500 employees companywide, with over 14,000 at the Bridgeport site and an output of war materials valued at more than $1.2 billion. Similarly, during the Korean and Vietnam conflicts Remington Arms Company helped meet the nation's needs.

Remington's Bridgeport plant is now one of the world's foremost

The 167-foot-high Shot Tower is used for the manufacture of shotgun shell pellets.

manufacturers of .22 caliber rim fire sporting ammunition. Remington has worked hard to maintain its long-standing reputation among sportsmen as the industry's standard for performance, quality, and dependability.

The personal foresight and genius of three individuals—Eliphalet Remington, Marcellus Hartley, and Eleuthère Irénée du Pont—have resulted in the Remington Arms Company of today—a corporation that surely has lived up to the strict guidelines set forth in that small New York shop more than 150 years ago.

The Remington Arms Company, Inc., in Bridgeport, circa 1920.

SIKORSKY AIRCRAFT

Igor I. Sikorsky (1885-1972), who in 1939 developed the first helicopter capable of sustained flight and satisfactory control. The VS-300 was the first in a long line of helicopters bearing his name.

The Sikorsky S-76 executive helicopter combines the latest in aircraft systems technology with the quiet comfort of a limousine.

On September 14, 1939, after years of serious study and research, Igor Sikorsky flew his first successful helicopter—the VS-300. The new, fragile-looking aircraft, built by the Vought-Sikorsky Division of United Aircraft Corporation in Stratford, was in sharp contrast to the sleek Navy scouts and bombers then being built at the plant.

A demonstration of the new aircraft in 1940 was attended by an enthusiastic visitor, Army Air Corps flier H. Franklin Gregory. He became the driving force that eventually brought the helicopter into military use.

On January 10, 1941, the U.S. Army gave Vought-Sikorsky a contract to build a two-seat helicopter for use as an observation trainer. Vought remained in the expanded Stratford plant mass-producing Corsair fighters for the Marine Corps and the Navy while the Sikorsky Division, with only a few hundred people, took over the renovated Crane Plumbing Building in Bridgeport. This Bridgeport plant was the first structure in the world to house the mass production of helicopters.

Many history-making flights of rotary-wing aircraft were made at the Bridgeport plant. Many of the most famous helicopters ever to have flown have been manufactured there. Not the least among them is the R-4, the first production helicopter. Delivered to the Army in 1943, it was the only helicopter to serve in World War II and was credited with the first combat rescue in Burma that same year. The R-4 is now on permanent display in the Smithsonian Institution's National Air Museum.

Today United Technologies' Sikorsky helicopters occupy a dominant international position in the intermediate-to-heavy range of helicopters (10,000 to 70,000 pounds gross weight). They are used by all U.S. military services, the Coast Guard, the military services of more than thirty countries, and by commercial operators worldwide.

The Bridgeport plant, with more than 500,000 square feet of floor space, has high-bay assembly areas, flight hangars, and flight fields, and also serves as Sikorsky's Northeast Service Center for its civilian S-76 helicopter. As Fairfield County's largest employer, Sikorsky has a total work force of 11,500 people.

Of all the firm's achievements since the early days of the VS-300, none gave the late Igor Sikorsky more satisfaction than the number of lives saved with his aircraft. The best estimates now put the total at well over one million. Many of those lives were spared because of the helicopter's special ability to hover and make rescues under conditions that were otherwise inaccessible. Those life-saving missions range from a wounded soldier rushed to medical aid or a lost child found wandering in a swamp to mass airlifts of hundreds of people in peril during natural disasters such as floods or earthquakes.

Igor Sikorsky, Orville Wright, and Lieutenant Colonel Frank Gregory, upon delivery of the first helicopter to the military services, an R-4 built in Bridgeport and received by the Army Air Corps at Wright Field, Dayton, Ohio, in 1943.

THE COCA-COLA BOTTLING COMPANY OF NEW YORK

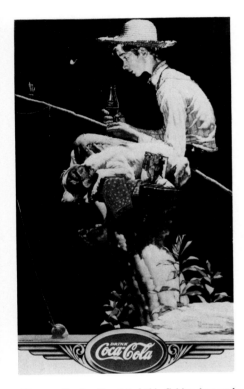

Norman Rockwell painted this fishing boy and his dog for the company's 1935 calendar.

Today the trucks of The Coca-Cola Bottling Company of New York deliver more than 20 varieties of soda in 127 different packages to the people of Bridgeport. Back in 1921, however, when Coke New York acquired the Bridgeport franchise, the consumer did not face such a dizzying array of choices. In those days The Coca-Cola Company sold one drink in only one package—the memorable 6.5-ounce Georgia green glass bottle.

In 1921 Coke was just beginning to emerge as the preeminent national soft drink. It had already conquered the South. The drink was invented in Atlanta in 1886. However, in the North people had not yet been convinced that any chilled soft drink should be consumed between October and April. Obviously, the early workers in Bridgeport made some headway against this regrettable notion,

and in the late 1920s the company was forced to seek larger headquarters at 286 Knowlton Street, at the corner of Barnum Avenue.

However, not until the Depression did sales of Coke really begin to take off in Bridgeport and other major cities in the Northeast. Bridgeport then quickly became one of Coke New York's strongest markets, so much so that in 1938 a bidding war developed over the franchise. Coke New York pondered many appealing offers, but as Bridgeport's sales continued to accelerate, it decided not to part with this prized territory.

In the 1950s and 1960s Coke New York introduced many new products, including Tab, Fresca, and Sprite, and packages, and their success ultimately changed the way the firm did business in Bridgeport. At first the company expanded within the city, leasing 18,000 square feet of warehouse space at 10 Maple Street in 1965. But the industry was changing, and it was gradually becoming less and less economical to produce soda on Bridgeport's antiquated machinery. The bottling line at Knowlton Street filled only 6.5-ounce bottles and at a rate of seventy-five per minute. The modern equipment Coke New York had installed elsewhere reached a speed of up to 500 bottles (or 1,300 cans) per minute and handled many different sizes of containers.

As a result, in 1970 Coke New York decided to stop production at the Knowlton Street plant. Nine years later the firm also outgrew the warehouse on Maple Street, and since then has been serving the city from a huge warehouse located five miles away in Fairfield.

For many years The Coca-Cola Bottling Company of New York has been an active participant in the Bridgeport community, contributing time, money, and free products to the Special Olympics, senior citizens'

groups, church activities, school programs, and other cultural events such as concerts by the American Wind Symphony. Many company employees are active in Bridgeport's community affairs, and one former employee, Leonard Paoletta, even served as the city's mayor.

The 1936 calendar, illustrated by N.C. Wyeth, observed the fiftieth anniversary of Coca-Cola.

293

MOORE SPECIAL TOOL CO., INC.

Moore Special Tool Co., Inc., has come a long way since 1924—as has the city in which the company has flourished. Founded that year by Richard F. Moore as a small tool and die shop—on the second floor of a building, above a diner, on John Street—the enterprise made tooling for the then-bustling clock and brass shops of the Naugatuck Valley.

Ten years later, with twenty employees, the firm moved to Remer Street, again on the second floor.

Moore Special Tool Co., Inc., marketed its first machine tool in 1932, the model No. 1 Jig Borer, and the stage was set for rapid growth.

Wayne R. Moore, president and chief executive officer of Moore Special Tool, stands next to one of the company's most advanced ultra-precise machining systems, the Moore M-18 Aspheric Generator.

In 1937 the company, with forty-five employees in the heart of the Depression, leased the Weed Manufacturing facilities on Union Avenue to provide needed production space.

Then, in 1940, Moore introduced a new machine tool it had invented, the No. 1 Jig Grinder. This first jig grinder overcame a perennial problem for tool and die makers having to jig bore parts in "soft" metals and alloys and somehow try to compensate for the distortions that resulted from subsequent hardening. With the jig grinder, holes could be ground precisely to location after hardening.

That same year, with employment at eighty-five, ground was broken for a new building on Union Avenue.

As more advanced jig borers and jig grinders came into production, and with the introduction of the firm's new universal measuring ma-

chines in 1957, the Belknap Building and adjoining land on Union Avenue were purchased. Plant capacity was now 150,000 square feet and employment stood at 270.

So successful were the measuring machines that the Measuring Machine Laboratory Building, a specially designed facility employing advanced concepts of temperature control, was constructed in 1964. That same year the Manufacturers Iron Foundry was purchased and razed to provide an additional 50,000 square feet of parking for Moore employees.

In 1966 the Reliable Steel Drum Company building next door was acquired. Most of it was torn down and a new, completely air-conditioned three-story structure was erected on its site.

By 1979 the number of Moore employees passed the 400 mark.

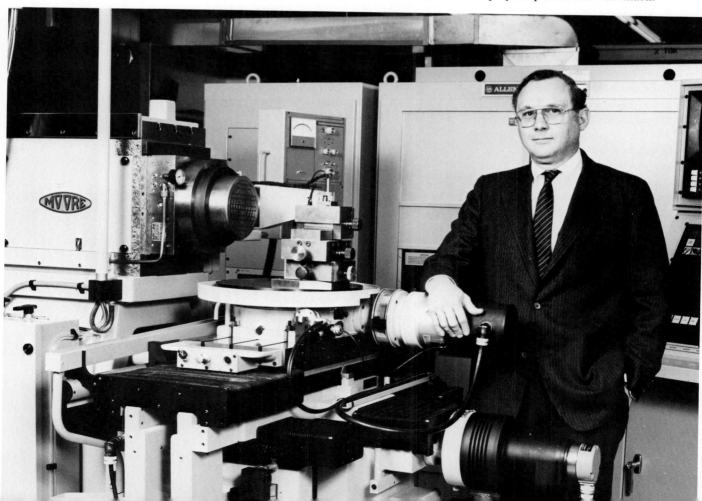

The latest addition, a three-story structure, was built in 1981 to provide needed manufacturing space to accommodate growing sales and to modernize offices. Total space then exceeded 295,000 square feet.

As a responsive, market-oriented company, Moore has led the industry with increasingly more accurate and more productive machines. In 1984 the firm introduced its G-18 computer numerically controlled (CNC) Series 1000 Jig Grinder, a highly automated machine tool that has rapidly become a new standard for the industry. One year later the company unveiled its latest CNC universal measuring machines, five-axis models with laser feedback and Moore's specially developed software.

The corporation also manufactures ultra-precise CNC diamond turning and grinding machines, called aspheric generators. These machines produce parts to optical quality measured in tolerances of millionths of an inch.

Among the company's most important metrology products are the 1440 Precision Index and 1440 Small-Angle Divider, which are ultimate standards for angular measurement. The accuracy of the 1440 spaces of the 1440 Precision Index is $\pm 1/10$th second of arc. The 1440 Small-Angle Divider permits direct reading of the circle to 12.96 million parts with an overall accuracy of $\pm \frac{1}{2}$ second of arc.

The firm also remanufactures and upgrades used Moore jig borers, jig grinders, and universal measuring machines. With remanufactured, warranted-as-new Moore equipment available for fast delivery, the organization thus offers its customers a broad selection of machines to meet their needs and fit their budgets.

Moore's strong commitment to automation and computers covers more than adaptation of these technologies to the advanced machines it designs and manufactures. A multi-year pro-

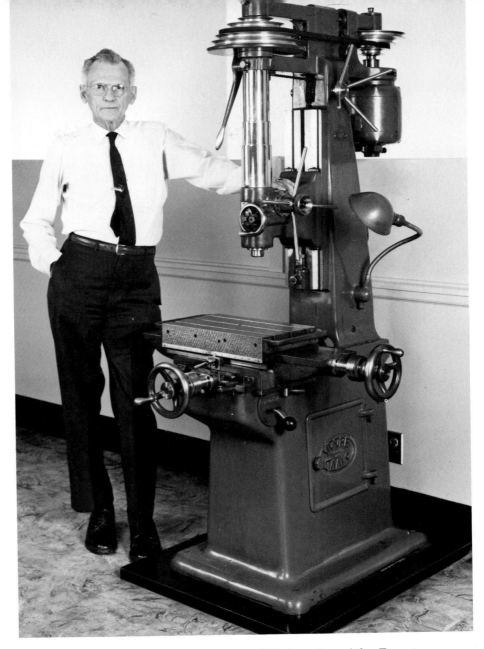

Richard F. Moore, founder of Moore Special Tool, with the Moore No. 1 Jig Borer, introduced in 1932. The machine employed hardened, ground, and lapped lead screws.

gram will also integrate computer technology into every facet of its business, including design, manufacture, finance, and purchasing.

Today the corporation successfully sells and services its products worldwide. A Moore subsidiary in Switzerland serves the European market, with distributors handling the Far East and other international areas.

The company's contributions to international trade were recognized first in 1971 with the President's "E" Award for Exports, and again in 1981 with the selective President's "E" Star Award for Exports.

Moore remains a "family" enterprise. Many of the immediate family members are a part of the operation. Wayne R. Moore succeeded his father in 1974 as president and chief executive officer.

There are numerous employee relatives—brothers, sisters, daughters, wives, uncles, and cousins—as well as neighbors. The result is a highly motivated and closely knit organization, thoroughly dedicated to precision and pride of workmanship.

As Moore Special Tool Co., Inc., confidently strides into its seventh decade, the firm is ready to meet the challenges of the future. Its commitment to the city of Bridgeport that nurtured it remains steadfast.

ANTHONY JULIAN RAILROAD CONSTRUCTION COMPANY

Anthony D. Julian, with a portrait of his father, Anthony F., in the background, who together founded the Anthony Julian Railroad Construction Company in 1946.

Italian-born Anthony F. Julian came to Bridgeport with his family when he was just a year old. As a young adult he worked for a railroad construction company, and after gaining the necessary experience started his own firm in 1946 with his son, Anthony D. Julian. The business was primarily concerned with adding spur lines and repairing tracks throughout Connecticut and New York.

In the following years Anthony's other sons, Raymond, Donald, and Dominick, joined the company as they came of age. They were later joined by Anthony's daughters, Mary Jane, Barbara, and Mildred, who also began working for the growing enterprise.

Business growth and venturing into new lines of work went hand in hand. Soon the firm's name no longer identified all the services it offered. The construction company began to undertake contract work for the local utilities, such as The Southern Connecticut Gas Company and the Bridgeport Hydraulic Company.

That work soon expanded into installing main storm and sanitary sewer lines and water and gas lines for municipalities and utility companies.

For the first nine years the business was run out of the Julian home on Lincoln Avenue in Bridgeport. Then, in 1955, the firm purchased the 1.5-acre Beachmont Dairy property nearby. The dairy warehouse, which is used for the storage and repair of equipment, still remains and Julian Railroad erected a one-story building for its offices.

In 1968 Anthony turned over the business to his four sons. His eldest son, Anthony, retired from the company in 1979 and is a consultant for his sons' construction firm. Raymond is now president of Anthony Julian Railroad Construction, Donald is vice-president, and Dominick is secretary/treasurer.

In the late 1960s and early 1970s the firm acquired additional adjoin-

The current owners and officers of the company (left to right) are Donald Julian, vice-president; Raymond Julian, president; and Dominick Julian, secretary/treasurer.

ing property in anticipation of its continued growth. In 1978 a new seven-room, two-story building was constructed on the now three acres of Julian property.

Along with the corporation's expansion came a further broadening of its services. Recent contracts include the Frances J. Clark Industrial Park in Bethel and the Wallingford Business Park. The firm continues to do extensive work for the utilities as well as sewer work for municipalities throughout the state. Recently it also reconstructed a pond in the town of Stratford. This unique project included deepening and widening the pond, building stone walls and walkway areas, and completing all landscaping.

Over the past four decades Anthony Julian Railroad Construction Company has grown considerably beyond the services implied by its name. And surely this trend will continue in the future. In the years to come the Julian children, and now their children's children, will continue in the firm's tradition of venturing into new areas and looking for new opportunities.

DEVAR, INC.

When the U.S. Navy needs highly sophisticated computing temperature transmitters for its new and retrofit ships, including aircraft carriers, it knows exactly where to turn. When nuclear power plants, chemical industries, and refineries need analog process control instrumentation, they know what Bridgeport company to contact. When major computer terminal manufacturers need CRT pens for computer-aided design and manufacturing (CAD/CAM), they know who to call. And, when manufacturers of military torpedos and fighter planes must have state-of-the-art, thick film hybrid microcircuits and optical detectors, the answer is the same. They contact Devar, Inc., a firm known worldwide for its analog electronic controls and hybrid microcircuits.

In 1976 chairman of the board Anthony Ruscito purchased Devar from Bell and Howell. Prior to the purchase Ruscito had developed three other high-tech electronic manufacturing companies into profitable enterprises, and he wanted to add this spin-off of Bell and Howell's to his list.

And so he did. Under the direction of his son, Anthony Ruscito, Jr., who serves as president, Devar is now a highly sophisticated, state-of-the-art electronic manufacturer. Ruscito Jr.

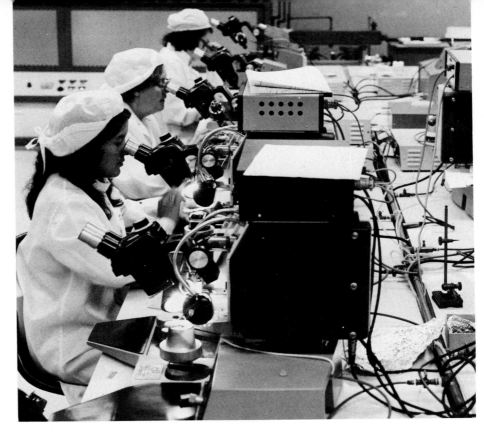

Devar, Inc., is known worldwide for its analog electronic controls and hybrid microcircuits. Shown here is the microcircuits assembly area.

follows his father's lead in having a strong engineering background. He received his mechanical engineering degree from Worchester Polytechnical Institute in 1970 and worked as an automatic machine design engineer for five years before joining Devar.

Other family members who aid in the company's success are wife Martha, secretary; daughter Marianne, treasurer; and Marianne's husband, Jeffrey Head, manager of production control. Also a factor in the firm's success is the expert guidance of chief engineer Andrew Gura and marketing manager T. Tomasko, who have been with Devar since 1968.

Devar is a class-one vendor for the process control instrumentation field. The company's reliable equipment has met such high safety standards that its instruments can go directly into the control centers of all major nuclear power plants.

The corporation is also the largest producer of CRT pens, manufacturing them in both the Bridgeport plant on Bostwick Avenue and at Information Control Corporation, a wholly owned subsidiary in Los Angeles. The CRT pens are used for design purposes on computer screens for medical, industrial, and military applications. In fact, Devar, Inc., is the only manufacturer with military-approved light pens.

Devar's thick film hybrid microcircuits and optical detectors have a variety of uses, including torpedo guidance, television cameras, fiber optics, telecommunications, blood-analyzing machines, and for controlling light intensity in the cockpits of military and private aircraft.

In 1980 the late Governor Ella Grasso named fifteen Connecticut companies that would join an industrial mission to China. The companies were seen as businesses with a bright future. Devar, Inc., was one of those chosen.

Control room instrumentation. Devar's equipment meets the highest safety standards so that its instruments can be used in high-reliability applications.

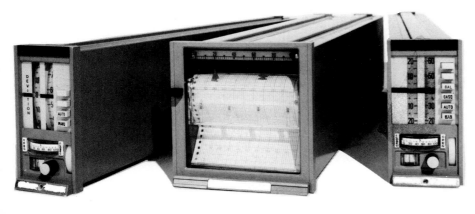

Patrons

BRIDGEPORT PATRONS

The following individuals, companies, and organizations have made a valuable commitment to the quality of this publication. Windsor Publications and The Business/Industry Council of the Bridgeport Economic Region gratefully acknowledge their participation in *Only in Bridgeport: An Illustrated History of the Park City.*

Louis A. Abriola & Son Funeral Home*
Alloy Engineering Company, Inc.*
The Bank Mart*
Blue Cross & Blue Shield of Connecticut*
The Bodine Corporation*
The Bridgeport and Port Jefferson Steamboat Company*
Bridgeport Hospital*
Bridgeport Hydraulic Company*
Seth O.L. Brody
Bryant Electric
A Division of Westinghouse Electric Corporation*
Bunker Ramo Corporation*
Cablevision Systems of Southern Connecticut*
Chapin & Bangs Company*
Chemical Connecticut Corporation-Affiliate of Chemical Bank
The Coca-Cola Bottling Company of New York*
Cohen and Wolf, P.C.*
Community Health Care Plan*
Como & Nicholson, Inc.*
Computer Processing Institute*
Conco Medical Co.
The Connecticut Bank and Trust Company*
Connecticut National Bank*
Elmer R. Craw Realtors*
Cummings & Lockwood*
Deloitte Haskins & Sells*
Devar, Inc.*
Diocese of Bridgeport*
Dresser Industries, Inc.*
The E&F Construction Company*
Fairfield University*

The First Connecticut Small Business Investment Co.
Fletcher Thompson*
General Electric Company*
Greater Bridgeport Transit District
Greenwood Insurance Agency
Hawley Industrial Supplies Incorporated*
Housatonic Community College
Harvey Hubbell Incorporated*
Anthony Julian Railroad Construction Company*
Kasper Associates, Inc.*
Lou Klein Associates*
P.J. Kuchma Construction Co., Inc.
Lafayette Bank & Trust Co.
Leake & Nelson Co.*
Lindquist Supply Company*
Mechanics and Farmers Savings Bank FSB*
Modern Plastics*
Moore Special Tool Co., Inc.*
People's Bank*
Physicians Health Services*
Post Publishing Company*
Rehabilitation Center of Eastern Fairfield County
Remington Arms Company, Inc.*
Rotair Industries, Inc.
Sacred Heart University*
St. Vincent's Medical Center*
The Schwerdtle Stamp Company*
Sikorsky Aircraft*
John L. Simpson Company, Inc.*
The Southern Connecticut Gas Company*
Sprague Meter Company*
Sturm, Ruger & Company, Inc.
The Swan Engraving Company*
Trefz Corporation*
United Illuminating*
University of Bridgeport*
University of Bridgeport Deans' Council
West End Lumber
West End Moving and Storage Company*
WICC 60*
Wright Investors' Service*
Karen E. Zavadsky
Zeldes, Needle & Cooper

*Partners in Progress of *Only in Bridgeport: An Illustrated History of the Park City.* The histories of these companies and organizations appear in Chapter X, beginning on page 224.

Bibliography

Barnum, Phineas T. *Struggles and Triumphs; or Forty Years' Recollections of P.T. Barnum.* Hartford: J.B. Burr, 1869.

Brilvitch, Charles W. *Landmark Architecture of Bridgeport, Connecticut: One Hundred Fifty Buildings Illustrating the Architectural Development of the City, 1663-1902.* Bridgeport: 1975. Typescript.

Brilvitch, Charles W. *Washington Park: A Guide to its Victorian Treasures.* Bridgeport: Upper East Side Neighborhood Housing Services, 1980.

Chance Vought Aircraft Corporation. *Wings for the Navy: A History of Chance Vought Aircraft.* Stratford, Connecticut: 1943.

Collier, Christopher. *The Pride of Bridgeport: Men and Machines in the Nineteenth Century.* Bridgeport: The Museum of Art, Science and Industry, 1979.

Connecticut National Bank. *Bridgeport's First Bank: The Story of Connecticut National Bank, 1806-1956.* Bridgeport: 1956.

Crispino, James A. *The Assimilation of Ethnic Groups: the Italian Case.* Staten Island, New York: Center for Migration Studies, 1980.

Curtiss, Lucy S. *Two Hundred Fifty Years: The Story of the United Congregational Church of Bridgeport, 1695-1945.* Bridgeport: 1945.

Danenberg, Elsie Nicholas. *The Story of Bridgeport.* Bridgeport: Bridgeport Centennial, 1936.

Desmond, Alice Curtis. *Barnum Presents General Tom Thumb.* New York: Macmillan, 1954.

Golovin, Anne Castrodale. *Bridgeport's Gothic Ornament: The Harral-Wheeler House.* Washington: Smithsonian Institution Press, 1972.

Guillette, Mary E. *American Indians in Connecticut, Past to Present. A Report Prepared for the Connecticut Indian Affairs Council.* Hartford: Connecticut Department of Environmental Protection, 1979.

Harris, Neil. *Humbug: The Art of P.T. Barnum.* Boston: Little, Brown, 1973.

Howell, Richard. *Tales from Bohemia Land.* Bridgeport: Bridgeport Herald Publishers, 1928.

Janick, Herbert F., Jr. *A Diverse People: Connecticut, 1914 to the Present.* Chester, Connecticut: Pequot Press, 1975.

Jones, Dick, ed. *Black Rock: a Bicentennial Picture Book: a Visual History of the Old Seaport of Bridgeport, Connecticut, 1644 to 1976.* Bridgeport: Black Rock Civic and Business Men's Club, 1976.

Koenig, Samuel. *Immigrant Settlements in Connecticut.* Hartford, Connecticut: Connecticut State Department of Education, 1938.

Municipal Register of the City of Bridgeport, Connecticut. Bridgeport: Controller, 1873-1961.

O'Dwyer, William J., and Randolph, Stella. *History by Contract: the Beginning of Motorized Aviation, August 14, 1901, Gustave Whitehead. Fairfield, Connecticut.* Leutershausen, West Germany: Fritz Majer and Son, 1978.

Olmstead, Alan. *Olmstead Papers on Jasper McLevy.* 1944. Historical Collections, Bridgeport Public Library.

Orcutt, Samuel. *The History of the Old Town of Stratford and the City of Bridgeport, Connecticut.* New Haven: Tuttle, Morehouse and Taylor, 1886.

Palmquist, David W. *Bridgeport: A Pictorial History.* Virginia Beach: The Donning Company, 1981. Revised edition, 1985.

Pearce, Arthur W. *The Future Out of the Past: An Illustrated History of the Warner Brothers Company on its 90th Anniversary.* Bridgeport: 1964.

Saxon, A.H. *Selected Letters of P.T. Barnum.* New York: Columbia University Press, 1983.

Stave, Bruce M. "The Great Depression and Urban Political Continuity: Bridgeport Chooses Socialism." In *Socialism and the Cities,* edited by Bruce M. Stave, pp. 157-183. Port Washington, New York: Kennikat Press, 1975.

Waldo, George C., ed. *History of Bridgeport and Vicinity.* New York: S.J. Clarke, 1917.

Others sources include numerous interviews and newspaper and magazine clippings, newspaper microfilm, maps, atlases, Bridgeport municipal records, pamphlets, and other materials available in the Historical Collections of the Bridgeport Public Library.

Index

BRIDGEPORT/FAIRFIELD COUNTY PARTNERS IN PROGRESS INDEX

Abriola & Son Funeral Home, Louis A., 267
Alloy Engineering Company, Inc., 229
Bank Mart, The, 263
Blue Cross & Blue Shield of Connecticut, 286-287
Bodine Corporation, The, 232
Bridgeport and Port Jefferson Steamboat Company, The, 280
Bridgeport Hospital, 258
Bridgeport Hydraulic Company, 244-245
Bryant Electric
  A Division of Westinghouse Electric Corporation, 236-237
Bunker Ramo Corporation, 262
Business/Industry Council of the Bridgeport Economic Region, The, 226
Cablevision Systems of Southern Connecticut, 281
Chapin & Bangs Company, 283
Coca-Cola Bottling Company of New York, The, 293
Cohen and Wolf, P.C., 233
Community Health Care Plan, 251
Como & Nicholson, Inc., 268
Computer Processing Institute, 273
Connecticut Bank and Trust Company, The, 239
Connecticut National Bank, 253
Craw Realtors, Elmer R., 289
Cummings & Lockwood, 242
Deloitte Haskins & Sells, 250
Devar, Inc., 297
Diocese of Bridgeport, 274-275
Dresser Industries, Inc., 256-257
E&F Construction Company, The, 246-247
Fairfield University, 285
Fletcher Thompson, 243
General Electric Company, 260-261
Hawley Industrial Supplies Incorporated, 254-255
Hubbell Incorporated, Harvey, 240-241
Julian Railroad Construction Company, Anthony, 296
Kasper Associates, Inc., 230
Klein Associates, Lou, 227
Leake & Nelson Co., 259
Lindquist Supply Company, 238
Mechanics and Farmers Savings Bank FSB, 290
Modern Plastics, 282
Moore Special Tool Co., Inc., 294-295
People's Bank, 288
Physicians Health Services, 271
Post Publishing Company, 248-249
Remington Arms Company, Inc., 291
Sacred Heart University, 285
St. Vincent's Medical Center, 228
Schwerdtle Stamp Company, The, 270

Sikorsky Aircraft, 292
Simpson Company, Inc., John L., 284
Southern Connecticut Gas Company, The, 276-277
Sprague Meter Company, 266
Swan Engraving Company, The, 272
Trefz Corporation, 278-279
United Illuminating, 234-235
University of Bridgeport, 264-265
West End Moving and Storage Company, 231
WICC 60, 252
Wright Investors' Service, 269

GENERAL INDEX
Italic numbers indicate illustrations

Aaron Turner's traveling circus, 71
Action for Bridgeport Community Development, 180, 194
Agriculture, 18, 19
Alexander, Dick, 64
Alhambra Music Hall, 35
American Graphophone Company, 128, *133*
American Museum, *75, 81*
American Revolution, 19
Ancient Order of Hibernians, 35, 41
Arendsen, Kathy, 148
Arsenal of Democracy, 41, 114
Atwater, Fred, 42, 155
Automobile Club of Bridgeport, *149, 203*
Avco, 121, 125

Bacon, Henry, 136
Baer, Arthur, 127
Bagley, John, 148
Bailey, George, 136
Bailey, James A., 90
Baldwin, Raymond, *164,* 164
Ball, Neal, 147
Banks: Bridgeport Bank, 98; Citytrust Bank, 96; Connecticut National Bank, 96, 98; Mechanics and Farmers Bank, 96; People's Bank, 96, *98,* 125, 193, 217
Barnum and Bailey Circus, 90
Barnum, Ephraim, 71
Barnum Festival, *91, 92,* 93, 121, 170
Barnum Museum, 68, 93, 194
Barnum, Phil, 71
Barnum, Philo, 81
Barnum, P.T., 12, 24, 34, 58, 64, 67-93, *69-70, 72-80, 82-83, 86, 88-89,* 112, 136, 152, 221; and Jenny Lind, *66, 77,* 81, *82,* 84; and Joice Heth, 71, *72;* and Tom Thumb, 68, *79, 80,* 81, *83, 86;* as mayor, 87-88, 90; contributions to Bridgeport, 68; establishment of Seaside Park, 87; family of, 71, 81, 87; home financing, 24, 68, 70-71; homes of, *75, 81, 85,* 87, 90
Barnum School, 93, 175
Barry, Joseph R., 132, 134
Barrymore, John, 128
Basset, Goody, 16

Bassick High School, 134
Beach, Lazarus, 63
Beardsley Dredging Company, 23
Beardsley, James, 136
Beardsley Park, 46, *126,* 136; Christmas Village, 200; zoo, 136, *138*
Behrens, William, 155, 157
Bellamy, Edward, 153
Bennett, Thaddeus, 19
Bethel African Methodist Episcopal Church, 53, *53*
Bifield, Daniel, 199
Big Chief Pan, 146, *147*
Billy Prince's bar, 151, 152
Birmingham, Eugene, 181
Bishop, Alfred, 22, *22*
Black and Tan saloon, 35
Blackham school, 57
Blanco, Jose, 148
Blizzards: of 1888, 184, *185;* of 1934, 184; of 1978, 184
Blodgett, William H., 155
Board of Education, formation, 54
Board of Trade, 98
Bohan, Ann, 60, 63
Bohemia, 35, 37, *38*
Bol, Manute, 149, *149*
Bon Ton, the, 46
Booth Memorial Park, *210*
Brakettes (softball), 148
Bramble, Mark, 93
Bresnahan, Roger, 184
Brewster, Pete, 151, *152,* 164
Bridgeport Bank, 98
Bridgeport Bears (baseball), 147
Bridgeport Bees (baseball), 147, 148
Bridgeport Brass Company, 25, 98, *99,* 101, 125, 199, *206, 211-213*
Bridgeport Deutsche Schulen, 41
Bridgeport Electric Light Company, 111
Bridgeport Gas Light Company, 111, 160
Bridgeport High School, *57,* 64, 147
Bridgeport Hospital, 60
Bridgeport Housing Company, 114
Bridgeport Hydraulic Company, *109,* 112, 160
Bridgeport image, 180, 191-200, 217-221; in films, 135-136; Up on Bridgeport campaign, 200
Bridgeport International Union of Firefighters, 121
Bridgeport Jets (football), 148
Bridgeport Machine Tool Company, 25
Bridgeport Public Library, 194
Bridgeport Schwaben Veiren, 41
Bridgeport Water Company, 112
Bridgeport Whaling Company, 22-23
Bridgescam, 189
Briggs, Warren R., 185
Brilvitch, Charles, 84
Brock, Louis, 146
Brooks, John, 23, 136
Brown, Alan, 64

Brunetto, Carl, 147
Bucci, Karen, *221*
Bucci, Thomas W., *221*, 223
Buckingham, Edward T., 64, 115, 116, 118, 154, 157, 158
Bullard, Edward P., 101
Bullard Company, 25, 101
Bumper rapist, 199
Bunnell High School, 58
Burns, Ellen Bree, 57
Burroughs home, 16
Butler, Jack, 170

Caldwell, J. Edward, *178*
Calhoun, Philo C., 58, 136
Callahan, Jim, 223
Candlelite Stadium, 147
Cantor, Eddie, 128
Capp, Al, 64
Captain's Cove Seaport, *215*, 217, *218*
Carlson, William and Philip, 58, 111
Central Avenue firehouse, 199-200
Central High School, 134, 147, 148, 149, 193, *222*
Chamber of Commerce, 41, 114, 120, 161, 200, 217, 221
Chance-Vought Division, 118, 121
Chauncey, Charles, 50
Chopsy Hill, 18
Christy, Earl, 148
Churches, 19, 49-53, *50-51, 53*, 63, *104*
Church Row, *50, 52*
Citytrust Bank, 96
Civil Service, 152, 154, 158, 163, 174, 179
Civil War, 25
Civil War Soldiers' Monument, 87
Clark, James G., 191, 200
Cleary, Joseph, 170
Cleveland, Francis Folsom, 101
Clifford, Arthur, 193
Cody, William F. (Buffalo Bill), 90
Cohan, George M., 127
Colchester reservation, 18
Colleges and universities: Fairfield College Preparatory School, 58; Fairfield University, 58; Housatonic Community College, 58; Junior College of Connecticut, 58; Sacred Heart University, 58; University of Bridgeport, 58, 87, 149, 177
Columbia Records, 128, 132, *133*, 192
Columbus school, 57
Commerce, 19, 20, 23, 25, *28, 29, 71*, 96-97
Congregational Church, 49
Congress Junior High School, 56, *57*
Connecticut National Bank, 96, 98
Connecticut Recording Studio, 134
Connelly, James, 57
Cooper, Ken, 65
Corbit, Lew, *47*
Cornell, John, 155, 158
Cortright, E. Everett, 57
Corum Hill reservation, 18

Coster, Frank Donald, 185
Coughlin, Patrick, *33, 35*
Country Road, 17
Cozza, Ernie and Frank, 188
Crane, Bob, 64, 65
Cross, Dean Wilbur, 157, 158, 163, *164*
Curcio, Francis, 188
Curcio, Gus, 188, *188*
Curran, Hugh, *156*, 177, 178, 179, 195
Curtis, Dan, 134
Curtis, Walter W., 52, *52*, 58

D'Addario, F. Francis, 148, *190*
Daly, T.F. Gilroy, 189, 195
Danenberg, Elsie, 113
Danenberg, Leigh, 63
Danish Benevolent Society, 41
Davis, George, 147, 148
Dean, Dennis, 135
Decerbo, Frank, 189
DePiano, Salvatore, 179
Depression, 115-116, *117*, 118, 121, 152, 158, 160-161, 167
Dewey, Thomas E., 187
Dictaphone Corporation, 125
DiJoseph, Gerald, 199
Dinan Center (Hillside Home Hospital), *60*
D.M. Read's, 128
Dockery, John, 148
Dolan's Corner, 46
Doolittle, Thomas B., 112
Doris, the, *25*
Dorsen's Modern Department Store, *29*
Downing, George "Needles," 37
Dunn, James L., 161
DuPont Company, 125
Dworkin, Sydney, 179
Dymaxion auto, 95, 111

Eagle's Hall, 147
Education, 18, 41, 53-59, *54-57*, 68, 101, 115, 116, 125, 154, 164, 217; desegregation, 57; formation of colleges, 57-58; formation of schools, 54, *55*, 56-57
Entertainment, 35, 37, 46, 64-65, *126*, 127-128, *129, 130-131*, 132-134, 136, *137-138*, 139, 146-149
Episcopal Church, 49, 52
Essen of America, 114
Ethnic Diversity. See Immigration

Fabrizi, Anthony, 188
Fairchild Wheeler Golf Course, 139
Fairfield College Preparatory School, 58
Fairfield County Courthouse, *8-9, 28*
Fairfield University, 58
Farley, Joseph, 31, 33
Father Panik Village, 194
Fayerweather, Nathaniel, 19
FBI sting attempt, 180, *181*, 188, 189, 199
Federal Express, wreck of, 184, *186-187*
Ferryboat Junction Restaurant, *198*, 200, 217

Fires, 25, 28, *28*, 90, 134, *142-143*, 181, 184, 185
First airplane flight, 103
First Baptist Church, 49, 52
First Church of Christ, 50
First Congregational Church (North Church), *50, 51*, 52
Fish, Nancy, 87
Fitton, Father James, 52
Flegenheimer, Arthur, 187-188
Florence, Wally, 148
Flying High Kite Shop, *215*
Flynn, Mary, 155
Fones, Alfred C., 57
Foote, Enoch, 11, 20, 22
Foxx, Jimmy, 148
French, Arthur, 136
Friend, David, 197
Frisbie Pie Company, 103, *104, 204-205*
Frisbie, William R., 103
Fuller, Buckminster, 95, 111

Ganim, George, 178
Gehrig, Lou, 147
Geller, Herb, 33
General Electric, 115, *116*, 121, *122*
Germania Singing Society, 41
Golden Hill reservation, *13*, 17-18
Goodie Shop, 128
Gould, Nathan, 84
Grant, W.E., 181
Grasso, Ella T., 184
Gray, Augustine, first woman exchange operator, 113
Greater Bridgeport Labor Council, 121, 125
Greater Bridgeport Old Timers Association, 149
Greater Bridgeport Symphony, 134
Greatest Show on Earth, 90
Green, Bert, 35
Greene, Nathaniel, 112
Gregorie, Richard, 188, 189
Grover's Hill, 19
Guardians, 195, 197
Guman, John T., Jr., 223

Hallet, Charity, 71
Hall, Lyman, 19
Halsey, James H., 57
Hamlin, Alanson, 58
Harbor development, 23-24, *25*
Harding High School, 121, 148
Harral, Henry, 193
Harral-Wheeler House, 193
Harrington, H.M., 54
Hawley, Samuel, 125
Haynes, John, 16
Hell's Kitchen, 46
Heth, Joice, 71, *72*
Hill, Albert, 193
Hillside Home Hospital, *60*
Hilton Hotel, 217

Hines, Johnny, 128
Hinks and Johnson Carriage Company, *113*
H.M.S. Rose, *15*, 217
Holy Rosary, *104*
Hospitals, 35, 60, *60-61*, 62, 63, 118;
    Bridgeport Hospital, 60; Dinan Center
    (Hillside Home Hospital), *60*; Park City
    Hospital, 63; Rehabilitation Center of
    Eastern Fairfield County, 60; St. Vincent's
    Medical Center, 60
Housatonic Community College, 58
Housatonic Museum of Art, 58
Housatonic Railroad, *21, 22, 23*
House of Happenings, 185-186
Housing, 41, 43, 46, 68, 70-71, 114, 121, 125,
    152, 167, 170, 191, 194, 200; suburban
    flight, 125, 191
Howard, Maureen, 134
Howe, Elias, 25, *26*, 28, 96
Howell, Richard, 35, 37, 63, 146
Howlands, 128
Hubbell, Harvey, 101
Hungarian Reformed Church, 52
Hunk Town, 46
Hurd, Frederick, 87
Hurricane Gloria, 139, *144*
H.W. Lochner Company, 193

Immigration, 28, 33-35, 37, 41, 52, 113, 116,
    153, 167; ethnic diversity, 33-34, 41, 43, 46,
    49, 127
Indians: conflict with colonists, 12, 16, 17-18;
    life, 12-16; Paugussett nation, 12, 18;
    Pequot War, 12; reservations, *13*, 17-18;
    Schaghticoke, 146
Industry, 19, 20, *24*, 25, 28, 37, 38, 41, 71,
    94-125, *124*, 221; auto, 95, 103, *108*, *110-
    111*, 111; aviation, 95, 118, 121; banking,
    96, 98; brass, 98; carriage, 96, 98, *113;*
    corset, 98, 101-102, *101*; electrical
    equipment, 95, 98, *99*, 101, 115, 192;
    Frisbee, 95, 103; machine tool, 95, 101, 118,
    121, 191, 192; mechanical trains, *102*, 103;
    munitions, 38, 41, 95, 96, 113, 114, *114*,
    155; records, 128, 132, *132-133;* sewing
    machines, 71, 96, 98
International Institute of Connecticut, 46
Italian Baseball and Softball Association, 149
Italian Community Center, 41
Ives Manufacturing Company, *102*, 103

Jai Alai Fronton, 197
Jasplanades, 167
Jerome Clock Factory, 71, 95
Jewish Community Center, 41
Jewish congregation, 49
Johnson, Geraldine, 57
Jolson, Al, 128
Joyce, Joan, 148
Junior College of Connecticut, 58

Keefer, William, 188

Kelly, Walt and Selby, 64
Kennedy, John F., *175*
Kennedy Stadium, 135, 148, 193
Kepshire, Kurt, 147
Kidd, Captain, 139
King, John T., 35, 154, 155, 157, 173, 174
King, Morris, 35, 37
King's Highway, 16, 17
Kinley, Frank C., 132
Kleinberg's Pawn Shop, *172*
Klein, Jacob, 134
Klein Memorial Auditorium, 134
Klein, Milton, 58
Knapp, Burr, 136
Knapp, Goody, 16, *17*
Knapp's Hotel, 19
Krolokowski, Edward, 132

Labor, 37-38, 71, 95, 98, 103, 115, 116, 118,
    121, 125, 155, 158, 192, 200, 221; disputes,
    41, 43, 57, 114-115, 121, *122*, 154;
    organized, *32*, 115, 118, 121, *125*, 167, 170;
    padrone and barracks system, 38
Lafayette Plaza, *198*
Lake, Simon, 114, *115*
Lake Torpedo Boat Company, *94*, 114
Lee, Richard, 193
Leka, Paul, 134
Leonardo da Vinci, 199
Libraries, formation of, 58, *59*, 60, *61*, 68;
    Bridgeport Public Library, 58, *59, 60;*
    Carlson Library, 58
Lighthouse, Bridgeport's first, 23, *24*
Lincoln, Abraham, 25, 87, 93
Lincoln School Band, *48*
Lind, Jenny, *66, 77*, 81, *82*, 84, 93
Locomobile Company, 103, *108, 110*, 111,
    114, *203*
Ludlowe, Roger, 16
Lutheran Church, 49
Lycoming Girls Club, *91*
Lyon, Hanford, 58

MacDonald, Thomas H., 128
Mandanici, John, 41, 57, *178*, 179, 180, *180*,
    197, 199, 200, 223
Maplewood School, 57
Marchand, Nancy, 87
Margolis, David, 189
Markle, Tiny, 64, *65*
Marra, Thomas E., 180, *181*, 189, *189*
Mathews, Wes, 148
McCormack, George S., 132
McCullough, James, 52
McKesson and Robbins case, 185
McKinley School, 134
McKinney, Stewart, 179
McLevy, Jasper, 12, 41, 57, 64, 118, 139, *150*,
    151-155, *153-154, 156-157*, 157-158, *159-
    160*, 160-161, *162-169*, 163-164, 167, 170-
    171, *171*, 174, *175*, 191, 193; and Vida
    Stearns, *156;* civil service, 152, 154, 158,

163, 174; dog Lassie, *159, 162*, 163, *169;*
    family, 153, *155, 156, 158*, 161, *169;*
    frugality, 151-152, 154, 155, 161, 164, 167,
    170, 171, *171*, 192; outlived vote base, 170;
    socialist, 152, 153, 154, 158, 161, 164, *165*,
    170
McLevy, Mabel, 161
McMahon, J.H., 139
McNally, Jimmy, 35
McNeil, Abraham A., 23
McNeil, John, 23-24, *25*
Mechanics and Farmers Bank, 96
Meekins, Ted, 195, *197*
Meskill, Thomas, 179
Messiah Baptist Church, 52
Methodist Church, 49, 52
Metro Truck, 111, *111*
Middlebrooks, Charles, 23
Middlebrook, Stiles, 58
Million Dollar Playground, 139
Milton Bond, *cover and 215*
Miska, Steve, 149
Mitchell, Chuck, 134
Mitchell, Doris, *176*
Mitchum, Robert, 134
Morton, Margaret, 179-180, *179*
Mount Trashmore, 217
Mucci, Henry, 41
Mulvihill, Cornelius, 170, 174, 175, *175*
Mulvihill, Denis, 35, *35*, 154
Murray, Mae, 128
Musica, Philip, 185
Mystic River, 12

Neighborhood Housing Service, 217
Neigher, Harry, 187
Newfield Park, 147
New Haven Electric Light Company, 111
Newman, Jon, 195
Newman, Paul, 128, 135-136, *135*
Newspapers, 19, 43; *American Telegraph and
    Fairfield County Gazette*, 63; *Bridgeport
    Chronicle*, 63; *Bridgeport Herald*, 35, 49,
    62, 101, 103, 146, 151, *152*, 166, 170, 187;
    Bridgeport Post, 63, 64, 103, 152, 157, 177,
    179, 185, 189; *Bridgeport Republican*, 63;
    Bridgeport Standard, 63, 68, 71, 93;
    Bridgeport Sunday Herald, 63, 64;
    Bridgeport Sunday Post, 33, 64, 136;
    Connecticut Courier, 63; *Fairfield County
    Advocate*, 64; *Herald of Freedom*, 71; *New
    Haven Palladium*, 28; *New York Tribune*,
    28, 93; *New York World*, 28, 93;
    Republican Farmer, 63; *Spirit of the Times*,
    63; *Telegram*, 64, 223; *Times-Star*, 63;
    Weekly Farmer, 58, 63
Newton, Wayne, 188
Nichols, Philip, 23
Nihill, J.B., 63
Nimrod, the, 23
Noble, William H., 24, 34, 68, 136
Nogert, Peter, 147

Nolen, John, 136, 146

Octagon House, 84
Odell, Goody, 16
O'Dwyer, William, 103
Oldest schoolhouse, *54*
Oliver, Myra, 46
Olmsted, Frederick, 136
Organized crime, *172,* 173, 180, 186-189
Organized Crime and Racketeering Strike
    Force, 188, 189
O'Rourke, James H., 146
Owens, Joseph, 179

Padrone and barracks system, 38
Paige, Allan, 154
Palliser, Charles and George, 84
Panik, Stephen J., 43, *44,* 167, *167;* Father
    Panik Village, 46
Panuzio, Nicholas, 136, 177, 178
Paoletta, Leonard, 41, 180, *180,* 200, 217, 223
Park City Dye Works, 136
Park City Hospital, 63
Park City, origin of name, 136
Park City Plaza, 217
Parks: Beardsley Park, 46, *126,* 136;
    Christmas Village, 200; fires, 139, *142-143;*
    Newfield Park, 147; Pleasure Beach, *6,* 46,
    64, *94,* 136, 139, *140-144,* 146, 197, *208-
    209;* Seaside Park, 35, 46, 58, 68, 87, *92,*
    136, 146, 184, 217, 221; Washington Park,
    24, 136; Wood Park, 139; zoo, 136, *138*
Patricelli, Alfred, 134
Peek, Charles D., 54
Peete, William, 22
Pelton, Robert, 93
People's Bank, 96, *98,* 125, 193, 217
Pequot War, 12
Perry Memorial Arch, 136, *137,* 217
Perry, William, 136
Pettengill, Catharine Burroughs, 58, 60, *61*
Piccolo, Frank, 188, 197, 199
Pilotti, Perry, 149
Platt, Edward A., 64
Pleasure Beach, *6,* 46, 64, *94,* 136, 139, *140-
    144,* 146, 197, *208-209;* fires, 139, *142-143*
Police department, formation of, 181, *182-183,*
    184; racial imbalance, 194-195, *196*
Poli, Sylvester Z., 128
Politics, 35, 87-88, 90, 118, 152-171, 173-181,
    223; charter revision, 177; patronage, 154,
    155, 173, 174
Polka Dot Playhouse, 134
Pool, George W., 84
Population, *34,* 41, 115; suburban flight, 125,
    191
Presbyterian Church, 49
Prohibition, 187
Propeller-powered balloon flight, world's first,
    103
Prospect Street school, 54, *55*

Quach, Tom and Kim, 31, 33

Radio, 64, *65;* WICC, 64; WJBX, 64;
    WNAB, 64
Randolph, Stella, 103
Rastas, Skirmantas, 46
Rattlesnake Club, 146-147
Read school, 57
Reagan, Ronald, 200
Recreation, 35, 136-139, 146-149, 155
Recreation, Board of, formation, 136
Redevelopment, 53, 121, 125, 167, 170, 191-
    200, 217-221; Congress Street project, 53;
    Gateway to the Sound project, 217; State
    Street project, 193, *198*
Reed, Carroll, 57
Rehabilitation Center of Eastern Fairfield
    County, 60
Reilly, Eddie, 149
Reinalda, Barbara, 148
Religion, 49-53
Remington Arms Company, 38, *38, 39,* 113,
    114, *114,* 115, *116,* 125, *203,* 221
Remington City, 113
Remington Nature Preserve, *114*
Republican Action League, 177, 179
Riker army trucks, 114
Ringling Brothers, 90
Ripper Bill, 157
Ritchel, Charles F., 103
Roberto, Fred, *125*
Rockwell, Charles, 23
Rodman, Perry, 161
Roosevelt, Franklin D., 118
Roosevelt school, 57
Rossetti, Anthony, *125*
Ruth, Babe, 147
Rylands, John, 181

St. Anthony of Padua, 52
St. Augustine Cathedral, 52
Sts. Cyril and Methodius Roman Catholic, 43,
    49
St. Georges, 52
St. James Church, 34, 52
St. John Nepomucene, 52
St. John's Episcopal Church, *50, 51,* 52
St. Joseph's, 52
St. Mary's, 52
St. Michael the Archangel, 52
St. Patrick's, 52, 63
St. Vincent's Medical Center, 60
Sacred Heart University, 58
Sandula, Edward A., 170, 174, 176, *176,* 177,
    178
Saxon, A.H., 68
Scandals: Merritt Parkway, 164; Stratford
    Avenue Bridge, 158; Teapot Dome, 174;
    Waterbury, 164; Yellow Mill Bridge, 157,
    158
Schaghticoke Indians, 146
Scheele, Jacob, 184

Schools: Barnum School, 93, 175; Blackham
    school, 57; Bridgeport High, *57,* 64, 147;
    Bunnell High, 58; Central High, 134, 147,
    148, 149, 193, *222;* Columbus school, 57;
    Congress Junior High, 56, *57;* Harding
    High, 121, 148; McKinley school, 134;
    Maplewood school, 57; Prospect Street
    school, 54, *55;* Read school, 57; Roosevelt
    school, 58; Warren Harding High, 64
Schultz, Dutch, 63, 187-188
Schwartz, Harry, 161, 163
Schwartzkopf, Fred, 161
Schwartz, Robert, 217
Scinto, Marie, 177, *177*
Seaside Institute, 101
Seaside Park, 35, 46, 58, 68, 87, *92,* 136, 146,
    184, 217, 221
Sea trade, 18, 19, 20, 22-23, 96
Second Congregational Church, *50,* 52
Segee, Lewis Christian, 128
Seres, William, 179
Settlements: Borough of Bridgeport, 19;
    Fairfield, 16, 17; Fairfield Village, 18, 50;
    Newfield, 18; Pequonnock, 16, 18, 54;
    Stratfield, 18, 54; Stratford, 17, 20;
    Uncoway, 16
Shamrock Pub, 46
Shanahan, Joseph, 167
Shehan, Lawrence J., 52
Sheridan, Bill, 35
Sherman, Issac, Jr., *10,* 11, 221
Sherman, Isaac, Sr., *19,* 19-20
Sherman, Neil, 217
Sherwin, Pat M., 170
Sherwood, Bob, 147, 148
Sikorsky Division, 118, 120, 125
Sikorsky, Igor, 95, 118, *118-120,* 121
Sikorsky Memorial Airport, 221
Simpson, William S., 148
Singer, 96, 125, 192
Singer Sewing Machine Band, *162*
Smith, Philip L., 173
Society of Jesus, 58
Sol's Cafe, 46
Sorrentino, Michael J., 121
Southern New England Telephone Company,
    25, *112,* 113, 160-161
Spaghetti Place, 128
Spillane, Emmett, 149
Staples, Goodwife, 17
Stapleton, James A., *176,* 176-178
Star Cafe, 37
Steam (rock group), 134
Stearns, Edmund, 161
Stearns, Vida, *155, 156, 158,* 161, *169*
Steeple Chase Island. *See* Pleasure Beach
Steinkraus, Herman W., 93, 121
Sterling, James H., 136
Sterling, W.C., 22
Stoccatore, Patsy, 64
Stokes, Charles J., 31
Stratfield Hotel, 187

Stratton, Charles. *See* Tom Thumb
Stratton, Lavinia, *79, 81*
Stratton, Sherwood E., 81
Success Hill, *114*
Sullivan, John L., 37, 146
Sullivan, P.B., 157, 158

Tedesco, Samuel, 132, 139, 170, 175, 192, *192,* 193
Telephone Dispatch Company, 112
Television, 65; WICC, 65
Theaters and ballrooms: Brooklawn, 132-133; Cabaret, 134; Club Howard, *203*; Globe, 128, 133; Hawes' Opera House, 128; Lyric, 132, 133; Majestic, 128, *130,* 133; Palace, 128, *129, 131,* 133; Pleasure Beach, 132; Ritz, 128, 132-134, *203*; Strand, 128, 133
Thomas, Norman, 154
Thompson-Houston and Brush Electric Company, 111
Thorne, Angus, 116
Thumb, Tom, 68, *79, 80,* 81, *83, 86,* 93
Tickey, Bertha, 148
Tisdale, Charles B., 148, 180, *180*
Tobin, Tom, 37
Tom Thumb Conservatory, 81
Topstone Cigars, *124*
Transportation: auto, 35, 41, 118, 121, *149,* 155, 163, 170, 191, 192-193, *194*; electric trolley, *36,* 114; horse-drawn trolley, *20,* 35; railroad, 20, 22, *23,* 84
Tremont Hotel, 37, 146
Trinacria Society, 41
Trumbull reservation, 18
Twain, Mark, 93

Uncle Chick (rock group), 200
Underwood Corporation, 125
Union Metallic Cartridge Company, 38, *39,* 96, 113, *114, 203*
United Aircraft Corporation, 118, 120
United Congregational Church, 50
United Illuminating Company, 23, 111, 193
Universalist Church, 49
University of Bridgeport, 58, 87, 149, 177
Utilities: electricity, 111-112, 115; gas, 111; telephone, 112-113, *112*; water and sewer, *36, 109,* 112, 152, 167, 170

Van Dykes, *160, 161*
Vastano, Thomas, 188
Vaux, Calvert, 136
Viera, Frank, 148
Visconti, Joseph, 46
Vogel, Anita, 177

Wall, Thomas, 64
Walsh, Joseph A., 180, *181,* 186, 188, 189, 194-195, 199, 223
Walsh, William J., 152
Warner Brothers Company, 25, 101, *101*
Warner, I. DeVer and Lucien C., 101

War of 1812, 19
Warren, Ed and Lorraine, 186
Warren Harding High School, 64
Washington, George, 18
Washington Park, 24, 136
Webster, Bruce, 149
Weicker, Lowell, 179
Well, George, 25
Wells, W.W., *182*
Wheeler and Wilson Sewing Machine Company, 25, *26,* 35, 71, *97*
Wheeler, Archer, 193
Wheeler, Charles E., 147
Wheeler, Nathaniel, 95, 193
Wheeler, Thomas, 17
Whiskey Hill, 187
White Eagles, 46
Whitehead, Gustave, 103, *106-107*; first airplane flight, 103
Williams, George, 146
Williams, Kaye, 217
Wilson, Allen, 95-96
Wilson, Clifford B., *30,* 35, 114, 136, 154, 174, *174*
Witch hangings, 16-17, *17*
Wood, Frederick, 25
Wood Park, 139
World War I, 38, 41, 113
World War II, 118, 128
Wren, P.W., 139
Wright, Orville and Wilbur, 103

Yellow Mill Village, 46

Zybyszko, Larry, 147